Seeing God Work Wonders in All My Situations

*I stepped out on the water and
learned to trust His Word,
let Him change my heart,
lean on His strength,
and live by His faith!*

Carole Seeling Tschumper

TRILOGY CHRISTIAN PUBLISHERS

TUSTIN, CA

Trilogy Christian Publishers
A Wholly Owned Subsidiary of Trinity Broadcasting Network
2442 Michelle Drive
Tustin, CA 92780

Seeing God Work Wonders in All My Situations

10 9 8 7 6 5 4 3 2 1

Library of Congress Cataloging-in-Publication Data is available.

ISBN: 978-1-68556-897-9

E-ISBN: 978-1-68556-898-6

Dedication

To my fabulous husband, Keith,
a major source of this book and my life!
To my faithful kids, Andrew and RaeAnn,
and my fantastic grandkids: Taylor, Dylan, and Kylie.

"That I may know Him and the power of His resurrection, and the fellowship of His sufferings..."
(Philippians 3:10)

Contents

Prologue

I want to see God in everything. I want to know what He's saying. I want to understand His ways. When I committed my life to Him, I saw Him in the blessings; it took longer to find Him in the trials until He showed me that hidden in every trial were treasures—and I don't want to miss any!

"I will give you the treasures of darkness and hidden riches of secret places, that you may know that I, the Lord, who call you by your name, am the God of Israel."

(Isaiah 45:3)

Before I saw God in anything, I remember thinking there had to be more to life than I was experiencing. I thought of the few goals I had and wondered what would happen when they were met. "And then what?" was the phrase that plagued my thoughts, leaving me apprehensive about the future. I was searching for what I didn't know, but in the fall of that year, I found the answer by praying a simple prayer, something like:

"Thank you, Jesus, for dying on the cross for me. Please forgive all my sins and make me the kind of person You want me to be. Come into my heart Lord, and live Your life in me..."

And He did! He was no longer way up there. This same Jesus, whom I'd learned about and loved in Sunday school as a child, came to live in me through the Holy Spirit. "Peace" and "Joy," words I'd seen on Christmas cards, were within me, along with a hope that my life could make a difference. I knew something incredible had happened, and I wanted to tell everyone about this awesome Savior I had met. Committing my life to Christ was only the beginning; God had so much more He wanted to show me. My devotionals are dedicated to "the rest of the story that has no end..."

Keith, my husband, dedicated his life to the Lord a few weeks later. At the end of that extraordinary year, we became adoptive parents of a son, who had been born on the day I was born-again. Two years later, while waiting to see our daughter, God quieted my anxious heart by whispering, "I picked her out just for you."

I was ready to live happily ever after, but God had other plans; after a few years, the spiritual honeymoon ended, and the "situations" began. Somewhere I read that God doesn't have any problems. He only has situations—I found His supply unlimited. As each adventure unfolded, I wrote down all that God was teaching me. When I followed His advice, it made a profound difference. When I didn't—nothing happened.

Somewhere in the above paragraph, life became mundane. I decided I needed a ministry. After several frustrating attempts at finding one, God finally got my attention with:

"The greatest calling I have given you is being a wife and mother. You can learn and grow faster in your own home than anywhere else on earth."

I went undercover, learning and unlearning how to be a parent from God's point of view. After a particularly trying day, I heard: "You can only discipline your children to the extent that you are disciplined."

"Oh, help!"

A year or so later, He tackled our marriage, and I mean tackled! He tore down all the old structures and began building our marriage according to His specifications.

"For He has torn, but He will heal us; He has stricken, but He will bind us up."

(Hosea 6:1)

God laid the foundation with parenting and marriage, but He didn't stop there. The one theme running through every devotional is faith. Like a never-ending stream, it is the heart of every situation—faith is what moves the Hand of God. Faith was the first lesson (devotional) God gave me, so I figured it must be important.

Before I understood His ways, I questioned His love; I was discouraged when I thought He'd let me down. I wondered more times than I can count if I'd ever get it right. But in spite of all my faults and failures, I had tasted His love, glimpsed His glory, and seen His power—I was captivated.

S-l-o-w-l-y, I began learning His mysterious ways. He opened my eyes and taught me ways I had read in His Word but had never truly seen. He amazed me with the simplicity of His lessons—simple yet profound!

It is my prayer that these devotionals—not written in any particular order—will inspire you to see God in all your circumstances, understand what He is saying, learn His ways, step out in faith and see Him work in new and wondrous ways.

The Lord wanted my mother to see Him in new ways. She had recently given her heart to Jesus and was diligently reading her Bible and praying daily. While doing dishes at her house one evening, she shared, "I was praying the other day, and I saw in my mind a picture of Jesus—like the one at church." (She was referring to Warner Sallman's Head of Christ.) Then she looked perplexed and said, "Only Jesus was looking right instead of left…"

"Mom," I interrupted, "Jesus is telling you He wants to show you a new side of Himself." And in time, He did!

Jesus has more facets (sides) than we could ever see in this lifetime, and I want to see as many as I can! I hope you feel the same.

"When You said, 'Seek My face,' my heart said to You, 'Your face, Lord, I will seek.'"

(Psalm 27:8, NKJV)

"Without faith it is impossible to please Him, for He who comes to God must believe that He is, and that He is a rewarder of those who diligently seek Him."
(Hebrews 11:6, NKJV)

1. Faith is a Bridge

Faith is a bridge between having and not having. Without faith, we get nothing; with faith, we have access to everything God has for us. Faith was the first lesson God taught me, so I reasoned it must be important.

One Sunday morning in church, I asked the Lord to come into my life, but I didn't know if He had, so I continued to ask Him, not knowing what to expect. Later that week, I was on the bus going to work, and I found myself asking again, "Lord, please come into my heart." We were crossing a bridge, and I looked down into the river when a thought came to me, *Why don't you thank Me for it?* So, I did. Somehow, I knew He had heard me, and I didn't ask again. Several days later, the Lord revealed a valuable lesson about faith.

"The bridge between doubt and faith
is thanking the Lord."

Many times, over the years, He has brought that lesson to mind, in things important and in things mundane. Saying "thank you" is not just an idle tack-on to every request I make. Rather, it is one way of expressing my faith by declaring I believe God has heard me and He will answer. Thanking Him before I see the answer is a scriptural act of faith.

"Be anxious for nothing, but in everything by prayer and supplication, with thanksgiving, let your requests be made known to God."
(Philippians 4:6, NKJV)

As soon as I acted in faith on the bus, my prayer was answered. But in the weeks to come, I found many requests weren't answered so quickly. When God chooses to make us wait, it's because He has a good reason, and while we wait on Him, our faith is being stretched. We can thank Him because we know the answer is coming—that's what faith is!

"But if we hope for what we do not see, we eagerly wait for it with perseverance."
(Romans 8:25, NKJV)

To persevere in this way is exercising faith. It takes effort to walk in faith, but when your faith is rewarded, and you see results, it not only increases your confidence, it makes you love Jesus all the more!

Persevering in faith is also refusing to listen to the doubts when they come—and they will come! Listening to doubts is a faith-killer. Between the enemy and my own mind, the list is endless: *Did He hear me? Did I put it in His hands? Why isn't God doing something? Did I do something wrong?* I'm sure you could add a few too. No matter how many times those questions trample through my mind, I've learned to tell the Lord something like:

> "Father, I refuse to listen to doubts; I trust You.
> I know You've heard my prayer, and I thank
> You for answering it."

If you find yourself listening to doubts, repeat your affirmation, but don't expect to feel faith. Sometimes you do, sometimes you don't. Yes, it's a bit scary, but eventually, you will find it's a tremendous relief NOT to rely on feelings which are so unreliable, but rather on what God says in His Word.

> "If having faith is a decision I can make and
> not a feeling I have to attain, then it's something
> I can do! Faith—which seemed so elusive before—
> becomes reachable."

As the personal representative for my mother's estate, I needed to travel on the only weekend I had available that month. A heavy snowstorm was predicted for that area, and so I prayed and asked God to either send it elsewhere or dissipate it altogether. I bolstered my faith by recalling other times He had changed the weather for me and by reading Scriptures about how Jesus changed the weather when He walked on this earth. Surely, if He did it, then He could do it now.

As I prayed, I thought I heard, *"Trust Me."* So I did. I wouldn't listen to the comments from those who knew I would be leaving during the storm. Instead, I kept saying, "Lord, I trust You...," kicking out thoughts of how will I look if my prayer isn't answered. Those are doubts masked with pride. We have to risk being wrong. Have you ever learned anything without making mistakes? Me neither. By the way, God sent the storm south, and thankfully, it wasn't as strong as predicted.

I've known Christians who stepped out in faith, and the things they wanted to see didn't happen, and they were hesitant to try again. Consequently, their faith hasn't grown much.

We have to give God room to be God. We don't always know how God will do things.

"Now this is the confidence that we have in Him, that if we
ask anything according to His will, He hears us."
(1 John 5:14, NKJV)

God used those times to stretch my faith when I had to say, "Lord, I know that You heard my prayer; I don't understand why You aren't answering, but I trust You anyway!" I learned that when He wasn't answering, He had a good reason. It's also important to listen—maybe God is saying something, something we need to do...?

In the beginning, there were too many times I doubted God, and those times I received nothing. One day I woke up and realized without faith (believing Him), I get nothing. When I diligently seek Him, believe from my heart, and it is His will, God rewards me as He promised.

*"The Spirit of the Lord came upon Jahaziel...and he said,
'Listen...King Jehoshaphat! Thus says the Lord to you: 'Do
not be afraid nor dismayed because of this great multitude,
for the battle is not yours, but God's.'"*
(2 Chronicles 20:14–15, NKJV)

2. God's Way &
God's Timing

There are times God tells us to do nothing—and every Christian knows "nothing" is the hardest thing to do—nothing but trust the Lord, that is.

*"You will not need to fight in this battle.
Position yourselves, stand still and see the salvation
of the Lord who is with you..."*
(2 Chronicles 20:17, NKJV)

I was a young Christian trying to quit smoking, feeling frustrated and discouraged after a dozen or so failures. After the last failure, the Lord impressed me with the above verses, but I wondered, if I do nothing, how long should I do it? At the time, I didn't understand how much I should do and how much God would do.

A friend, also a new Christian, and I were in a restaurant talking about our struggles when she said, "Why don't you just trust the Lord to help you quit smoking?" Her remark wearied me as if I hadn't tried that!

"I will," I answered, "when you tell me how you trusted the Lord to lose weight." She nearly choked on a french-fry, but she got the point. My friend was right about trusting the Lord, but at the time, neither of us knew how to trust Him.

One unforgettable morning my son (around nine) left for school and seconds later came into the house, ran into his room, and came out with a small heart-shaped box of chocolates. He stuffed the box in my hand and said, "This is for you, Mom. I'm sorry," referring to a disagreement we had earlier. He smiled and ran out the door to catch up with his friends.

His gift touched me deeply. He had bought it the day before when he and his dad were shopping. He said he didn't know why he had bought it when I asked him later. For whatever reason, it made me want to quit smoking, so I would be alive and well for my kids. They had viewed those cancer-related films at school and had begged me to quit. I had tried and tried, prayed and prayed, but my determination lasted only until the second or third upset of the day.

What made this day any different? Three days earlier, I was watching the 700 Club, listening to a woman who lost over 150 pounds by doing nothing! Well, not exactly nothing. She had prayed and tried everything. Then one day, she stopped trying and started praying:

> "Lord, help me to want to do Your will, help me to
> want to do Your will more than I want to eat."

Then she stopped trying and started trusting God to do what she couldn't. As she waited on God, resisting the temptation to try one more thing, He gave her the want-to and the power to lose weight!

I listened to her testimony in tears, with an incredible feeling of freedom, finally understanding God's part and mine. I didn't know how or when, but I had faith that He would give me the power to quit—the power to work out what He promised to work in.

> *"For it is God who works in you both to will*
> *and to do for His good pleasure."*
> (Philippians 2:13, NKJV)

Three days and a box of chocolates later, God delivered me from smoking. This time it was different: I really wanted to quit. I still had the temptations to smoke, but I had the strength and the power to resist! God had worked both the "will" and the "do" in me just like He promised.

Doing nothing and having faith that God will do something may sound too simple, but it works—God responds to faith. When we stop trying and start trusting Him, He will do what we cannot do. God's power comes through faith, not works.

> *"...and be found in Him, not having my own righteousness,*
> *which is from the law, but that which is through faith in*
> *Christ, the righteousness which is from God by faith;"*
> (Philippians 3:9, NKJV)

Did you catch that? "...the righteousness, which is from God by faith." I have read those verses before, but I equated them strictly with salvation, not with how God wanted to work in me in my life today. Paul admonished the saints in the book of Galatians, who had begun "in the spirit" but were now trying to be righteous by works.

> *"Are you so foolish? Having begun in the Spirit, are you now being made perfect by the flesh?"*
> (Galatians 3:3, NKJV)

In order to receive what God has for us, we need to know what God's part is and what is ours. Our part will be doing the things we can do. God won't do our part, and we can't do His. I've tried to do his part many times, failed miserably, then blamed Him for not helping me. I didn't understand the meaning of Galatians 5:5 (NKJV).

> *"For we through the Spirit eagerly wait for the hope of righteousness by faith."*

God defines our part and His part in 2 Chronicles, Chapter 20, when Jehoshaphat learned that several armies were coming to battle against him.

- "Jehoshaphat feared, and set himself to seek the Lord, and proclaimed a fast..." (vs. 3)
- Jehoshaphat gathered together to ask for help from the Lord... (vs. 4)

- Then Jehoshaphat stood in the assembly of Judah and Jerusalem in the house of the Lord (vs. 5)...and said, "Oh Lord God of our fathers, are You not God in heaven, and do You not rule over all the kingdoms of the nations, and in Your hand is there not power and might, so that no one is able to withstand You?" (vs. 6)

- "Are You not our God, who drove out the inhabitants of this land before Your people Israel, and gave it to the descendants of Abraham Your friend forever?" (vs. 7)

- "O our God...we have no power against this great multitude that is coming against us; nor do we know what to do, but our eyes are on You." (vs. 12)

- "Then the Spirit of the Lord came upon Jahaziel..." (vs. 14)

- "And he said...'Do not be afraid nor dismayed (discouraged) because of this great multitude, for the battle is not yours, but God's.'" (vs. 15)

- "You will not need to fight in this battle. Position yourselves, stand still and see the salvation of the Lord, who is with you..." (vs. 17)

- And Jehoshaphat bowed his head with his face to the ground, and all Judah and the inhabitants of Jerusalem bowed before the Lord, worshiping the Lord. (vs. 18)

- Now when they began to sing and to praise, the Lord set ambushes against the people...who had come against Judah; and they were defeated." (vs. 22)

While we don't follow Jehoshaphat's *specific* plan, we can learn from it. He prayed, sought the Lord, fasted, looked to God for help, encouraged himself, asked others to pray, listened to what God said, believed (had faith in) what He said, followed it, and praised the Lord.

"So then faith comes by hearing,
and hearing by the word of God."
(Romans 10:17, NKJV)

God has a part for us, and when we do our part, we need to trust God to do His.

"...for the battle is not yours, but God's."
(2 Chronicles 20:15, NKJV)

I have read this chapter over and over and would recommend you read it until the words are settled in your heart, so you can trust God to do what we can't. Too often, we try to handle things alone when we have a God in heaven...,

"...who is able to do exceedingly abundantly above all that
we ask or think, according to the power that works in us..."
(Ephesians 3:20, NKJV)

"For if you forgive men their trespasses, your heavenly Father will also forgive you. But if you do not forgive men their trespasses, neither will your Father forgive your trespasses."
(Matthew 6:14–15, NKJV)

3. Learning to Forgive

"Mom, you always taught us to love," my daughter reminded me over the phone from across the country. My daughter was being the mother today, and I the child. She went on, "I want you to buy some flowers and a fruit basket and take them to her."

Take her a fruit basket and flowers? She had to be kidding; I gave her several reasons why I shouldn't, but my daughter persevered. I thought I heard a faint voice telling me she was right, but I dismissed it. Yet the thoughts persisted after we hung up. Reluctantly, I told the Lord I'd go, but He'd have to change me. I couldn't see how it was possible, but I gave Him permission to try.

I did take her the flowers and the fruit basket. It was a beginning. We had a long way to go, but the visit opened a door of discussion between us, and through much prayer and time, the situation—and my heart—slowly changed.

Things didn't always go smoothly. Whenever I was ready to "call it quits," I would hear my sister's advice: "Don't burn any bridges you will be sorry for." Then I would run to God for help.

One day, I lost it. I got angry and slammed the phone down. I was on my knees asking God for help, certain that I'd gone too far when the phone rang—it was my friend. We both apologized and then talked for over an hour, sharing our feelings on a deeper level than we had before.

It always amazes me after I take that first step and obey the Lord how things come together; not only do I change, but the people around me change as His marvelous love unfolds, smoothing out the most impossible situations.

I am so grateful God initiated the restoration, kept me from giving it up, held it together, and built it into a firm friendship. The important things the Lord taught me in rebuilding relationships is:

- It's more important to get the relationship right than to be right.
- It's not about fixing blame; it's about working things out.
- If you are wrong in some ways, admit it without expecting a reciprocal apology.
- It's about accepting others where they're at without expectations.

"For with what judgment you judge, you will be judged; and with the measure you use, it will be measured back to you."
(Matthew 7:2, NKJV)

That verse was a wake-up call. I don't want to stand before God on Judgment Day in defeat. If I don't embrace what He's teaching me now, the rest of my life will be adversely affected.

Learning to forgive is a lot like learning to love. God has since placed several people in my life that I found impossible to love. But the good news is He doesn't expect me to love them, but He does ask me to allow Him to love them through me. It's good for us to know we can't love like Him—it humbles us—and teaches us that whatever good comes through us is from Christ alone. The fruit is of the Spirit, not of us.

> *"The fruit of the Spirit is love, joy, peace, longsuffering,*
> *kindness, goodness, faithfulness, gentleness, self-control."*
> (Galatians 5:22, NKJV)

And when I'm not willing, I have prayed, "Lord, make me willing; make my heart like Yours." He will! I've also prayed, "Don't let me go until You have what You want from me." He won't! If you think I find that easy, look behind me, and you'll see deep heel marks! But after God does the work and my heart is changed, I am so grateful that He doesn't give up on me.

Some situations He works out in a day, sometimes it takes weeks or months, and it is never quite the same way, but through it all, we learn more about His ways as we witness the restoration of relationships. Jesus came to build our relationship with Him first! Then He tells us to go to others—first.

> *"We love Him because He first loved us."*
> (1 John 4:19, NKJV)

Is there someone you need to build a bridge with? Ask God what you can do, then sit back and see what He can do...you'll be amazed!

"Surely the wrath of man shall praise thee;
the remainder of wrath shalt thou restrain."
(Psalm 76:10, KJV)

4. The First Step: Accept

The shrill sound of the smoke alarm jolted my husband and me out of bed around four a. m. and sent us running down the hallway into the living room. An eerie glow framed one of the windows; Keith yanked the drapes aside to see my car engulfed in flames—and parked dangerously close to the house.

My face felt the scorching heat as I stood on the front lawn watching the fire roar upwards of twenty feet while Keith hosed the side of the house. Thoughts roared in my mind. *This can't be happening to us! Why God? Did I do something wrong?* The Word of God constrained me:

"No evil shall befall you, nor shall any plague
come near your dwelling;"
(Psalm 91:10, NKJV)

God, this is mighty close to our dwelling!

I knew in order to stop the confusion, I had to accept what was happening. I've stumbled through too many perplexing situations with no answers in sight, not to have learned that if I don't accept my circumstances and look for God in them, the confusion only gets worse.

I can't stop the initial thoughts from coming, but I have learned to take a leap of faith, forcing myself to say something like: "Lord, I don't understand what's happening, but I accept it, knowing You are in it somewhere, so help me to trust You." I said it that morning as I waited desperately for help to come.

Neighbors, awakened by the noisy fire alarms, came to see the charred mess of melted, twisted iron. They stepped carefully over the glass shards strewn over the driveway by the explosion of heat. I gratefully accepted their company, comfort, and cups of coffee. The detective at the scene informed us several other cars in the area had been torched.

Even though I had accepted the ordeal in my heart and felt no malice for whoever was responsible, I still had to deal with a psychological alarm set in my brain that would go off every morning around four o'clock. I would get up and look out all the windows to make sure everything was all right, even though I knew it was unlikely anyone would return. Yet fear is rarely logical. This happened for several nights.

Fearful at night and tired during the day, I prayed about it earnestly and put it in God's hands. Early the next morning, I woke up on cue, got out of bed, and took a step towards the window when the Lord halted my steps with: "Don't look out, go back to bed."

You've got to be kidding, Lord! He wasn't. I did go back to bed reluctantly, but I didn't go back to sleep. I repeated the words,

"Lord, I trust You," not sure if I did, or even if it was God's voice I'd heard, though it sounded like something He would say.

It wasn't easy lying there doing nothing—nothing but trusting the Lord and repeating verses that I had written down during the day. God was stretching my faith, but at the time, it didn't feel like it. It never does while I'm in the middle of a situation.

> *"Meditate within your heart on your bed, and be still."*
> (Psalm 4:4, NKJV)

I was doing that. Occasionally I would fall back to sleep. Then one night, I woke up after sleeping all night long.

> *"I will both lie down in peace, and sleep; for*
> *You alone, O Lord, make me dwell in safety."*
> (Psalm 4:8, NKJV)

When my car was bright and shiny, I watched over it like a mother hen. I inspected it regularly for those dreaded door dings; I walked long distances to avoid subjecting my car to the "metal abuse" of too-close cars and careless drivers.

We bought another car, and the first time I parked it at the grocery store, someone next to me backed out, dented my back fender, and of course, didn't leave a forwarding address. But an amazing thing happened! Somehow—and I still don't know how—God loosened me from the inordinate affection of my car. A far cry from the time I was upset with my daughter when a little ding was discovered after she had driven it. God was in the process of shaking a few things out of me.

"Yet once more I will shake not only the earth, but also heaven...that the things which cannot be shaken may remain."
(Hebrews 12:26–27, NKJV)

When we accept our circumstances, the trial that seemed so dreadful becomes a blessing. God uses it to increase our faith, deepen our understanding, and change our hearts. He allows only what we need and not one iota more so that the "wrath of man will praise Him;" anything more "He will restrain" (Psalm 76:10, KJV). What a Savior we have!

By the way, we inadvertently left the living room window open an inch or two on that cool October night, just enough for the smoke to drift through the window and trip the alarm. The siding of the house had to be replaced, the kitchen and living room were scrubbed from floor to ceiling, but who knows what might have happened if the window had been shut? But with God, there are no *what-ifs*; He always leaves a "window" open.

Is there something in your life that you need to accept? Something you don't understand? Do questions gyrate in your head like: *Is God angry at me? Did I do something wrong? Is God really in control? Does He care?* Or maybe you're blaming the people involved and not seeing God's Hand? The first step is to accept. It's a step of faith, but when you take it, God will respond in His timing.

"God is in the midst of her, she shall not be moved; God shall help her, just at the break of dawn."
(Psalm 46:5, NKJV)

"Open rebuke is better than love carefully concealed. Faithful are the wounds of a friend..."
(Proverbs 27:5–6, NKJV)

5. Blind Spots

I was preparing dinner when my husband stuck his head in the kitchen and said, "If you don't close those cupboard doors, someone is going to get hurt." I glanced up to see two doors open.

"I always close them," I protested. "I just forgot today." I could tell I hadn't convinced him. As I reached up to close the doors, a question tumbled into my mind, *Don't I, Lord?*

Much to my chagrin, in the next several days, I noticed the doors were open quite often. A few days later, the cupboard-door scenario came to mind while I was praying, and my next thought was from God.

"There are times you need to see yourself through the perspective of others."

God weaves His truths through the mundane things in life— even cupboard doors. All of us suffer from blind spots, so God uses people closest to us, who see what we can't see, to tell us what we need to hear. He designed His children to be interdependent; one of those ways is making us see the real us.

"As iron sharpens iron, so a man sharpens
the countenance of his friend."
(Proverbs 27:17, NKJV)

Insecure people have the hardest time accepting reproof. I know because I was one of them. If I agreed with others, my already low self-esteem would plummet even lower. But God, through His word, instilled in me the hope that dealing with my "blind spots" would be for my good. What you don't know can hurt you!

"Let the righteous strike me; it shall be a kindness.
And let him rebuke me; it shall be as excellent oil;
let my head not refuse it."
(Psalm 141:5, NKJV)

When I cooperated with God and let Him work on those areas, my self-esteem increased! The truth—though it hurt at first—eventually set me free!

"You shall know the truth, and
the truth shall make you free."
(John 8:32, NKJV)

So, when Keith informed me I lacked "maturity and aplomb" when it came to making decisions, I had to admit he was right— my indecisiveness happened way too often. He wasn't referring to just important decisions, but the mundane, everyday kind of decisions as well. I knew it was a problem, but not knowing how to deal with it, I ignored it. Now God was showing me how He and I could overcome it. I prayed something like:

> "Lord, give me the grace to make decisions without floundering; help me to pray first, make a decision, then trust You for the outcome. If doubts come to my mind, help me to cast them out. And if my decision was wrong, show me how to handle it..."

One prayer will not remove inherent weaknesses, nor will a single act of faith free them from our feeble frames. It is accomplished through numerous experiences of coming face to face with our infirmities, placing them again and again at His feet, repeating and believing God's promise:

> *"For it is God who works in you both to will and to do for His good pleasure."*
> (Philippians 2:13, NKJV)

Some of the ways God deals with our habits, hang-ups, hurts, and fears, is by pushing us into circumstances that reveal our infirmities. We can blame others, or even our circumstances, when in reality, the weakness was in us all along; it just needed the right "ingredients" to bring it out.

Others may not be right, but it's our responsibility to bring it to Jesus: "Lord, is there something You are trying to tell me?" became a prayer of mine.

After I started listening to Keith, in time, he began listening to me. One fine day he overwhelmed me with, "You see my problems so much better than I do; you bring out all the things I never think of; you are a real helpmate."

What a contrast to the days we competed with each other, defended our agendas and avoided our problems. And now we have God's promise:

"He who regards a rebuke will be honored."
(Proverbs 13:18, NKJV)

We can bring out each other's weaknesses, but it is God who has to change us from the inside out, and we have to be willing to listen and want to be changed.

There are too many people in the Bible who refused to listen to God's "messengers;" I don't want to be one of them. I hope you don't either!

"And we know that all things work together for good to those who love God, to those who are the called according to His purpose."
(Romans 8:28, NKJV)

6. No Answers, Yet

I felt so helpless. All I could do was hold her in my arms and cry with her. Our daughter had crawled into our bed that morning and, between the tears, asked me, "Why is God allowing this?" I had no answers; I wondered myself.

Our daughter was in the seventh grade—the year that changed everything. The group she hung out with began experimenting with alcohol, watching late-night cable movies, and conducting séances at sleepovers. Our daughter spoke up. She tried to do it in a non-judgmental way, but some of the girls made fun of her values.

For years she had taken her friends to church activities; now they were calling her a Jesus freak. Some ignored her at school functions, others tried to remain friends, but peer pressure pulled them back into their group.

One of the mothers called me the day after a séance sleepover. She didn't see anything wrong with the séance but said she was impressed with my daughter for taking a stand because of her beliefs and for speaking up in a "very gracious way."

It all came to a head one evening at a school dance. Her dad had volunteered to pick up the girls after the dance. Just as he approached the school, he saw our daughter sitting on the curb and a car full of girls driving away. They had left her. It broke his heart to see her alone, but he was grateful God had led him there.

She recorded her pain in journals, drawing cartoon-like characters that depicted what her friends had done and said and her feelings about it. It was heartbreaking to read these and see her "character" flooded with tears.

Then she began having severe headaches. We took her to several doctors, and they couldn't find anything wrong. Finally, the head physician at a Children's Hospital diagnosed it as "psychosomatic due to problems at school." Unknown to us, she also struggled with bulimia in her effort to become acceptable.

That same year she was crowned Honor Star, the highest award for the Missionettes group at church. A few of the requirements included reading the entire Bible, memorizing dozens of Bible verses, reaching out to people in need—all this helped her get through the rejection.

She found new friends, the headaches went away, the bulimia was in check, but she never got over what happened. But that's not the end of the story. No, with God, that's never the end!

Her high school years were far from ideal. After graduation, she decided to work full-time for a year, saying she wasn't ready to leave home yet. She applied to a university in the southwest with one of her friends and was accepted. Her friend backed out later.

When friends and family heard she was going so far away, they questioned it. I would have been hesitant, too, if God had not assured me that she would bloom there "like a rose in the desert."

> *"And the desert shall rejoice and blossom as the rose;*
> *it shall blossom abundantly and rejoice,*
> *even with joy and singing."*
> (Isaiah 35:1–2, NKJV)

We came home one day and found her in tears. She told us she had been mistakenly assigned to a co-ed dorm. Keith called the university and was told it was too late to change. We prayed...then Keith remembered one of the counselors we met during enrollment, who was originally from our area and had told us to call if we ever needed anything. Keith called—and our daughter was transferred to an all-girls dorm. It was the first of many miracles she would experience. We prayed, and God worked out the problem—every time!

Even though I never doubted it was God's plan, it was incredibly difficult for us to leave as we watched her walk towards the dorm all alone. Our tears watered the desert and several states on our long way back to the Midwest.

Our daughter was determined to make a difference. She became the Dorm President and later a Resident Assistant in the dorms. She spoke to groups by sharing her pain, the problems she encountered, and how she overcame them. We received letters from those who served with her praising her attributes. After having a lackluster high school record, she graduated from college summa cum laude and several years later received her master's degree magna cum laude.

Her first job was with fifth graders in an oppressed area. She stayed at least a couple of hours every day, helping them achieve academically. She did her best to make them feel good about themselves. She drove one boy home daily so the gangs wouldn't get him. On the last day of school, she was saying her goodbyes, trying to hold back the tears. She praised one boy who had a rough start but a great ending, who responded, "That's because of you, Teach," and the tears came.

As she related the above over the phone and across the miles, we talked again about her pain and how God had turned it into good. She summed it up by saying, "I believe God allows everything for a reason. If it weren't for all the problems I encountered, I probably wouldn't be here today."

Instead of becoming overly sensitive or bitter, she senses things others don't always see—people who need a word of encouragement or praise, a prayer, a meal, a hug, or someone to talk with. She will go the nth mile to make sure someone isn't left out. While attending a seminar in her second year of teaching, she met another teacher who said, "I remember you. In my freshman year, you saw me sitting alone and said, 'Come eat with us.'"

God cares about today—He has promised comfort. It's real; you can feel it. Receive it!

"Blessed be the God...of all comfort, who comforts us in all our tribulation, that we may be able to comfort those who

are in any trouble, with the comfort with which we our-
selves are comforted by God."
(2 Corinthians 1:3–4, NKJV)

"As one whom his mother comforts, so I will comfort you..."
(Isaiah 66:13, NKJV)

And if your mother or father isn't able to comfort you,
God has thought of that too:
"When my father and my mother forsake me,
then the Lord will take care of me."
(Psalm 27:10, NKJV)

"He will gather the lambs with His arm,
and carry them in His bosom."
(Isaiah 40:11, NKJV)

God's word is overflowing with comfort. He has many verses for you to uncover with your name on. Give Him your time; He will meet you, strengthen you, and cover you with His never-ending love.

I started this devotional with Romans 8:28, "All things work together for good..." Most of you have heard that as an expression or a verse. Let's skip to the next verse that explains why and how all things really do work together and why it's important to understand.

"For whom He foreknew, He also predestined to be con-
formed to the image of His Son, that He might be the
firstborn among many brethren."
(Romans 8:29, NKJV)

God knew before the world began who would come to Him, and so he predestined our life so that every situation we encounter could make us more like Jesus, depending on how much we let God work in us.

As a young Christian, I didn't understand why some things happened, but the more I studied the Bible, the more God taught me His ways, the more I understood how important it is to embrace situations and learn from them because all things (good and not-so-good things) really do work together for good.

"What then shall we say to these things?
If God is for us, who can be against us?"
(Romans 8:31, NKJV)

No one!

"How sweet are Your words to my taste,
sweeter than honey to my mouth!"
(Psalm 119:103, NKJV)

7. "The Book!"

I have lifted my Bible to the heavens—
Hugged it close to my heart;
I've kissed those hallowed pages
When His words have spanned the ages,
Reached into my now and warmed my heart.

I can still see Alice, one of my mentors, sitting on her sofa, lifting her Bible heavenward, quoting Jeremiah 15:16 (KJV).

"Thy words were found, and I did eat them; and thy word
was unto me the joy and rejoicing of mine heart;"

God's words were woven in and through her life, giving her gift of teaching, an anointing that made her listeners hungry to know more about Jesus. Her predominant theme was: *The Book. Let everything be judged by the Book.* Because of that, I learned to love God's Word, revere it, study it, rely on it, and trust it.

She taught me to rely on the Holy Spirit for interpretation of God's Word, not some preconceived notion or religious dogma, but to keep my mind open as I studied His word, prayerfully reading all the verses on a particular subject while trusting the Holy Spirit to give me understanding.

"Trust in the Lord with all your heart,
and lean not on your own understanding."
(Proverbs 3:5, NKJV)

"When He, the Spirit of truth, has come,
He will guide you into all truth;"
(John 16:13, NKJV)

"Read, listen, and consider what others say, but remember the Holy Spirit is the final authority," she would remind us.

"The anointing which you have received from Him
abides in you, and you do not need that anyone teach you;
but as the same anointing teaches you concerning
all things, and is true..."
(1 John 2:27, NKJV)

"Don't put God in a box," she cautioned—a forerunner of today's out-of-box expression. "He is too big to fit into our little minds." Then she quoted one of her favorite verses:

"Now to Him who is able to do exceedingly
abundantly above all that we ask or think,
according to the power that works in us."
(Ephesians 3:20, NKJV)

I like to think the above verse implies "according to the power" that we let "work in us."

A young family member questioned my expressed thoughts concerning the accuracy of the Bible and said: "I wouldn't trust anything that was written by man."

I answered, "I agree, except the Bible wasn't written by man alone. Scripture assures us,

> *"No prophecy of scripture is of any private interpretation,*
> *for prophecy never came by the will of man, but holy men of*
> *God spoke as they were moved by the Holy Spirit."*
> (2 Peter 1:20–21, NKJV)

I know God wrote it because I see Him in it. He speaks to me through it, and when I commit His words to memory (not always perfectly), He brings them to mind wherever I am, whenever I need them. And because I believe what He says on those holy pages, He has done some pretty amazing things for me.

The Bible is the most magnificent, glorious, awe-inspiring book ever written. What's astounding is that so many men under the inspiration of the Holy Spirit could write such a profound book that spanned several thousand years, doesn't contradict itself, and continues to be a bestseller today.

> *"All Scripture is given by inspiration of God, and is profit-*
> *able for doctrine, for reproof, for correction, for instruction*
> *in righteousness, that the man of God may be complete,*
> *thoroughly equipped for every good work."*
> (2 Timothy 3:16–17, NKJV)

Another family member, around seven years old, picked up his Bible and said, "I am going to read my Holy Bible." Holy? I don't think I've ever heard anyone call it what is written on many Bibles—but I liked it!

> *"Out of the mouth of babes...You have ordained strength..."*
> (Psalm 8:2, NKJV)

Do you like finding treasures? Psalm 119 is a treasure-trove with over thirty references to the Word of God. But the treasures in that Psalm aren't inclusive; the whole Bible is full of treasures that can be found as we diligently search for them.

> *"My heart stands in awe of Your word. I rejoice at Your word as one who finds great treasure."*
> (Psalm 119:161–162, NKJV)

Do you like secrets? God has some that He yearns to tell us, and we don't have to keep them; we can tell everyone! Let's listen closely as we read our Bibles, so we don't miss His whispers.

> *"The secret things belong to the Lord our God, but those things which are revealed belong to us and to our children forever..."*
> (Deuteronomy 29:29, NKJV)

I don't want to just read His words. I want to embrace and embody them, so His word descends from my head into my heart, then I can believe what God is saying in His word—making it mine.

"So then faith comes by hearing,
and hearing by the word of God."
(Romans 10:17, NKJV)

I want to hear His words, like the two men on the road to
Emmaus did when they "ran" into Jesus. They didn't recognize
Him as He expounded Scriptures concerning Himself until He
sat at their table, blessed the bread, gave it to them, and—

"Their eyes were opened and they knew Him; and He van-
ished from their sight. And they said to one another, 'Did
not our heart burn within us while He talked with us on the
road, and while He opened the Scriptures to us?'"
(Luke 24:30–32, NKJV)

When I read in Scripture that Jesus gave up everything to
come to earth, how he was mistreated, misunderstood, aban-
doned by most, endured the shame, crucified and died...I am
awed by the extent of His love. For us to take so few of His
promises, to believe such a limited number of His blessings,
to use so little of His power somehow lessens the value of the
enormous price He paid.

"Lord, burn our hearts as we read Your Holy Scriptures—
Give us faith to believe Your every Word,
Open our ears to hear Your voice,
Touch our eyes to see Your beauty and
Free our minds to understand Your wondrous ways."

"When the Lord brought back the captivity...we were like those who dream. Then our mouth was filled with laughter, and our tongue with singing...the Lord has done great things for us, and we are glad."
(Psalm 126:1–3, NKJV)

8. My God, I Don't Love Him

I glanced at my watch as we pulled up in front of our house. I had left a note, hired a sitter, and went with friends to a Christian fellowship meeting that afternoon; it was late, and I knew my husband would be waiting for me. As I walked to the house, I found myself thinking about the meeting, not what the speaker had said, but testimony from a young housewife telling us how God was working in her home.

The house was quiet. I walked to the back door and looked out. The kids were playing, and Keith was sitting in a lawn chair reading the newspaper.

This was the second summer my teacher-husband had been working on his master's degree 300 miles out of town, coming home on the weekends. A fleeting thought crossed my mind: I wasn't very excited about seeing him after being apart for nearly a week. Last summer, I had eagerly anticipated his weekend "visits," giving our marriage a needed shot in the arm. But this summer: *What had happened to us?*

As I reached for the screen door, the Lord suddenly turned—as it were—a searchlight on in my soul, and over and over, these words repeated themselves.

My God, I don't love him! I don't love him! I don't...

That revelation sent me to my knees. I prayed fervently in the days ahead: "Lord, help me to love my husband, *really* love him, as a wife should love her husband..." As I prayed, the Lord showed me how shallow our relationship was, how little we had in common, our lack of communication, and how competitive we were.

Somewhere through the years, we had drawn lines of demarcation; we dropped our swords and set up limits and boundaries, being careful not to step over the imaginary lines of our individual lives—we built walls instead of bridges.

God heard and answered my prayer, but His way of answering was totally unexpected: He tore down all the faulty structures we had constructed before He began building our marriage according to His specifications.

"For He has torn, but He will heal us;
He has stricken, but He will bind us up."
(Hosea 6:1, NKJV)

Summer turned into fall, and Keith began refinishing the kitchen cupboards. All the contents were packed in boxes on the floor, and I was tired of cooking out of them and tripping over them while Keith found endless excuses not to commence work.

My passive nature would do anything to avoid conflict. Instead of speaking up, I suppressed my feelings, modeling what I thought was the biblical submissive wife. But something was amiss: instead of loving my husband more, I loved him less. Suppressed feelings have a way of bursting forth, and God knew exactly how to put the pressure on.

One evening during a heated discussion over the kitchen's lack of progress, my usually controlled demeanor slipped. I don't remember how I veered from the kitchen to our relationship, but years of buried resentments burst forth in painful recollections as I told him how I felt about our relationship, our marriage, and him. When I finished, we were both crying; then we cried in each other's arms.

My outburst proved to be cathartic, for springing up from within us flowed a refreshing honesty. With childlike freedom, we expressed our likes and dislikes, our disappointment and dreams. What seemed to be the end became the beginning as God planted a seed of love in our hearts that night—but seeds need to grow…

I was so sure that after such a beautiful reconciliation, we would live "happily ever after," but like Israel's triumphant departure out of Egypt proved to be only the *beginning* of her journey, God had a shock in store for us: most of our work was ahead of us.

In the midst of all the problems that surfaced over the weeks and months to come, I recall saying, "Lord, all I prayed for was a happy marriage." I smile now, and I think Jesus did then as I heard:

"That's what I'm trying to give you, but it's *through*
these problems that will bring about my promises."

There were no easy ways, no shortcuts or bypasses—though
God knows I looked for them. His perfect path led straight
through the problems that forced us to deal with the areas in our
lives that needed changing. We spent hours talking, praying,
and working out our difficulties, digging deeply into our pasts,
trying to understand our actions and reactions. As our masks
slowly came off, we learned to know one another intimately as
we shared our fears, hurts, and hang-ups. As we changed—our
marriage changed.

> *"Unless the Lord builds the house,*
> *they labor in vain who build it;"*
> (Psalm 127:1, NKJV)

God had started this pilgrimage—making us one—and He
would finish it. Occasionally we encountered an impasse. I recall Keith praying, "Lord, help me to love my wife; I just don't
know how." We learned our own love is never enough. God
wants us to let *His* love come through us.

> *"The fruit of the Spirit is love, joy, peace..."*
> (Galatians 5:22, NKJV)

Notice, the fruit is of the Spirit, not us. Our love is never
enough. We just need to step aside, by faith, and trust the Holy

Spirit to love through us. That way, He deserves all the praise. He can handle praise. We can't!

God began to prod me to bring up situations to Keith. I protested, "But Lord, he won't listen to me."

"Tell him anyway." I did, but I was right. He didn't listen. God was in the process of tearing down my passive nature and teaching me to speak up. Not every situation went smoothly. When it didn't, He would tell me not to get angry but put it in His Hands and let Him deal with it. I had to trust God to do what I couldn't. Sometimes Keith would apologize. Sometimes I had to apologize to him—both of us had to change.

But it wasn't all work. We were forced to begin talking about our situations, but happily, it progressed to an enjoyable pastime that I thought had died about the third year of marriage: laughter, sometimes until our sides ached, became an integral part of our relationship.

> *"For it is God who works in you both to will*
> *and to do for His good pleasure."*
> (Philippians 2:13, NKJV)

Mistakes? Lots. But "love covers a multitude of sins" (1 Peter 4:8, NKJV).

Situations? Many. But "the Lord delivers us out of them all" (Psalm 34:19, NKJV).

Through it all, we are becoming true helpmates. Instead of putting each other down, we learned to lift each other up. On a day I especially needed Keith's encouragement, he told me:

"If holding you up in prayer is a way of expressing
my love, then you're right there at His Feet."

Sigh! Does every woman yearn for a romantic husband? I
did. Early in our marriage, I reluctantly laid to rest my youth-
ful dreams and settled for a magazine article's description of
"mature love": settled, non-demonstrative, faithful, and a good
provider. Keith was all of that, But God wouldn't let us settle for
little when He had so much more, He wanted to give us.

> "*Eye has not seen, nor ear heard, nor have entered
> into the heart of man the things which God has prepared
> for those who love Him. But God has revealed them
> to us through His Spirit. For the Spirit searches
> all things, yes, the deep things of God.*"
> (1 Corinthians 2:9–10, NKJV)

As God continued to work in us, Keith began likening me to
flowers, rainbows, and violins. For someone who for years had
two stock answers: *just fine* and *pretty good*, he started telling me
daily how much he loved me, that I was beautiful (remember,
beauty is in the eye of the beholder), and even called me his
bride!

When the Lord told me to reciprocate, my mouth felt like it
was full of peanut butter. I had never complimented him before. It's hard to praise someone you are competing with; if I
had built him up, I wouldn't have looked so good. I was waiting
for his approval of me first, and then I would give it back. But

when God's love invaded our existence, I learned that I could lift Keith up without feeling threatened. In fact, I loved telling him how much I appreciated him.

We've come a long way over the years, so when problems arise, one of us will say, "Let's talk," and we listen, *really* listen. I learned to ask God, "Lord, if I'm wrong, show me." After a while, "being wrong" wasn't so bad because I no longer felt I had to compete with Keith. God impressed me with the thought:

"It's more important to 'get it right' than to 'be right.'
When we get it right, we both win, but when we try
to be right—nobody wins."

Marriage is about change. No one is exempt. But the best part is: the more I change, the happier I am, and the closer I am to God. He keeps showing me ways I need to improve—often through my husband—and change will go on until I see Jesus.

I thank God for opening my eyes to see what we could have through Him; I want to share what He has taught us with everyone who has ever dared to hope that the honeymoon is only the beginning. And it all started with a desperate prayer years ago:

"Lord, help me to love my husband, *really* love him, as a wife should love her husband."

And God is still answering...

*"I have loved you; therefore I will give men for you, and
people for your life. Fear not, for I am with you;"*
(Isaiah 43:4–5, NKJV)

9. God Provides

What a trip! I was at the airport, pushing my big suitcase
and pulling a smaller one with an old and heavy computer on
my shoulder—struggling to get in line—when the guy behind
the counter left. I saw another line, so I strapped my smaller
suitcase on top of the bigger one, and as I turned, the small
one fell off, pulling the larger one to the floor. I reached for the
suitcases, and my computer bag slid off my shoulder and hit
the floor along with my purse. I caught myself before joining
the melee. *"Lord, I need Your help!"* And help He did!

I managed to get to the other line; there was only one man
ahead of me. The woman behind the counter said, "You need a
baggage claim to get into this line."

"Where do I get one?"

"On the machine," she said.

"I don't know how."

The man who was *still* standing there said, "I will help you." I
started to pick up my bags, and he said, "I'll get them." We went
through the machine questions, put the baggage claims on my
suitcases, and he carried them back to the counter.

I thanked him profusely and said, "God bless you..." The line was longer; I picked up my baggage to go to the end of the line when I heard the man say, "Wait! The people in front will let you go ahead." *Really? Really!* I thanked the couple as the man put one of my suitcases on the scale; I thanked the man again before he left.

The woman behind the counter said, "That was your angel today." I heartily agreed! I praised the Lord all the way to my gate, asking Him to bless those who blessed me, thoroughly amazed at the way He took care of me through the people He had positioned at the right time and place.

"I will bless those who bless you."
(Genesis 12:3, NKJV)

God is so faithful! He has helped us so many times...my husband and I had gone to a movie out of town, and it was dark when we came out. The lighting wasn't good, and Keith didn't see the curb, fell onto the street, and couldn't get up. Two men ran over and picked him up. The younger one went to get a chair for him, and the woman with them called 911. The family stayed there, talking to us until the rescue squad came. The woman said if I wanted to go with Keith, she would pick me up at the hospital no matter what time it was. I elected to drive there; it was only a couple of miles away. We thanked the family over and over.

Having that family there eased the pain and gave us comfort. When God says, "I will be with you," He is with us through the people He faithfully provides.

"The preparations of the heart belong to man,
but the answer of the tongue is from the Lord."
(Proverbs 16:1, NKJV)

10. Letting God Speak

"I don't understand why it happened..." My daughter had called me from across the country, voicing her pain and distress with God. "It's not fair," she said, concerning the miscarriage she had experienced a few months earlier. Two of her friends had recently told her they were expecting, "Although I am happy for them, it brings back the hurt."

I couldn't think of a thing to say that would help her. Wishing I were there to put my arms around her, I prayed silently, *Lord, please give me Your words to comfort her.*

She continued, "And all this stuff about how it will be a comfort for someone else someday doesn't help me *now*." She told me she had asked God to send her someone who had lost a baby and could understand her loss. "Most people think I should be over it, but it was my baby—it was a *real* baby to me."

Most of her friends were sympathetic; a few reacted shallowly: "Oh, you'll have more," as though it shouldn't mean much, but it had meant a lot to her. I could feel her pain, and I prayed again for the right words.

Not knowing anyone close who had experienced a miscarriage, I didn't know how to respond except to tell her we loved her; her dad and I were sorry, and we were praying for her.

My words seemed inadequate. Then I shared how disappointed we were when all our friends were having babies, and her dad and I were unable to conceive. Eight years later, we became adoptive parents. "It was worth the wait. God picked our kids better than we ever could."

She didn't seem to hear. She sighed and then recited her favorite childhood verse:

> *"Have faith in God."*
> (Mark 11:22, NKJV)

"It was so easy to believe when I was young; the faith was just there." She lamented her lack of faith now and then started to cry. My heart ached for her; I began praying out loud *that God would put His arms around her, comfort her and send someone who could understand her loss...*

Then I thought of my father, who died of lung cancer fourteen years earlier, and how my mother felt that God was unfair. God had told her to "pour out her anger at His feet." I shared that with my daughter and the verses God gave me when her grandpa was ill.

> *"Though He causes grief, yet He will show compassion*
> *according to the multitude of His mercies. For He does not*
> *afflict willingly, nor grieve the children of men."*
> (Lamentations 3:32–33, NKJV)

"Grandpa committed his life to the Lord during that time, and because of that, we will see him again. Grandma felt that God was unfair; I believed He was compassionate. Who's right? It was the same incident, yet two different opinions of God. This I know: until we are willing to accept our circumstances, we are unable to receive the comfort God has for us, nor can we understand His ways. Life is hard, and sometimes it seems unfair. But His comfort can ease our pain. His strength can see us through when we 'have faith in God.'"

As we continued to talk, my daughter sounded more peaceful, more accepting of what had happened. Then she offered a welcome insight, "Mom, God answered your prayer. You prayed He would send someone—He did; He sent me you!"

Thank you, Lord. Thank you for speaking through me,
for giving me the words to comfort her. I don't have the
words or the wisdom, but YOU always do!

Within months she was expecting again, and God blessed them with a beautiful, healthy baby boy.

God will speak through us and give us the words to say if we ask. He tells us to be "prepared," walking close to the Lord, so when a need arises, we need to take a few moments and ask the Holy Spirit to speak through us. He will. He promises that—

"The preparations of the heart belong to man, but the an-
swer of the tongue is from the Lord."
(Proverbs 16:1, NKJV)

"And He said to me, 'My grace is sufficient for you,
for My strength is made perfect in weakness.'"
(2 Corinthians 12:9, NKJV)

"Therefore most gladly I will rather boast in my
infirmities, that the power of Christ may rest upon me.
Therefore I take pleasure in infirmities, in reproaches,
in needs, in persecutions, in distresses, for Christ's sake.
For when I am weak, then I am strong."
(2 Corinthians 12:9–10, NKJV)

11. My Infirmities

A mid-life crisis uncovered several weaknesses in me that were hidden under the surface for years. I had a vague awareness of them, but I didn't realize how much they hindered me from God's best until He forced me to look at them square in the face.

I can still see the scene and remember the fear that overwhelmed me as I approached the school I was assigned to work in that day. I wanted desperately to turn the car around and go home; instead, I cried out, "Lord! Please deliver me from this..."

Why were these things happening? I experienced them at work, in church, during meetings—anywhere I was resigned to one place. I tried everything I could think of to make them go away: I persevered in prayer, asked others to pray for me, fasted (once for three days!), resisted the enemy as the Lord teaches in James 4:7, reluctantly took medication—but nothing worked. The harder I tried, the worse it got. Desperation often gives way to faith because I heard Him speak on my way to work that morning:

> "I don't want to deliver you *out* of it because
> I have many things to teach you *in* it."

His words brought little comfort that day. I went into work terrified, but at least I knew He was in it—somewhere.

God was waiting for me to run out of my ideas, and when I stopped trying and started listening, He spoke. My first lesson was to accept the fact that it was God who had brought me into this trial, and the quickest way out was to cooperate with Him, no matter how long it took or what it took from me.

> *"You brought us into the net; You laid affliction*
> *on our backs. You have caused men to ride over our*
> *heads; we went through fire and through water;*
> *but You brought us out to rich fulfillment."*
> (Psalm 66:11–12, NKJV)

Did you read that? "Rich fulfillment!" The enemy said that God had forgotten me and that I'd never get out of this, but the enemy is a liar. The truth was that God wanted to deliver me from some of the bondages of the past that contributed to my fears, and knowledge is the first step to freedom.

"And you shall know the truth,
and the truth shall make you free."
(John 8:32, NKJV)

The second lesson was to:

"Be still, and know that I am God;"
(Psalm 46:10, NKJV)

"Rest in the Lord, and wait patiently for Him;"
(Psalm 37:7, NKJV)

I was being schooled in "being still" and "learning to wait." I resisted when everything progressed at an excruciatingly slow pace. I soon learned God was not in a hurry while He was...

"...working in you what is well pleasing
in His sight, through Jesus Christ..."
(Hebrews 13:21, NKJV)

But the work *did* progress. My first "assignment" was to reduce my stress-load and rest. I was overly involved in church activities; my husband was a deacon, and that added to my responsibilities. God was saying I needed time to listen, so I hid away in that "secret place of the Most High...under the shadow of the Almighty" (Psalm 91:1), searching His Word, "He is my refuge and my fortress; my God in Him will I trust" (Psalm 91:2). His Word ministered to me through many verses over the weeks and months to come, but my lifeline was and still is:

*"My grace is sufficient for you, for my strength is made
perfect in weakness. Therefore most gladly I will rather
boast in my infirmities, that the power of Christ may rest
upon me...for when I am weak then I am strong."*
(2 Corinthians 12:9–10, NKJV)

I have repeated those two verses hundreds of times. Experientially, I learned those words are true. But like the children of Israel whose manna fell fresh from heaven but rotted the next day (Exodus 16), our faith fades and must be fresh every morning. There's nothing like a few falls to remind me to seek the Lord before I face my giants because it's His strength I am relying on, not mine.

Running out the door with a quick "Lord, help!" may have its place, but in this case, it didn't cut it. I had to be willing to lay aside *things* that I thought were important and take time to listen, read and repeat scripture, pray and paraphrase His word to fit my infirmities:

"Lord, I lay my weakness at Your feet, and I exchange it for Your strength. Your grace is more than enough for me. You said Your strength shows up best in weak people—that's me Lord—weak! But I'm not trusting in me, Jesus, *I am trusting in You*, and when I take that step of faith, I believe that the power of Christ *will* rest upon me, and I *will* be strong in You, just like You promised. Thank you, Father, for Your faithfulness..."

Deliverance was a process happening and a promise waiting. After dwelling many weeks "taking refuge under His wings" (Psalm 91:4), praying fervently, I stepped out in faith—somewhat wobbly—while repeating my verse emphatically: "Your grace *is* sufficient for me; Your strength *is* made perfect in weakness..." as I waited in faith for "the power of Christ to rest upon me" (2 Corinthians 12:9). I didn't feel strong, nor did I feel His presence, but when I got to wherever I was going, the fear subsided—at least enough to deal with it.

If I looked at the circumstances and anticipated what might happen—I would start to sink like Peter did when he took his eyes off Jesus and looked at the wind and the waves (Matthew 14:24–31).

"And immediately Jesus stretched out His hand
and caught him, and said to him, 'O you of little faith,
why did you doubt?'"
(Matthew 14:31, NKJV)

But even when I succumbed to fear, He caught me and set "little helpers" in place to ease my mind, allowing me to sit it out and not run. God knew what I could do and what I couldn't.

When I received a summons for jury duty, I asked three doctors if they would write an excuse—none would. "Lord, *help!*" No answer. "Okay, Lord, You must know that I can handle this." I prayed fervently, quoted verses, and each night I would call to see if I had to go in. There was not one case in court for the entire time. Not one! I praised the Lord, knowing He was in control and would not give me more than I could handle—and in the process, my faith was tested and tried.

I wanted to sense His presence whenever I went out, but it didn't work that way. I perceived that if I sensed His presence, I wouldn't need faith, so I stepped out trembling but trusting. And through it all, I didn't make a fool of myself like the enemy said I would. Jesus said:

> *"The young lion and the serpent you*
> *shall trample underfoot."*
> (Psalm 91:13, NKJV)

I learned to say, "Get thee behind me, Satan, in the Name of Jesus..." and then drawing near to God, telling Him: "Lord, I know You are faithful and that 'You will never leave me nor forsake me...'" (Hebrews 13:5)

> *"Surely He shall deliver you from the snare of*
> *the fowler...He shall cover you with His feathers,*
> *and under His wings you shall take refuge:"*
> (Psalm 91:3–4, NKJV)

Can you think of a safer and more comforting place than "under His wings?" Little by little, step by step, I learned to trust Jesus more each time I stepped out in faith and found Him faithful. I would tell Him, "Lord, I can't do this. You know I can't, but I'm trusting You to take over..." as I waited for the "power of Christ to rest upon me." And it did just like He promised! I didn't sense His presence as much as I noticed calmness within me. I would tell Him: "Lord, this is a miracle that I am sitting here without being afraid."

"His truth shall be your shield and buckler.
You shall not be afraid of the terror by night,
nor of the arrow that flies by day..."
(Psalm 91:4–5, NKJV)

As my faith grew, I became more confident that God would be there for me each time I stepped out in faith. But I still had to spend time in His presence in order to trust Him.

God allowed me to take a low-dose beta-blocker to keep a lid on the adrenalin. He allowed me to use it, not lean on it. It didn't work unless I was trusting Him. As my faith grew and my insecurities lessened, I rarely needed it, but I will never outgrow my need to rely on the faithfulness of God and His never-failing word.

"Because he has set his love upon Me, therefore I will deliver
him; I will set him on high, because he has known My name.
He shall call upon Me, and I will answer him; I will be with
him in trouble; I will deliver him and honor him, with long
life I will satisfy him, and show him My salvation."
(Psalm 91:14–16, NKJV)

As I continued leaning on His word, God showed me why these "situations" were happening: I was overly concerned with what people thought—or what I thought they thought; I grappled with acceptance, my self-esteem was low. I was passive, overly dependent, fearful, and carried a host of other weaknesses. I had done little to advance the few talents and abilities I possessed. I over-compensated in the spiritual realm and ended up unbalanced.

When I began seeing the truth in what God was showing me, I told Him, "Lord, I don't want to be a people-pleaser. I want to be a God-pleaser!" But I wondered, *How will I ever change?* God said, "Let *Me* change you."

I liked being in control, so God and I went round and round many times. But thankfully, He won every time. I was learning the hard way that His way was the best way, and I don't need to be in control. Slowly, He pushed, encouraged, corrected, and taught me to lean on Him instead of myself. I thank God that He didn't let me go and that my faith grew stronger as His love pursued me through the rough times.

"Not my way but Yahweh!"

"The lines have fallen unto me in pleasant places;
yea, I have a goodly heritage."
(Psalm 16:6, KJV)

12. Who Will Go First?

When I was growing up, I frequently boasted to my friends, "My parents have the perfect marriage." It was truly a made-in-heaven kind. As kids, we never grew tired of hearing stories of their early years—they had little money but lots of love. As I grew older, I was in awe of how they never argued, how well they communicated, and how much they enjoyed being together. It was no wonder I wanted to find a man like my father, get married, and live happily ever after.

By the third year of our marriage, I knew my dreams weren't even close to coming true; we argued about everything. I thought our problems were Keith's fault, and he thought they were mine. Looking back on our condition, I believe however much our spouse needs changing, that's about how much we need to change as well—because we tend to choose a mate with about the same maturity level as ourselves.

Will Rogers said, "Everybody is ignorant, only on different subjects;" it is my conviction we are all immature, only in different areas. But those areas we've made excuses for, defended, and learned to live with don't seem as bad as our spouse's immature areas.

The end of the third year of marriage, we went to a counselor twice; he said we had to learn to accept each other. We stopped arguing, but we didn't have a meaningful conversation.

During the eighth year of marriage, we committed our lives to the Lord, adopted our son, and two years later adopted our daughter. We got along well as a family. In my pursuit of God, I did much to widen the gap between us. It was sometime later that I discovered what God meant when He said,

> *"She who is married cares about the things of the world—*
> *how she may please her husband."*
> (1 Corinthians 7:34, NKJV)

I had mistakenly thought that "the things of the world" were synonymous with "worldly things" and should be avoided. But God says we should care for the *practical* things of the world if we have chosen the married life. I had totally ignored practical things, and marriage, I have learned, is *terribly* practical.

About that time, God started shaking the foundations of our marriage. I was praying about our marriage one day when God startled me with the thought: "I will change your marriage if you allow Me to change you first."

I was pondering what that meant when I heard Him continue, "Listen to your husband's complaints."

"*Ouch!*" God knows how to make it hurt. For years I'd heard my husband's complaints: I didn't encourage him, I wasn't observant, had too few interests, too religious, indecisive, overly-dependent, prudish, and...*Oh, help!*

If I had agreed Keith was right, my fragile self-image would have plummeted even lower, so I either defended myself or ignored his complaints. But this was God talking, and my way wasn't working, so what other option did I have?

> *"And you shall know the truth,*
> *and the truth shall make you free."*
> (John 8:32, NKJV)

The truth may hurt in the beginning, but as I allowed God to extricate me from some of those child-like areas that had plagued me for years—the ones that kept me from really liking myself—my self-esteem slowly began to rise.

God would bring out the area He wanted to work on, usually through circumstances, and if I didn't see it right away, it came back until I did, or until I was willing to pray, "Lord, help me want to change." I still find it amazing how He works in me the "want to." Not the old way of "I should," but the new way that enables me to say, "I really want to!"

> *"For it is God who works in you both to will*
> *and to do for His good pleasure."*
> (Philippians 2:13, NKJV)

Too often, we lean on our own strength instead of leaning on God's—it doesn't work. I had tried to change on my own, failed, and then blamed God for not helping me. He was a patient teacher, but He wasn't about to let me shuffle through until I learned His ways.

Somehow, He got through to me, and I got it! "Lord, I can't change myself, but You can change me, so I'm going to trust (have faith in) You to do it." And He did! I am still amazed at the power of simply believing God. It's called faith, and the Bible says it moves mountains, but for me, some of my "childhood ghosts" disappeared. Not all at once, but through a lot of prayer, faith, and determination to see my problem and then allow God to work on it.

> *"Being confident of this very thing, that He who*
> *has begun a good work in you will complete it*
> *until the day of Jesus Christ;"*
> (Philippians 1:6, NKJV)

Somewhere in the process, my husband and I fell in love again, but this time God was at the helm. The more I allowed God to work in me, He allowed me to speak up and bring my own complaints to the table, except I had to bring them to Keith "in the Spirit." That meant not reacting in the flesh.

I recall one of the first times I stayed "in the Spirit" after bringing a situation to Keith's attention. I prayed inwardly, *Lord, let my words be Your words, help me to stay in the Spirit.* Keith didn't accept what I said, but I didn't react! Feeling so good about it, I said inwardly, *Lord, this is in Your hands, and I trust You.*

Later that day, I was at the kitchen sink, and Keith came up behind me, put his arms around me, and said, "You know I've thought about what you said, and I think you're right." *Gasp!* It was a good thing his arms were around me, or I think I would have exited to the floor.

When I needed to confront Keith about an issue, I prayed for the fruit of "gentleness" in Galatians 5:22. Before long, Keith said things like, "Thanks for not giving up on me." I cried when he said, "You see my problems so much better than I do; you bring out all those things I never think of. You are a real helpmate."

> *"Counsel in the heart of man is like deep water,*
> *but a man of understanding will draw it out."*
> (Proverbs 20:5, NKJV)

I learned that when I stayed "in the Spirit," sooner or later, God worked our situations out. When I didn't, He couldn't— because He wanted to work through me, it was that simple. It wasn't simple to stay in the Spirit; it took time on my knees and a resolve to move beyond the failures. God never condemns us when we fail; instead, He faithfully sets up another test.

"What do you think the Lord is saying to us?" I asked Keith after another unfruitful search for a car. A thought whisked through my mind, *Maybe the Lord is trying to tell me something?* I swept it out. Neither of us came up with a good explanation. During prayer later that day, the same thought came to me. I've learned not to ignore that voice; no matter how faint, it could be God. "Lord, are you trying to tell me something?"

Sometimes wisdom settles in gradually over time. Other times it comes apple-falling fashion. *Ouch, it hit!* I had been criticizing my husband's handling of the negotiations. I labeled it good advice; God called it criticizing. "Lord, I blew it again. Help me to keep my mouth shut!" He did...and we found our car.

There seemed to be no end to the opportunities to learn this lesson. I, who had been the passive/submissive wife for years, now saw my aggressive side emerging.

Our family was on vacation and looking for a restaurant in a busy tourist town. It was late, we were hungry, and the nice restaurants were getting filled. We finally settled around a well-worn, red and white checkered tablecloth, complete with loud guffaws coming from the counter. I wanted to look further, but Keith said emphatically, *"We're staying here!"* I could feel the anger rising in me. It's times like this I have to submit cheerfully, and it takes the Holy Spirit to do it. "Lord," I muttered, "change me; I need your help!" And He did! I am always amazed at how He changes my attitude—the anger is gone, and I feel peace. The atmosphere in the place wasn't the best, but around our checkered table, it was à la special.

God kept His promise. Our marriage was changing as long as I allowed God to change me first. When I complained about always being first, God said it was a privilege. He reminded me that He came to me—just as I was—*first!*

> *"God demonstrates His own love toward us, in that*
> *while we were still sinners, Christ died for us."*
> (Romans 5:8, NKJV)

Being first was my opportunity to let God's love flow through me and touch my husband. In time, it did. Keith not only began loving me more—he reached out to God because the love he felt coming through me was God's love.

The Lord needs just one person to start the process. Whoever is willing to change, to be first, He will use that one to begin making that made-in-heaven kind of marriage.

Will you be that one?

"For we walk by faith, not by sight."
(2 Corinthians 5:7, NKJV)

13. Keep Believing

It was Saturday night, and my husband and I were going to review our lesson for the adult Sunday school class we were leading when Keith (a teacher) discovered he had forgotten to bring home the lesson materials he had taken to school the day before, and, he had given his keys to his assistant who was coming in to work over the weekend. We called her, but there was no answer.

We were standing outside the school, pounding on the door, asking God to send a custodian walking by. None came. We prayed again and waited...after several more tries, Keith said, "Let's go." I banged a little louder, prayed a little harder...then reluctantly followed him to the car. As I opened the car door, I heard that taunting voice, *"God didn't hear your prayers."* The enemy wants us to doubt, but God wants us to trust Him.

I was leading a women's group at the time, and we were discussing a chapter in the book entitled *Putting Things in God's Hands and Leaving Them There.* I thought this was a good time to test my faith, so inwardly, I said, *Lord, I don't understand, but I am going to trust You; maybe You have something else in mind for our class.*

"Above all, taking the shield of faith with which you will be
able to quench all the fiery darts of the wicked one."
(Ephesians 6:16, NKJV)

We started driving home when a case of indigestion nearly doubled me over. My husband suggested getting an antacid at the store near the school; I quickly agreed. We drove down the lane looking for a place to park when walking in front of us was Keith's assistant—*and* she had the keys with her! We praised the Lord, drove back to school, and picked up our materials.

The indigestion? It left as mysteriously as it came. Proving again that no matter what the situation looks like, no matter how serious or how mundane, God is in it. And when we refuse to doubt, God honors it.

It is just as easy to choose to believe as it is to decide to doubt. For all the times I've doubted, I received nothing.

"But let him ask in faith, with no doubting,
for he who doubts is like a wave of the sea driven
and tossed by the wind. For let not that man suppose
that he will receive anything from the Lord;"
(James 1:6–7, NKJV)

Does God always answer like that? Yes and no. Not always that dramatically. Sometimes He thinks Plan B is better. That, too, takes faith, especially when we have set our hearts on Plan A. It's not easy to keep believing; it takes effort to kick out the doubts when our faith is being stretched. Whether it's Plan

A, B or Z, when we trust God, we win. He isn't going to let us have something that He knows isn't good for us or when He has something better in mind.

> *"Now this is the confidence that we have in Him, that if we ask anything according to His will, He hears us. And if we know that He hears us, whatever we ask, we know that we have the petitions that we have asked of Him."*
> (1 John 5:14–15, NKJV)

"According to His will" is our safeguard!

The next week our group was still studying the chapter "Leaving Things in God's Hands," and I was trying unsuccessfully to get the contractor we hired to replace several cracked tiles he had installed in the basement ceiling. I prayed, called him several times, and even threatened him with "further action," which I had no idea what that would be. So, when all else failed, I put it in God's hands and told Him I was trusting Him to do what I couldn't.

The next morning, I felt led to call the contractor one more time, but to take a different tact: "Lord," I prayed, "I'm trusting You to give me the words."

"Good morning, Mr. _____. How are you today? He mumbled something. "I was reading your estimate, and it said your work was guaranteed. I believe you are a man of your word and..." he interrupted me and said he would be over at six pm that night. "Praise You, Lord," I didn't know it would be that easy. Six o'clock came and went that night, and no contractor. Now what? I could listen to all those voices in my head demanding attention, or I could "fight the good fight of faith" (1 Timothy 6:12, NKJV). I decided to fight!

I picked up that "shield of faith" and told the enemy (like Jesus did), "Get behind me, Satan! You are an offense to me" (Matthew 16:23, NKJV).

I told Jesus I was still trusting Him and

- Refused to ruminate on the situation.
- Affirmed it was still in God's hands.
- Continued to tell Jesus, "I trust You, Lord, I trust You..."

Perhaps I didn't hear the contractor correctly because he came at six p.m. the next night and cheerfully replaced the broken tiles. Even so, my faith was stretched. It took God two days to do what I couldn't do in thirty.

So, what do you have in your hand that should be in His? He's waiting to do what you can't. And when He does it, He gets all the glory—where it belongs.

Go ahead, take that step of faith *now!*

"I will give you the treasures of darkness and hidden riches of secret places, that you may know that I, the Lord, who call you by your name, am the God of Israel."
(Isaiah 45:3, NKJV)

14. Treasures of Darkness

I was wrong. I misinterpreted the guidance I received on my way to work several weeks into the job. I was praying desperately for strength that morning when God's peace filled the car, and I arrived at work with new confidence, assuming it was confirmation that everything would work out—even though the job was way over my head. It did work out for a day or so, but it didn't last.

The job's stress factor was out of control: huge red blotches appeared everywhere on my body except my hands and face—even on the soles of my feet. Soon after retiring for the night, my legs started aching, my body started itching, and I spent the remainder of the night on the couch so I wouldn't keep my husband awake.

Nothing helped. Not prayer, fasting, medications, or even tranquilizers. It was either "quit or be let go," my boss nicely informed me. I quit. Then I became a red-blotchy, legs-aching, depressed and confused Christian without a job. My self-esteem plummeted. I couldn't understand why God was allowing this.

While I was looking for answers, the Lord kept telling me to accept the situation. But I didn't want to accept it; *I wanted it changed!* Depression deepened. When I finally got tired of being miserable, I yielded. I'm so glad God didn't let me go until He got what He wanted from me.

I've never won an argument with God—thankfully. If I knew what God had in mind, I wouldn't want to, but that's where faith comes in. My husband says I must be from Missouri—because I ask a lot of questions. I want all the details. But God doesn't have to give me details, nor does He have to answer my questions. Most of the time, He says: "Trust Me," *period!* He seldom answers right away—but His timing is perfect. I have had to learn this, and it hasn't been easy.

I told Him I accepted the job failure, the misguidance, the aching legs, and even the blotches. And then an amazing thing happened: that night, I slept *all* night long. I got up the next morning, opened up Charles Stanley's booklet, *God's Power through Prayer*, and the first thing I read was:

> *"I will give you the treasures of darkness and hidden riches*
> *of secret places, that you may know that I, the Lord, who*
> *call you by your name am the God of Israel."*
> (Isaiah 45:3, NKJV)

"Treasures of darkness?" I didn't know "darkness" held treasures, but I found them after I accepted my situation just as it

was: the Lord healed my legs, gave me peace for my mind, and wisdom (through my mother's advice) to heal the blotches. And the peace that morning in the car was His assurance that He was in control.

The greatest blessing came as He led me in a new direction to pursue a field I loved, one that fit my talents and abilities. Only God could've seen those "hidden riches" in me. Going back to school had crossed my mind several times, but I didn't act on it. God had to convince me to get moving.

Looking back, I could see how God was trying to get my attention. I was working as a temp in Special Ed in a school district and hoping to find a permanent job. Three times I had been given assurance I would be hired as an assistant, and three times the job offer fell through. I told the Lord how upset I was, and I heard Him say, "The employment office is not in control of your life; I AM!" Of course, what was I thinking? Jesus is the "Door."

> *"He who has the key of David, He who opens and*
> *no one shuts, and shuts and no one opens."*
> (Revelations 3:7, NKJV)

I had taken a *Strong Interest Test* and registered high in four fields, but I didn't pursue any of them. Instead, I continued to work as a temp until I went to work for an attorney as an "ill-fated" assistant.

Have you noticed that God sometimes has to push us into uncomfortable circumstances to get our attention? I'm so glad He doesn't let us settle for little when He desires to give us much more. Like young birds ready to come out of their nest but desperately trying to stay in it, God lovingly kicks us out, convincing us that we can fly higher and farther than we dreamed.

A few months after I started school, things weren't going well, and I wondered if I had made a mistake. Believing God had led me there, I decided to stick it out. I am sooooooo glad I did because I am seeing God's "treasures" and experiencing His "hidden riches." Although the money is considerably less, I absolutely love what I am doing.

Why do I think that when I am following God, everything has to work out perfectly? It doesn't. Even in my field of choice, I need perseverance, determination to learn, and continued trust in God.

We don't always understand what God is up to; Peter questioned Jesus when He began to wash His feet, and Jesus answered him,

> *"What I am doing you do not understand now,*
> *but you will know after this."*
> (John 13:7, NKJV)

And so will we if we accept what is happening and decide to trust God. He has treasures for us in whatever darkness we find ourselves. The more we trust Him, the greater our faith will be. The greater our faith, the more we will see Him work wonders in our lives.

Are you in darkness today? Take the time to listen to what God is saying...

"Therefore do not cast away your confidence,
which has great reward. For you have need of endurance, so
that after you have done the will of God,
you may receive the promise."
(Hebrews 10:35–36, NKJV)

"He has put a new song in my mouth—praise to our God;
many will see it and fear, and will trust in the Lord."
(Psalm 40:3, NKJV)

15. The Message of Christmas: God's Love

Christmas Eve found the family sitting around the kitchen table singing Christmas Carols—an annual tradition at our parent's home. Except for this year, it was far from the idyllic picture of yesteryear: some were talking, one was singing in an irreverent way, and I was getting angry at the whole situation.

I had committed my life to the Lord several months earlier, and this Christmas had taken on a deeper meaning, but the atmosphere around the table was hardly conducive to meaningful singing. I decided to get up, throw my songbook on the table, and march into the living room. As I started to rise, I heard: *"Sit down, and you sing to Me!"*

I sat down and started to sing; the words of the old familiar carol took on a profound newness as I sang to the Lord, and before long, I looked around, and everyone was singing along.

It was the first of many lessons I needed to learn about showing God's love to my family—and in time, they wanted to know more about this Jesus who had "put a new song in my mouth" (Psalm 40:3).

We lived about four hours from our hometown; my husband was a teacher and was off at the same time as our kids, so we were able to spend a lot of time with our families. We were at my family get-together a few weeks later when someone suggested playing a game that I didn't feel comfortable with, and I asked the Lord silently, *What do I do?* I didn't hear anything. Just then, another family member (the one I thought would be the least likely to object) said he didn't want to play it, and the game was forgotten.

"Wow, God, You can do anything!"

I have heard Christians criticize their family for their beliefs, their actions, what their church teaches, and then wonder why they do not want to hear about Jesus. I'm not saying we shouldn't stand up for what we believe, but the Lord impressed on me how important it is to stand up in His love.

Whenever I would talk to one of my sisters about salvation, she said that the church we had grown up in was enough for salvation, quoting one of the few verses we had learned. The Lord cautioned me not to criticize anyone's church because they will just defend it.

"Be swift to hear, slow to speak..." warns James, 1:19 (NKJV).

"Listen to them carefully..." He would remind me. "Tell them what I have done for you." As I listened, I prayed that the Lord would give me the words to say. His word promises wisdom, if we ask.

"If any of you lacks wisdom, let Him ask of God,
who gives to all liberally and without reproach,
and it will be given to him."
(James 1:5, NKJV)

So, when the same sister showed me a book that held all the answers to the world's problems—it preached love and being good, but not the cross, I asked her, "If being good is all we need, why did Jesus have to suffer on the cross?" Surprisingly, she agreed.

I was sharing with my other sister, the nurse, how God had healed my broken toe. I had stubbed it on a chair leg during the night, and by morning it was swollen, black, with a red ring around it, and the pain was shooting up my leg. Keith was on the phone trying to find a doctor on Saturday—this was before emergency rooms—when God told me to step on it. I did, and when my foot hit the floor, it was healed. I was dancing around the kitchen as Keith looked at me with his mouth open.

My sister said it was probably out of joint, and when I stepped on it, it slipped into place. I know the Lord gave me the answer when I responded, "Maybe so, but it was the Lord who told me to put my foot down."

"The preparations of the heart belongs to man,
but the answer of the tongue is from the Lord."
(Proverbs 16:1, NKJV)

My niece paged through a book on astrology, telling me how it promised peace, fulfillment, and successful life. I listened—praying for the right words—as she related chapter after chapter. Nothing came, so I kept listening. When she finished, I said, "It sounds good, but does it work?" She thought for a few seconds and said, "No." I told her I had found something that *did* work and shared with her some of the things Jesus was doing in my life. She listened but didn't ask any questions.

Not everything turned out positive. I listened to another niece expound on the theories of Karl Marx. I said nothing, and nothing came to me. I recalled an author/mentor who had written: "If God isn't saying anything, that makes two of us."

In time, most of my family turned their lives over to the Lord—it was contagious. There were some holdouts. My grandmother told my mother to tell me she didn't want to hear about religion—that is, until the day my sister came to visit her and found her on the floor, called for help, and led her to the Lord.

My father was a good man, the best I have ever known. Everything He put his hand to worked out well. He believed in God and gave generously to the church but never felt He had a need for anything more—until cancer came to stay. Then he listened; sometime later, my husband led him in the prayer of salvation.

My brother buried two wives; both of them were led to Jesus shortly before they died. He, too, told my mother to tell me not to talk about God to him. With two wives waiting for him in heaven, I don't think he has a chance!

Years later, he was in the hospital undergoing a serious test. He told me over the phone he was worried, and I asked him if I could pray for him. He said, "Yes." I prayed; then I asked him if he remembered the twenty-third Psalm, I started saying it, and he joined in. Afterward, he said he had felt a touch on his neck, felt peaceful, and wasn't going to worry about the test anymore. It turned out negative.

Sometimes God calls us to plant, sometimes to water, and other times to reap, but always He calls us to love.

> *"Love suffers long and is kind...does not behave rudely,*
> *does not seek its own, is not provoked...bears all things...*
> *endures all things... Love never fails."*
> (1 Corinthians 13:4–8, NKJV)

"You will keep him in perfect peace, whose mind is stayed on You, because he trusts in You."
on You, because he trusts in You."
(Isaiah 26:3, NKJV)

16. Let Go and Let God

The new millennium, amidst all the controversy, arrived and survived without a glitch. My own experience was quite different: it started out quietly enough, but the year ended in disaster. What happened?

Growing up, we were a close family. We knew families who were estranged for one reason or another, but we were confident it would never happen to us. *But it did!*

It was an avalanche of accusations and misunderstandings between my two sisters that turned it into a major conflict. For several years I tried to put out fires with prayer and reason, some successful, some not so, but in the end, my intervention only exacerbated the situation and nearly leveled it.

We were at our mother's house dividing up the estate when yet another controversy arose. In my attempts to calm the storm—and not being successful—I, the peacemaker, totally lost it.

Hoping to put the family problems behind me, I was looking forward to getting away with my husband on our annual

December trip to Arizona, visiting our daughter and family. I buried myself in Christmas activities, but I couldn't relax; I had a burning in my chest that several over-the-counter meds didn't help. In fact, it got worse. A trip to the emergency room, some tests, and a couple of prescriptions didn't alleviate the growing discomfort in my chest.

We resumed holiday activities while the anxiety continued to rise and the burning increased. Back to the emergency room—this visit lasted three days with many more tests and still no answers. We prayed, but either God was silent, or I couldn't hear Him. Keith blamed it on the problems at home; I wasn't sure. We cut our vacation short and returned home.

I prayed, "Lord, show me what You're saying in this..." I thought I heard God say "rest," so I took off work for the remainder of January and rested. I wrote my sisters and apologized for my outburst, yet I continued to replay the scenarios of the past year over and over in my mind, unable to deal with the mixture of anger and grief I felt over the split in our family.

Then one cold February morning, God spoke, and my heart was warmed. I was in church half watching an excerpt from a *Time-Out for Women's Seminar* when I heard these words from one of the women: "Let go and let God..."

That's what I need to do!

It suddenly sounded so simple: *let go and let God!* Inwardly I let it go. Immediately, I felt a measure of peace which continued to grow in the days ahead.

The temptation to ruminate on the family situation knocked frequently on the door of my mind, but after all that I had gone through, there was no way I was going to let it in. I resisted every thought with an emphatic prayer,

"Lord, I am trusting You! I am not taking this out of
Your hands. I'm letting You take care of it..."

The Lord told me to stop blaming myself. *I should have said
this*, or *I should have done that*, as if it all depended on me. I had
to accept it just the way it was. That was the hardest part. I
wanted so badly to see our family healed and back together, just
like old times. But if I wanted to know peace, I had to continue
to "let go and let God."

Putting things in God's hands was a lesson I had learned
and practiced in many situations, but that Sunday morning in
church, when I heard God speak, I realized I wasn't trusting
Him at all in this one.

Most situations change after I put them in His hands and
leave them there, this one has not, but I am learning to keep my
mind focused clearly on Jesus—that's where I find that "perfect
peace" God promises us—not in the absence of problems but
right in their midst. I no longer worry about it, replay it in my
mind, feel anger, or try to work it out. I'm not doing anything
unless God tells me to.

*"You will keep him in perfect peace, whose mind is stayed
on You, because he trusts in You."*
(Isaiah 26:3, NKJV)

Is there something in your hands right now, something
that's robbing you of peace? Something you can't control but
keep trying? Put it in God's hands now, and when it comes back

to your mind—*and it will*—don't accept it. Tell Him, "Lord, I'm trusting You to take care of it; I can't." He may tell you to do something. If not, then...

"Let go and let God..."

Update:

One beautiful Easter morning, several years later, my husband and I were in church with my sister and her family in our hometown. After the service, we ran into our estranged sister and her family in the foyer (they always attended the first service, but not that day). They inquired about Keith's recent surgery, and after some small talk, I felt I had to say something before we parted. I walked around our family circle to my other sister, put my arms around her, and said, "If you and your family would come to the family picnic, it would absolutely make my year!" The whole family came. One of my nieces called it "our Easter miracle." Glory to God, He resurrected our family. It is now as though it never happened!

A million thank-yous to You, Jesus!!!

"My son...was lost and is found."
(Luke 15:24, NKJV)

17. Persevering Hope

How many prayers?
How many tears?
How many hopes?
How many years?

Hoping to receive divine wisdom concerning our son, we stopped on our way home from vacationing out East at a church, supposedly experiencing a "move of God." It was a huge disappointment! After much prayer and a variety of unpleasant circumstances, we both sensed God was saying, "You won't find what you're looking for here, go home and put your house together."

We left a couple of days earlier than planned, confused and wondering what God meant. Each mile closer to home made me more depressed. I felt like God had let us down. I voiced my thoughts to Keith in a loud un-Christ-like manner. Keith didn't agree; he accepts things much better than I. He tried reasoning with me, but I was listening to no one—except maybe the enemy.

I had been down this "road" before. I knew if I wanted any peace, I'd have to change my attitude and ask God to forgive me. It took several miles to muster the prayer:

Lord, help me to want to give up my anger. Work in me.

After some time, and in ways I never understand, I sensed a shift in my thinking; I wanted to change my attitude. I asked God to forgive my childish outburst, my unbelief, and then I put my disappointment in His hands, telling Him I trusted Him. God changed me from the inside out just like He promised:

> *"For it is God who works in you both to will*
> *and to do for His good pleasure."*
> (Philippians 2:13, NKJV)

For years I tried to change myself and failed until I began to believe the above verse—that God works *in* me, and only *then* can I "work it out."

> *"...work out your own salvation with fear and trembling;"*
> (Philippians, 2:12 NKJV)

Looking back, I was putting way too much hope on circumstances *I* had mapped out. It had taken over a couple of hours to find the church. The directions we received from several sources were extremely confusing. I had said to Keith, "Either God doesn't want us to find this church or the devil is trying to keep us away."

Less than an hour after we arrived back home, a call from the ER informed us our son had been in an accident. Three days later, we learned that he had struck a car while trying to pass, flipped his car over on the driver's side, skidded down the road, and hit another car. But while he was skidding, he told us later, "God came into the car and reclaimed me."

You might be thinking it's been smooth sailing since then. I have learned that "happily ever after" exists only in fairy tales and other people's books. We contended with many unrelenting problems as our son vacillated and eventually walked away from his commitment.

During this time, Keith and I were *forced* to stay close to the Lord, spending many hours praying and trusting God. We finally buried that *"I wish I'd done things differently"* syndrome, accepting the fact we did the best we could. We cannot alter the past, but God isn't restricted by the past. He is the God of the *Now!*

Yes, there were some things we had to change—not concerning parenting but our lives in general, things that kept us from committing our lives totally to the Lord. But today, we are holding on to His promises; I am confident there will be another devotional to write someday.

> *"Thus says the Lord: Refrain your voice from weeping, and your eyes from tears; for your work shall be rewarded, says the Lord, and they shall come back from the land of the enemy. There is hope in your future, says the Lord, that your children will come back to their own border."*
> (Jeremiah 31:16–17, NKJV)

I believe God's word. If you're walking in shoes like ours, I encourage you to believe it too!

*"Be anxious for nothing, but in everything by prayer
and supplication, with thanksgiving, let your requests be
made known to God; and the peace of God, which surpasses
all understanding, will guard your hearts and minds
through Christ Jesus.*
(Philippians 4:6–7, NKJV)

18. Be Anxious for Nothing

Four weeks after surgery and wondering why my foot was still swollen, the words from the above verse came to mind. *Be anxious for nothing...*"But Lord," I countered, "I'm not anxious, I'm just concerned—"

He interrupted, "Then be concerned for nothing!" I got it! I was using a euphemism to describe my worrying. I confessed my unbelief and handed over my, uh, "concerns."

Five weeks after surgery, that verse came to me again. I had taken my foot back.

"Lord, teach me what it means to be 'anxious for nothing.' I want to live out that verse every day of my life!"

Tired of worrying about my health, I said it slowly and with conviction. After engaging in some dialogue with Jesus, I was convinced He was using this situation to put some depth into that verse.

When God says "be anxious for nothing," it's because He is in control, and we don't have to be anxious about anything. (I know that, I just don't always know it.) Having everything in His hands doesn't mean—like we sometimes think and pray for—that everything will go beautifully, perfectly, and quickly. Occasionally it does, but for all those times it doesn't, God has some walking-in-faith lessons He wants to teach us.

I was talking to the Lord about trusting Him in these situations, and a question rose up:

"Do you want to be Carole the Worrier
or Carole the Warrior?"

"Lord, I want to be a Warrior! I want to 'fight the good fight of faith.' I want to 'take the shield of faith and quench all the fiery darts of the wicked one' (from 1 Timothy 6:12 and Ephesians 6:16). I want to trust You in everything and 'be anxious for nothing' (Philippians 4:6). Lord, work that in me no matter what it takes."

In the beginning, when I allowed my worries to remain too long, I asked the Lord to forgive me; then, I began kicking my concerns out sooner. I told Him to keep working in me until I learned. He did!

Eight weeks after surgery, and I'm not worrying, nor am I concerned about my foot. Doubts continue to sneak in, but I keep asserting,

"Lord, I am trusting You. I don't know what's
keeping my foot swollen, the doctors don't know,
but You know, Lord, and I believe You are using it
to teach me to 'be anxious for nothing.' Thank You,
Lord. I don't know how long it will take, but I
want to trade my anxiety for Your peace..."

I have no serious health issues, but even the small stuff left unchecked in my mind can give the enemy a chance to blow it out of proportion, take aim, and bring me down.

Ten weeks and nothing has changed. God seems silent. In the past, I would have questioned Him, but I've learned that His silence sometimes speaks louder than His words. If He isn't saying anything, everything must be okay. My foot is in His hands, and I am trusting Him.

Above my desk, I have a sign: "Half of being smart is knowing what you're dumb at." My unwritten version reads: "Half of being strong is knowing what you're weak at." And worrying about my health is a major weakness. Thank God He is changing that!

Have you noticed that when you've passed a few heavenly *tests* things begin to change? During prayer, I feel impressed to soak my foot in an old-fashioned recipe my mother suggested—and it helped! Soon I was comfortable in something besides sneakers. "Thank You, Jesus!"

Looking back and trying to understand when and why my health fears started, I recalled the day I went back to work after major surgery. I had taken a couple of aspirins for pain, and within minutes, I felt like I was going to pass out. Unknowingly, I had an infection from the surgery, and a week or so later, I learned I was allergic to the antibiotics. The fear of pills was ingrained into my thinking patterns, compounded by the fact my temperament is given to fears. From pills it evolved into health problems in general. I wasn't a Christian then, so I easily succumbed to fear. I was a captive. But God sent Jesus...

"...to proclaim liberty to the captives..."
(Luke 4:18, NKJV)

After all those years, having a taste of not worrying about my health feels wonderfully freeing, yet I know there will be more health situations to overcome because "being anxious for nothing" isn't easily learned by an inveterate worrier like me. But I will learn! I am repeating His words until they become part of me, such as:

"For God has not given us a spirit of fear,
but of power and of love and of a sound mind."
(2 Timothy 1:7, NKJV)

"You did not receive the spirit of bondage again to fear,
but you received the Spirit of adoption by whom
we cry out, 'Abba, Father.'"
(Romans 8:15, NKJV)

The enemy wants to keep us in bondage through fear, but when God our Father adopted us, He broke that bondage. We need to know it, believe it, and act on it!

Our God is in control of all things that touch our lives: every situation, every problem, every sickness, every trouble, and every-thing!

> *"And we know that all things work together for good to those who love God...For whom He foreknew, He also predestined to be conformed to the image of His Son..."*
> (Romans 8:28–29, NKJV)

The above verses are of great comfort, knowing that He planned every situation so that we could be more like Jesus as we work on our weaknesses. Our situations are not just haphazard—though we may not always sense God's presence—He is still there! If we always sensed His presence, we wouldn't need faith—now, would we? And if everything went well, we wouldn't need Jesus. God is looking for people who trust Him when we can't see; we still believe when we can't feel, and when God doesn't answer prayer, we wait on the Lord—and our faith grows stronger, our peace is greater, and our relationship with Jesus deepens.

So, when a fear of pills or a health problem comes to me, I may feel some trepidation in the beginning—then I realize I can't handle it, but He can, and I lay my fears at His feet.

> *"and the peace of God, which surpasses all understanding, will guard your hearts and minds through Christ Jesus."*
> (Philippians 4:7, NKJV)

"Wives, likewise, be submissive to your own husbands, that even if some do not obey the word, they, without a word, may be won by the conduct of their wives.…let it be the hidden person of the heart, with the incorruptible beauty of a gentle and quiet spirit, which is very precious in the sight of God."
(1 Peter 3:1 and 4, NKJV)

19. A New Perspective on an Old Situation

I have a friend whom I admire in many ways. She faithfully meets with the Lord every day. She is by nature dove-like, sweet and gentle. She is also passive. My friend is waiting for the above verses to become a reality; she's been living it for years, and nothing has changed. I've seen it work for other wives; why not her?

What if God has something else in mind? What if He has another principle working when things aren't going the way we think they should? Maybe we should ask ourselves why we keep doing the same old thing, hoping the result will be different.

Benjamin Franklin said, "The definition of insanity is doing the same thing over and over, expecting different results."

Are we too close to the problem to see the solution? Perhaps a new perspective on an old situation holds the answer we seek.

"Help us to think 'out of the box' today, Lord.
Open our minds to think Your thoughts. Lord, You
said we have 'the mind of Christ' (1 Corinthians 2:16);
help us to believe it and use it!"

It was my goal to have a great marriage. I thought one way to accomplish it was to "be submissive to my husband" (1 Peter 3:1). I was passive, so it wasn't too difficult to submit—except it wasn't working. I found myself loving my husband less, not more.

I recall an overwhelming impulse to throw what I had in my hand at Keith during a heated discussion on an out-of-town trip. Usually, I backed down, but this issue was important to me, so I desperately tried to contain myself—and managed to do so—but I still felt anger and resentment within. That is what I thought submission was: restraining myself from the act, even though my inner feelings (heart) had not changed, nor did any good come out of the situation. Then God gave me a whole new perspective on submission.

Man's way is to suppress the outward, hoping to change the inward. It doesn't work. God's way works: He remakes us from the inside, so we find ourselves wanting to do what we made ourselves do before. When we do it our way—by suppressing the outward—we invariably take some of the credit. God's way gives Him all the glory where it belongs. We need to believe that He will do what He says He will do—

> *"For it is God who works in us both to will*
> *and to do for His good pleasure."*
> (Philippians 2:13, NKJV)

I prayed, "Lord, work in me to will and to do..." And He did, but it wasn't easy changing a lifetime of passive behavior. But first, I had to see my pseudo-submissiveness was not from God. Rather, it was a weakness I hid behind. My first step was to read several books on assertiveness, pray much, and take some baby steps in faith.

"Speak up. Tell Keith how you really feel," God said. I was afraid Keith wouldn't understand. I was right; he didn't. God would say, "Tell him anyway." I learned to speak up in faith because my desire to have a good marriage became greater than my fear of what Keith would say. In the process, God taught me a powerful lesson in communicating:

> "When I tell you to speak up, stay in the Spirit, and
> do not react in the flesh."

When I reacted in anger, nothing was accomplished. God simply wouldn't honor it; I had to apologize to Keith for losing my cool. When I stayed in the Spirit, God worked it out every time!

God said that it is more important to *get it right* than to *be right*. When we try to be right, no one wins. When we try to get it right, we both win. Almost every situation we encountered was for both of us to learn.

I could have prayed for a good marriage until Jesus came back, but I don't believe it would have changed until I changed. God chose to use me, but first, He taught me to stay in the Spirit and trust God to work our situations out.

"Unless the Lord builds the house,
they labor in vain who build it;"
(Psalm 127:1, NKJV)

And Keith? He has told me many times how glad he was that I pressed on. He was forced to acquire a sensitivity he never had, a depth of understanding—not only for me—but for understanding his own feelings as well. He has affectionately (I think) likened me to a pitbull because of my tenacity.

Is there something you've been doing in the same old way and not getting the results you've been praying for? Let God give you His perspective on the situation. Spend time in prayer, waiting on Him until your soul is at rest, then listen...If you don't hear anything, keep praying, reading the Word until you do—be tenacious! God loves it—and eventually, your spouse will too!

"As iron sharpens iron, so a man
sharpens the countenance of his friend."
(Proverbs 27:17, NKJV)

20. Remember Cain

Last night I called an old friend whom I haven't seen in a long time. We talked for quite a while; actually, she did most of the talking—what God was doing in her life and the blessings He was pouring out. Frankly, I was in awe.

I felt envious after we hung up, along with a feeling of rejection rising up in me, exclaiming: *God isn't blessing me like that!*

"Remember Cain," I heard in my mind. *That's strange,* I thought. *How can I be linked with Cain?* Nevertheless, I looked up the account in Genesis and read how God accepted Abel's offering but rejected Cain's. Cain was angry because he thought God was favoring his brother. God took the initiative, sought him out, and said:

> *"Why are you angry? And why has your countenance*
> *fallen? If you do well, will you not be accepted?"*
> (Genesis 4:6–7, NKJV)

But Cain refused to "do well" and decided to solve the problem his way, and you know how that ended!

And then there was the Prodigal son who returned home after spending his inheritance on riotous living? (from Luke 15:11–32) His father was overjoyed and threw a party for him. The older brother was angry and refused to celebrate. His reaction? *My father isn't blessing me like that.* Once again, the father took the initiative—

> *"His father came out and pleaded with him...'Son, you are always with me, and all that I have is yours.'"*
> (Luke 15:28 and 31, NKJV)

He didn't listen to his father.
The solution for Cain and the older brother was:
- They had to give up being envious/jealous.
- Be willing to change their way of thinking/doing.

Cain and the older brother wanted to be blessed, but on their terms—without change. God doesn't work that way. If I am serious about walking close to God, I have to be open to what He is saying and be willing to change my thoughts and my ways.

I was leading a group of women, and our chapter from the book that day was "Faith—Asking God for Things." I had shared how I asked God to give me a verse in January that highlighted what He was going to be teaching me that year when one of the women said I shouldn't have shared that because it might make others feel inferior. She said she hadn't received any verses. I certainly wouldn't want anyone to feel inferior, and I know there are some things I shouldn't share, but I'm not sure if that was one of them. But I do know that God has enough blessings/

verses for all the Cains, the older brothers, and for every one of us!

> *"What man is there among you who, if his son asks for*
> *bread, will he give him a stone?"*
> (Matthew 7:9, NKJV)

> *"How much more will your Father who is in heaven give*
> *good things to those who ask Him!"*
> (Matthew 7:11, NKJV)

I thought of my friend on the phone and remembered that she started spending an hour in prayer and Bible study every day prior to being blessed. The realization came to me: I had been cutting short my time with Jesus, too busy to read His word—causing our relationship to lose its edge.

Like Cain and the older brother, I had a choice: when I see someone being blessed, it could make me thirsty for a closer walk with Jesus, decide to seek the Lord daily, and be willing to change whatever is necessary, *or* I could continue feeling rejected.

I took the way of blessing!

> "Thank You, Lord, for using my friend as the "iron"
> to "sharpen my countenance" (from Proverbs 27:17).

> *"And bless my friend, Lord, for she has blessed me."*
> *"I will bless those who bless you..."*
> (Genesis 12:3, NKJV)

"Oh, that I knew where I might find Him (God).
That I might come to His seat!"
(Job 23:3, NKJV)

"Look, I go forward, but He is not there,
and backward, but I cannot perceive Him...
I cannot behold Him...I cannot see Him."
(Job 23:8–9, NKJV)

21. Searching for God

Job was searching for God, but God seemed to be nowhere around. Can you identify with that? I can. There was a time I lived in the book of Job. I not only read it—I devoured it. I knew it held answers to mysterious questions, and if I searched diligently, I would find them.

Job lived in the land of Uz. He was revered, respected, and honored; he had no trouble doing all the right things. (Now that part I couldn't identify with!)

God said of Job:

"There is none like him on the earth, a blameless and
upright man, one who fears God and shuns evil."
(Job 1:8, NKJV)

Then one day Job awoke to his worst nightmare: he lost his servants, his livestock, his sons and daughters.

> *"Then Job arose...and he fell to the ground and worshiped.*
> *And he said: 'Naked I came from my mother's womb, and*
> *naked shall I return there. The Lord gave, and the Lord has*
> *taken away; blessed be the name of the Lord.'"*
> (Job 1:20–21, NKJV)

That was impressive! Then God takes us behind the scene, and we learn that Satan had challenged Job's commitment to God, so God had allowed Satan to touch all that he had. Job proves his integrity as he accepts his losses and worships the Lord.

Satan counters God, "But stretch out Your hand now, and touch his bone and his flesh, and he will surely curse You to Your face!" (Job 2:5)

The Lord responded, "Behold, he is in your hand, but spare his life" (Job 2:6). So Satan "struck Job with painful boils from the sole of his feet to the crown of his head" (Job 2:7).

If that wasn't bad enough, his wife said, "Do you still hold fast to your integrity? Curse God and die!" (Job 2:9) Job reproved her and said,

> *"Shall we indeed accept good from God,*
> *and shall we not accept adversity?"*
> (Job 2:10, NKJV)

Wow! That's some kind of faith. But a week or so later, Job "cursed the day of his birth" (3:1). Though he still loves God, he doesn't agree with Him:

> *"Though He slay me, yet will I trust Him. Even so,*
> *I will defend my own ways before Him."*
> (Job 13:15, NKJV)

As I searched this enigmatic book, I noticed a striking similarity between his situation and mine. No, I didn't have family or possessions taken away, nor was I covered with boils, but I certainly encountered problems that seemingly had no answers, and like Job, I would say:

> *"Even today my complaint is bitter; my hand is listless*
> *because of my groaning. Oh, that I knew where I might*
> *find Him...I would present my case before Him, and fill my*
> *mouth with arguments."*
> (Job 23:2–4, NKJV)

In my own vernacular, it sounded like:

> "Lord, I don't understand these problems; You are
> giving me more than I can bear. I've prayed and
> prayed, but nothing changes. *God, where are You?*
> *Why aren't You doing something?"*

I lacked depth in my experience with God; I *knew* Him, yet there was so much about Him I didn't know. Like Job, I felt helpless and afraid—

> *"He performs what is appointed for me, and many such things are with Him. Therefore I am terrified at His presence; when I consider this, I am afraid of Him."*
> (Job 23:14–15, NKJV)

Before Job was tested, his life was close to ideal—almost perfect. He logs an impressive list of works in Chapters 29–31. He was right; there wasn't anything anyone could find against him. He was, as God said, "there is none like him on the earth, a blameless and upright man, one who fears God and shuns evil." Job 1:8 So what was God after?

Job could see God in his past, but he couldn't see Him in the present.

> *"Oh, that I were in months past, as in the days when God watched over me; when His lamp shone upon my head, and when by His light I walked through darkness*
> (Job 29:2–3, NKJV)

> *...when the Almighty was still with me..."*
> (Job 29:5, NKJV)

"Still with me?" Like Job, I looked back to the days when God was answering my prayers, when I sensed His presence, and saw His works—life was good. *"What happened, God? Did I do something wrong? Where-are-You?"* I petitioned, but the heavens remained silent.

Job revisited the "days of his prime" (Job 29:4, NKJV):

*"When my steps were bathed with cream, and the rock
poured out rivers of oil for me! When I took my seat in the
open square, the young men saw me and hid, and the aged
arose and stood; the princes refrained from talking, and
put their hand on their mouth; the voice of the nobles was
hushed, and their tongue stuck to the roof of their mouth...I
delivered the poor...the fatherless...I caused the widow's
heart to sing for joy. I put on righteousness, and it clothed
me...I was eyes to the blind...feet for the lame..."*
(Job 29:6–15, NKJV)

Job continues on with all he has done in Chapter 31 while questioning God,

*"Oh, that the Almighty would answer me,
that my Prosecutor had written a book! Surely I would
carry it on my shoulder, and bind it on me like a crown;
I would declare to Him the number of my steps; like a
prince I would approach Him."*
(Job 31:35–37, NKJV)

I think God was trying to get Job's attention long before his world fell apart. Perhaps Job sensed something was amiss because he admits:

*"For the thing I greatly feared has come upon me,
and what I dreaded has happened to me."*
(Job 3:25, NKJV)

Even though Job couldn't see God, He was keeping Job in His sites. God looked where no man can look and heard what no man can hear—a cry deep inside of Job that sounded something like: *"God, I long to know You in a deeper way."* God answered that cry by allowing some hard things to come in his life.

How about you? Are there some hard things in your life too? Know this—God is working to give you a closer walk with Himself, but it will take greater faith. That's something I didn't have back then—and that was part of my problem.

Job's faith wavered under extreme testing—more extreme than most of us will ever encounter. He didn't understand what was happening to him, so he assumed God was no longer with him. Does that sound familiar? It does to me.

My faith wavered under much less testing many times until I made the decision to believe in my heart that what God does is always for my good—because He said so in His Word—even though I can't see it at the time. But when I take that step of faith to believe Him, it is then I begin to understand His ways and eventually know what He is doing.

Faith is not stretched when all is going well. It is only when circumstances are confusing and the way ahead is dark that faith takes its finest bow.

Job was not bowing; he was looking for God to justify him; He accused God of being "an unjust judge." If you've ever argued with God, you know winning isn't even a remote possibility. Job didn't have the faintest idea of what God was after. He understood "works" more than he understood "grace." Still, Job loved God. Some of his words are drenched in devotion and oft-quoted:

"The Lord gave, the Lord has taken away;
blessed be the name of the Lord."
(Job 1:21, NKJV)

"But He knows the way that I take;
when He has tested me, I shall come forth as gold."
(Job 23:10, NKJV)

"Though He slay me, yet will I trust Him..."
(Job 13:15, NKJV)

Job should have stopped there, but he continued,
"...Even so, I will defend my own ways before Him."
(Job 13:15, NKJV)

If you find yourself in a Job-like experience, watch out for friends like Job's three "comforters;" they had more head knowledge than heart experience. I think they meant well, but they could not discern what God was after. They used high-sounding platitudes like: "If something bad happens to you, God must be punishing you." No wonder Job said,

"...miserable comforters are you all!
Shall words of wind have an end?"
(Job 16:2–3, NKJV)

Their words ended, but God's words were just beginning as the wind shifted and the scenery changed. Elihu, God's man in the wings, had waited until the three older men had spoken before he took the stage and introduced himself:

> *"Truly I am as your spokesman before God."*
> (Job 33:6, NKJV)

As Elihu spoke, a breath of fresh air overpowered the stench of Job's boils. The wisdom of his words rose above the din of textbook advice from the three "comforters." Elihu was angry with Job's friends "because they had found no answer, and yet had condemned Job" (32:3), and he was angry with Job "because he justified himself rather than God" (32:2).

Elihu offered hope and encouragement without mincing God's words. He proceeds to teach Job about God's justice, His goodness, and His majesty while condemning Job's self-righteousness (Chapters 32–37). Within that dissertation, Elihu challenges Job:

> *"Why do you contend with Him? For He does not give an accounting of any of His words."*
> (Job 33:13, NKJV)

> *"Has anyone said to God, 'I have borne chastening; I will offend no more; teach me what I do not see; if I have done iniquity, I will do no more?'"*
> (Job 34:31–32, NKJV)

"...teach me what I do not see." Oh, if we would repeat those powerful words and stop questioning God, He would teach us what we do not see—and we would find that it is a lot!

Elihu continues:

*"Bear with me a little, and I will show you that there are yet
words to speak on God's behalf. I will fetch my knowledge
from afar; I will ascribe righteousness to my Maker."*
(Job 36:2–3, NKJV)

Elihu implores Job to hear and consider what he has to say,

*"Listen to this, O Job; Stand still and
consider the wondrous works of God."*
(Job 37:14, NKJV)

Elihu recites some of God's mighty works as He prepares Job
for an audience with the Almighty! Think of it: *Almighty God is
going to talk with him!*

*"Then the Lord answered Job out of the whirlwind, and
said: 'Who is this who darkens counsel by words without
knowledge? Now prepare yourself like a man; I will question you, and you shall answer Me.'"*
(Job 38:1–3, NKJV)

God reveals His omnipotence as He continues to question
Job (Job 38:4–39:30).

*"Moreover the Lord answered Job and said: 'Shall the one
who contends with the Almighty correct Him? He who
rebukes God, let him answer it.'"*
(Job 40:1–2, NKJV)

Job finally gets his chance to declare his righteousness, to tell His Maker He is unjust and that God counts him as His enemy...but Job didn't repeat his accusations. Instead, he acknowledged and finally understood his insolence:

"Behold, I am vile; what shall I answer You? I lay my hand over my mouth. Once I have spoken, but I will not answer; Yes, twice, but I will proceed no further."
(Job 40:4–5, NKJV)

God continues to challenge Job (Job 40:6–41:34), asking if he can do all the things that God does.

"Would you indeed annul My judgment? Would you condemn Me that you may be justified? Have you an arm like God? Or can you thunder with a voice like His? Then adorn yourself with majesty and splendor, and array yourself with glory and beauty."
(Job 40:8–10, NKJV)

And if so, God says...

"Then I will also confess to you that your own right hand can save you."
(Job 40:14, NKJV)

There it is! No one is righteous enough to save themselves, and once saved, no one can obtain righteousness by good works. Job finally gets it—and He humbly answers God,

"I know that You can do everything...Therefore I have ut-
tered what I did not understand, things too wonderful for
me, which I did not know...You said, 'I will question you,
and you shall answer Me.' I have heard of You by the hear-
ing of the ear, but now my eye sees You. Therefore I abhor
myself, and repent in dust and ashes."
(Job 42:2–6, NKJV)

Job had "heard" about God, but now he "sees" Him. What a divine difference!

"Now the Lord blessed the latter days of Job
more than his beginning;"
(Job 42:12, NKJV)

How about you? Do you feel like you're in the "land of Uz" and God is nowhere around? I have good news: God planned your "trip," and He has a purpose in it, just like He did for Job; it may be somewhat different than Job's,

"But He knows the way that I take;
when He has tested me, I shall come forth as gold."
(Job 23:10, NKJV)

Like Job, I learned that God wanted to get my attention. First, He taught me to believe that it's not what I do; it's what I trust God to do through me that counts. It's not my trying, not my works, not my righteousness; it is His righteousness, His works, attained only by trusting Him to work through me. That way He gets all the glory—where it belongs!

"Without Me, you can do nothing."
(John 15:5, NKJV)

Nothing!

"If any of you lack wisdom, let him ask of God, who gives to all liberally and without reproach, and it will be given to him. But let him ask in faith, with no doubting, for he who doubts is like a wave of the sea driven and tossed by the wind."
(James 1:5–6, NKJV)

22. Coming Out of Confusion

Have you ever asked God for wisdom, searched your Bible for a verse, talked to your spouse, family, or friends, and received different opinions? Or maybe you think you heard from Jesus, but as the days go by, you're not sure, and eventually, you end up thoroughly confused? I have.

Then God began teaching me the importance of the above verse and how to "ask in faith with no doubting." I can't keep the doubts from coming, whether they are from the enemy or my own mind, but I can choose not to listen to them by lifting up the "shield of faith."

"Above all, taking the shield of faith with which you will be able to quench all the fiery darts of the wicked one."
(Ephesians 6:16, NKJV)

How do I take up the shield of faith? How do I quench all the fiery darts of the wicked one? I tell the Lord something like: "Jesus, I refuse to listen to doubts. I know my situation is in Your hands, because I gave it to You, and I know You took it because You are faithful, and I can trust You. I believe You will give me wisdom—in Your time and in Your way."

His word has a lot of waits. Here's a couple:

> *"Rest in the Lord and wait patiently for Him;"*
> (Psalm 37:7, NKJV)

> *"My soul, wait silently before God alone,*
> *for my expectation is from Him."*
> (Psalm 62:5, NKJV)

A friend came to me about an important decision she had to make. She was engaged to a man whom her pastor and others were discouraging her from marrying. She was confused. She told me she had prayed and prayed but couldn't discern God's voice. She really wanted to do God's will, which was half the battle, but she didn't want to make a mistake.

I advised her to put the entire situation in God's hands: to picture laying it at His feet, seeing Him pick it up, then thank Him for taking it. "And this is important," I said, "when the situation returns to your mind, or if doubts come, affirm your faith by saying something like: 'Lord, I'm not going to think or worry about it; I've put it in Your hands, and I am trusting You to let me know Your will just like You promised.'"

"I will instruct you in the way you should go;
I will guide you with My eye."
(Psalm 32:8, NKJV)

It's important not to try and figure it out but to wait for the confusion in your mind to settle down. Compare your confusion to a winter scene in a glass globe after you've shaken it. For a time, you can't see the scene until the snow settles. That's like trying to hear from God when our mind is full of confusion. Waiting in faith will settle our minds, stretch our faith, and enable us to hear Him. God has called us to live by faith, not by sight.

He has tested me on that principle many times, and I am learning to not look at circumstances because they look confusing, but if I look to Jesus, He honors it, and in His time, I will know His answer.

A few weeks later, my friend shared that she had put the situation in His hands and refused to mull it over in her mind. And as the days passed, she sensed a quietness developing in her heart. As confusion gave way to peace, she was able to hear God. "The answer," she said, "came not in words but in a deep knowing in my heart." Even though she wasn't happy about the answer, she knew it was from God, and she broke off the relationship.

It is good to listen to advice from others because God often speaks through people—in this case, her pastor and friends—but it's still God's voice we ultimately need to hear. There are many voices in the world; that's why it's crucial to hear from the Lord.

"And when He brings out His own sheep, He goes before them; and the sheep follow Him, for they know His voice. Yet they will by no means follow a stranger, but will flee from him, for they do not know the voice of strangers."
(John 10:4–5, NKJV)

The end of my friend's story? It wasn't long after she followed God's leading that she met and later married a wonderful Christian man. God gives us happy endings when we follow His advice.

"The Lord will give grace and glory; no good thing will He withhold from those who walk uprightly. O Lord of hosts, blessed is the man who trusts in You!"
(Psalm 84:11–12, NKJV)

A brief reminder:

1. Put the situation in God's hands. Thank Him for taking it.
2. Be willing to accept His will; you can be assured it will be the right one for you!
3. When the situation (or doubts) comes to mind, no matter how many times, kick them out and tell God (in your own words), "Lord, I trust You; it's in Your hands, and I refuse to worry about it."

"The Lord is good to those who wait for Him,
to the soul who seeks Him."
(Lamentations 3:25, NKJV)

4. You will know when God speaks.

"My sheep hear My voice, and I know them,
and they follow Me."
(John 10:27, NKJV)

"I drew them with gentle cords, with bands of love.
And I was to them as those who take the yoke from
their neck. I stooped and fed them.
(Hosea 11:4, NKJV)

23. Wilderness Wandering

Tucked away in the minor prophets is a rather obscure but beautiful book of the Bible called "Hosea," whose name means "salvation." A couple of years after I asked the Lord to come into my life, I began experiencing more confusion than peace, and the Book of Hosea revealed why.

"Therefore, behold, I will allure her, will bring her into the
wilderness, and speak comfort to her."
(Hosea 2:14, NKJV)

It was suddenly clear! The trials weren't happening because God was angry with me because I wasn't measuring up; rather, He had allured me into the "wilderness" to get my attention. He had something important to say.

"I will give her, her vineyards from there,
and the Valley of Achor as a door of hope;"
(Hosea 2:15, NKJV)

He promised as I walked through the Valley of Achor (which means trouble) that He would turn my trouble into a door of hope. So, instead of running from it, I needed to seek God in my troubles and listen to what He had to say.

"She shall sing there, as in the days of her youth, as in the
day when she came up from the land of Egypt."
(Hosea 2:15, NKJV)

I recalled the joy I experienced when I had committed my life to the Lord and left my old life (Egypt) behind me.

"It shall be in that day, says the Lord, that you will call Me
'My Husband,' and no longer call Me 'My Master.'"
(Hosea 2:16, NKJV)

The Lord wants to show us a new dimension of Himself. He does not want to be our Master that we have to obey; rather, He wants to be a Husband that we want to follow willingly. He's describing law vs. grace.

My mindset told me, "It can't be that easy," and yet part of me hoped it would be. In the beginning, I hopped back and forth—in and out of grace.

I constantly wondered where I was spiritually. I never felt like I measured up. From there, I fell into condemnation and then into depression. Until one day, I heard God say:

"Forget about where you are or where you think you should be. Rather, be concerned where I AM!"

Slow but sure (and mostly slow), I learned to keep my eyes on Jesus. When I started thinking about how I was doing spiritually or bemoaning my inadequacies, I would reach for my Bible and/or put on Christian music and pray something like: "Lord, help me to look to You for strength. I can't change myself, but I know You can..." There wasn't a lot of good teaching back in the seventies, and the church we attended at the time, believed in salvation by grace. Beyond that, it emphasized "works."

About that time, God sent a mentor who had experienced the workings of the Holy Spirit and whose teaching from the Bible was like a fresh breeze on a sweltering day.

"Sow for yourselves righteousness; reap in mercy, break up your fallow ground, for it is time to seek the Lord, till He comes and rains righteousness on you."
(Hosea 10:12, NKJV)

Did you catch that? Seeking the Lord is our part, and it takes effort. We have to let Him "break up our fallow ground," and that means accepting whatever trouble God puts in our path, teaching us more about Himself, as well as making us more like Him.

"I will take from her mouth the names of the Baals (idols),
and they shall be remembered by their name no more."
(Hosea 2:17, NKJV)

Idols in the Old Testament were images made by hand and worshipped in temples as though they were alive and had power over a person. It sounds foolish in this day and age, and yet idols still exist in foreign lands, and yes (gasp), even in Christians.

Anything in us that we desperately try to hold onto can be an idol. I was sure the idol the Lord eradicated from me would eradicate me first! But I lived through it, amazed that I felt more alive and freer than ever!

Doesn't it put our trials in a different perspective when we perceive that it is in the wilderness that we begin to taste the deeper things of God? I love the way He describes the unprecedented, incomparable, unparalleled consummation between Christ and His Bride:

"I will betroth you to Me forever; yes, I will betroth
you to Me in righteousness and justice, in lovingkindness
and mercy; I will betroth you to Me in faithfulness,
and you shall know the Lord."
(Hosea 2:19–20, NKJV)

Who could turn away from the One who "drew us with gentle cords, with bands of love," then laid down His life to "take the yoke from our necks," and if that wasn't enough, He "stooped and fed us" (from Hosea 11:4), with the living bread from heaven

for His own people, and for a people who did not know Him—
He declared:

> *"Then I will sow her for Myself in the earth, and I will have*
> *mercy on her who had not obtained mercy; then I will say*
> *to those who were not My people, 'You are My people!' And*
> *they shall say, 'You are my God!'"*
> (Hosea 2:23, NKJV)

Yes, Lord. You are our God!

"I (Jesus) have glorified You on the earth. I have finished
the work which You have given me to do."
(John 17:4, NKJV)

24. Finishing My Work

We took turns reading various verses assigned to us at our Friday night Bible study. It was my turn, and I read the above verse and then said, "Would to God we could all say that—that we have finished our work."

I pondered that verse the next day until the conviction became personal, "Lord, *I* want to be able to say *I* have finished the work You gave *me*," knowing in my heart I was falling far short.

The message in church Sunday morning was on seeking the Lord. I wrote down relevant verses that morning and more in the afternoon from my concordance—reading them prayerfully, so they would sink deep in my spirit:

"And you will seek Me and find Me, when you
search for Me with all your heart."
(Jeremiah 29:13, NKJV)

*"I love those who love Me, and those who
seek Me diligently will find Me."*
(Proverbs 8:17, NKJV)

*"When You said, 'seek My face,' my heart said to You,
'Your face, Lord, I will seek.'"*
(Psalm 27:8, NKJV)

*"O God, You are my God; early will I seek You; my soul
thirsts for You; my flesh longs for You in a dry and thirsty
land where there is no water."*
(Psalm 63:1, NKJV)

Seeking Him regularly has been the greatest challenge of my spiritual life. When I do, everything changes: I sense His peace, see more answers to prayer, hear His voice more clearly, step out in faith, and have the power to walk in the Spirit.

I've had seasons of highs when God is blessing and seasons of drought—when I've wasted days on "stuff" and then lamented the fact that the "desires of my heart," that God promised, were out of reach.

I have let the vicissitudes of life: vacations, illnesses, projects, meetings, and so on, crowd my schedule and weaken my resolve. It's not that I ignore Him. I talk to Him off and on during the day. I listen to worship songs, read and study the Bible, and so on, but not consistently.

God sent Haggai to speak to His people about "stuff." The Jews had started rebuilding the temple, and sixteen years later, the work was not finished because they were too busy doing their own thing.

Haggai's prophetic utterance connected with me frequently whenever I inadvertently (which seemed to be a lot!) turned to these verses in one of the shortest books of the Bible:

"You looked for much, but indeed it came to little; and when you brought it home, I blew it away. Why?" says the Lord of hosts. "Because of My house that is in ruins, while every one of you runs to his own house. Therefore the heavens above you withhold the dew, and the earth withholds its fruit. For I called for a drought on the land and the mountains, on the grain and the new wine and the oil...and on all the labor of your hands."
(Haggai 1:9–11, NKJV)

It took me too long to realize I was the only one holding me back. God wanted to continue the building of His temple—*me*—and to eliminate some "strongholds" that would be conquered only by seeking the Lord diligently, consistently, and with my whole heart.

My prayer became: "Lord, bind me to the altar; don't let me go until You have what You want from me." Morning by morning, I met with Him. Many times I had to force myself. He said to me one morning,

"The hardest thing you will do today
is to start praying!"

There was always "stuff" to do, and I had to make the decision to ignore it until after I prayed. It got easier as the weeks turned into months, and rewards were being reaped.

> *"So the Lord stirred up the spirit of Zerubbabel...*
> *and the spirit of Joshua...and the spirit of all the remnant of*
> *the people; and they came and worked on the house*
> *of the Lord of hosts, their God."*
> (Haggai 1:14, NKJV)

About a month later, God spoke through Haggai, and He tells the leaders and the people that even though the temple isn't even close to its former glory, they should—

> *"'Be strong...and work; for I am with you,' says the Lord of*
> *hosts...'My Spirit remains among you; do not fear!'"*
> (Haggai 2:4–5, NKJV)

God is patient with us when we begin to seek Him. Our "temple" needs work, but when our hearts are set on following Him wholeheartedly, God forgives and forgets our failures and encourages us to keep going.

> *"'Once more (it is a little while) I will shake heaven*
> *and earth, the sea and the dry land; and I will shake*
> *all nations, and they shall come to the Desire of All*
> *Nations, and I will fill this temple with glory...the glory*
> *of this latter temple shall be greater than the former,'*

says the Lord of hosts. 'And in this place I will give peace,'
says the Lord of hosts."
(Haggai 2:6–9, NKJV)

Three months after they started to work on the temple, they hear the word from the Lord, through Haggai:

"As yet the vine, the fig tree, the pomegranate,
and the olive tree have not yielded fruit, but from
this day I will bless you."
(Haggai 2:19, NKJV)

Oh, how I want the blessings of the Lord in my life to continue, so when the King (Jesus) comes to His temple—we are that temple—I can say,

"I have glorified You on this earth. I have finished
the work which You have given me to do."
(John 17:4, NKJV)

"I know your works, your labor, your patience,
and that you cannot bear those who are evil..."
(Revelations 2:2, NKJV)

"Nevertheless I have this against you,
that you have left your first love."
(Revelations 2:4, NKJV)

25. Contentment—
That Great Thief

When the pastor asked if anyone wanted to come to the altar for prayer, I didn't hesitate. I told the one who took my hands to pray, "I want to walk close to the Lord again; I want to love Him with all my heart, with all my soul, and with all my mind..." (from Matthew 22:37). Those were Jesus' words, and they expressed what my heart was feeling. The person prayed for me in like manner.

Where had my "first love" gone? My quiet times with the Lord had become sporadic; His words sat waiting in my Bible. My lack of discipline was evident. I still talked to God throughout the day but was overly involved with church committees, too occupied with "stuff" to listen for that transcendent voice that once had thrilled my heart whenever I heard it.

Where was the passion and enthusiasm that had once captured my entire being but now was passive and content? It happened so gradually I hardly noticed—until that morning in church when I sensed deep loneliness, a longing for the closeness that once was.

It had been over ten years since I had given my heart to the Lord. God had done so many things for me; I'd seen miracles, answers to prayer, my extended family had come to the Lord, but lately...there wasn't much happening. What was God saying? I guess I never asked.

After early church, my husband and I went to Sunday school between services. We hadn't gone for some time, so I picked the closest class, the one meeting in the sanctuary. After the usual preliminaries, the leader put us in groups of five or six and gave each group a different scripture to read along with questions to ask. Someone handed me the slip of paper; I looked up the verse, Deuteronomy 6:5 (NKJV), and read it to our group:

"You shall love the Lord your God with all your heart, with all your soul, and with all your strength."

I wondered if anyone noticed the tear in my eye or the catch in my voice. God was speaking. He was saying, "I've missed you too."

"When You said, 'Seek My face,' my heart said to You,
'Your face, Lord, I will seek.'"
(Psalm 27:8, NKJV)

In the *Book of the Revelation*, Jesus appeared to John, telling him to write a letter to seven churches, pointing out what was wrong in each one. The Church of Ephesus was the first, and it nailed my negligence.

> *"...you have persevered and have patience, and have labored*
> *for My name's sake and have not become weary. Nevertheless*
> *I have this against you, that you have left your first love."*
> (Revelations 2:3–4, NKJV)

It is a familiar trap of the enemy: to keep us overly busy with works, without realizing our times with Jesus are shorter, less frequent, and without depth. The time we spend in His Book dwindles; we haven't heard His voice much, nor sensed His presence, or got on our face. We pray, but the "peace that passes understanding" isn't as real, and our prayers aren't answered as much—the worst thing is we don't always notice it.

> *"Remember therefore from where you have fallen; repent*
> *and do the first works, or else I will come to you quickly and*
> *remove your lampstand from its place—unless you repent."*
> (Revelations 2:5, NKJV)

"Whatever it takes, Lord, whatever it takes."

> *"He who has an ear, let him hear what the Spirit says to the*
> *churches. To him who overcomes I will give to eat from the*
> *tree of life, which is in the midst of the Paradise of God."*
> (Revelations 2:7, NKJV)

"Thank you, Jesus, for speaking to me, for opening my eyes, for sensing Your love and Your peace. Don't ever let me go; Lord, break down every wall. Help me to seek Your face, devour Your word, and love You with all my heart and soul, mind and strength."

*"It is vain for you to rise up early, to sit up late, to eat the
bread of sorrows; for so He gives His beloved sleep."*
(Psalm 127:2, NKJV)

26. Leaving Things in God's Hands

A few years after my husband had given his heart to the
Lord, he found himself in a deep valley of despair. I was holding
onto the Lord with all my might simply because I didn't know
what else to do. I knew if I let go, I'd fall apart—the situation
was that serious.

In the middle of the third night, I woke up surrounded by
fear. I got up, made my way into the kitchen, and sat down at
the table, feeling my fears escalating out of control.

Dealing with situations in the middle of the night is difficult for most people—the mind is hazy, making situations
loom like giants—this night was no exception. The realization
of what was happening and what could happen swept over me,
and all I could manage was a weak "Jesus, I trust You." I said it
again, a little stronger.

Still trying to clear my mind, I thought of the women's sup-
port group I was leading and what we had been discussing the
last two weeks—putting things in God's hands and leaving
them there. I decided to take a leap of faith:

"Lord, I'm putting these fears in Your hands. I refuse
to listen to them. I trust You, Lord, I trust You…"

I said it over and over. As I continued to pray, I saw—in my
mind's eye—a black cloud hanging over the table. Then the
cloud parted, and I saw light behind it. I heard in my spirit:

"This valley will be the answer to your prayers."

I had been praying for Keith's walk with the Lord for several weeks, and God was allowing this trial for Keith's good! It
would be a beginning, not an end. There wasn't any reason to
"stay up late and eat the bread of sorrows; for He gives His beloved sleep" (Psalm 127:2). So I went back to bed, praising the
Lord!

"I will bless the Lord who has given me counsel;
my heart also instructs me in the night seasons."
(Psalm 16:7, NKJV)

In the days and weeks ahead, God gave Keith a new desire
to please Him as he prayed frequently and searched the Bible
for answers. I encouraged him whenever I felt led, praying for
the right words. When we understand what God is doing and
cooperate with Him, He turns the valley of despair into a ver-
dant valley.

"Lord, teach us to trust You when we cannot see
Your hand or understand Your ways. Help us to take
a step of faith without any feeling, and prove your
faithfulness as we put our fears in Your hands and
wait for Your response."

We affirm our faith, and then we see. When we put a situation in His hands, we believe it's there because we put it there. That's the kind of faith Jesus wants to find in us. We don't have to feel faith before we act in faith.

As we wait—and we must learn to wait—we can tell Jesus we trust Him when circumstances look just the opposite of good. We must refuse to listen to the enemy's doubts by singing praises, quoting scripture, and kicking out doubts in the name of Jesus. There is power in that Name. God will respond to our faith because He is faithful. He doesn't always respond immediately, but His timing is perfect. As we wait, our faith is being stretched.

"Fight the good fight of faith..."
(1 Timothy 6:12, NKJV)

And it is a fight! The enemy wants us to fail. He wants us to question God's faithfulness. Don't listen to him; kick out his doubts. Resist him in the faith.

*"Therefore submit to God. Resist the devil and he will flee
from you. Draw near to God and He will draw near to you."*
(James 4:7–8, NKJV)

That is a promise!

Do you remember "doubting Thomas?" He was the disciple who wouldn't believe Jesus had risen from the dead until he saw Him. Jesus told him,

> *"Thomas, because you have seen Me, you have believed.*
> *Blessed are those who have not seen and yet have believed."*
> (John 20:29, NKJV)

Whenever I have decided to take that step of faith and trust God, He has blessed me. Yes, it's scary, but it beats the times I've doubted and received nothing. There isn't any other way than faith, as recorded four times in scripture (NKJV): Habakkuk 2:4, Romans 1:17, Galatians 3:11, and Hebrews 10:38. *"The just shall live by faith."*

Not my way, but Yahweh!

"My sheep hear My voice, and I know them,
and they follow Me."
(John 10:27, NKJV)

27. Hearing God's Voice

While reading Hannah Hurnard's *The Hearing Heart*, a deep hunger formed in my heart to hear God's voice. In the days ahead, I prayed frequently, "Lord, I want to hear You, I want to know what You are saying; teach me how to know Your voice..." I had recently asked Jesus to come into my life, and I wanted to know all about this awesome Savior I had just met.

I started searching the Bible—God spoke to Samuel when he was a child. Samuel thought Eli, the priest, was calling him. Eli perceived it was the Lord and told Samuel to say:

"Speak Lord, for your servant hears."
(1 Samuel 3:9, NKJV)

Samuel said it, and then he knew it was the voice of God.

In the beginning, that was my prayer, "Speak Lord, your servant hears." If persistent prayer is the first step, then taking the time to listen is next. As a new Christian, I knew very little about hearing His voice, so I decided to experiment. After praying about purchasing a particular item, I waited quietly before Him, listening when a positive phrase came to mind; believing it was from God, I purchased the item, and it proved to be a good buy.

That was many years and many *hearings* ago. Since then, I have learned He speaks in numerous ways—through His Word or a book, a sermon or a song, a dream or a vision, through a friend, or a spouse, or...His ways of speaking cannot be numbered, limited, or directed. If you think because He spoke a certain way yesterday, He will speak the same way today, He will often change it because He doesn't want us to rely on methods *but on Him.*

After my husband graduated from college, we moved to another state, rented an apartment for a couple of years, and then bought a house in another section of town. I had promised my son I would take him to a park, but I wasn't familiar with the area. As a young Christian and full of newfound faith, I asked God to lead us there—and He did! I didn't hear a voice giving me instructions, but I seemed to know what direction I should take and when I should turn. However, halfway there, I hit a dead end. I was even more determined, I told the Lord I wasn't going to give up, and from there, I knew where to turn and found the park.

The next day I asked Him to lead me to a grocery store. To make a long story short, I ended up asking a neighbor for directions to the store. I learned:

- It's okay to ask God first.
- He doesn't always do the same thing the same way.

Instead of doubting God's willingness to help, I asked Him to teach me what I did not know—which was a lot!

"The Helper, the Holy Spirit, whom the Father shall send
in My name, He will teach you all things, and bring to your
remembrance all things that I said to you."
(John 14:26, NKJV)

Through experience, I have learned His voice sounds different. It makes sense; it sounds right. No one can tell us exactly how it sounds because God put within us the Teacher—the Holy Spirit—He will teach us. That's God's promise.

If I'm uptight, stressed out, or trying too hard to get Him to speak, I either hear nothing or my own voice. I have learned at those times to put the matter in His hands, leave it there and go shopping, or whatever. When it's in His hands, and my mind is clear, and I wait on God's timing, I can hear Him.

There are times I have prayed, "God, I need some answers *now!*" when a decision has to be made. God doesn't dangle the answer above me, waiting for the last minute to drop it. But sometimes, getting down to the wire forces me to release my faith, then I am able to hear Him.

And when He speaks, I've learned to:

- Act on what I hear; if He wants me to do something right away, and I wait, doubts will arise, and the opportunity may be lost. (I speak from experience.)
- Take a step in faith, and then you will know if it's His voice when doors begin to open up or close.

In learning to know His voice, I struggled with acting in faith because I wanted to be sure it wasn't my imagination. I'm sure I've made mistakes. Probably the most mistakes were not acting on what He said. By understanding this, I can throw out the doubts and take a step of faith, trusting God to close the door if it's not from Him.

"Your ears shall hear a word behind you, saying, 'This is the way, walk in it,' whenever you turn to the right hand or whenever you turn to the left.'"
(Isaiah 30:21, NKJV)

Did you notice He said He would tell you when you are going the *wrong* way, but when you are going the *right* way—straight ahead—and you don't hear anything, you have to keep walking in faith, believing all is well.

We tend to want to say, "God, am I doing okay?" But He would say: "Keep walking in faith; I will let you know when you are going the wrong way."

At first, this caused me concern. I told Him, "I don't think I like this 'walking in faith stuff,' I don't know if I can trust myself." My next thought was,

"You don't have to trust yourself; you can trust Me."

"Ah, yes, Lord."

"For we walk by faith, not by sight."
(2 Corinthians 5:7, NKJV)

If we want to hear God's voice when He blesses us, we must be willing to hear God's voice when He corrects us.

"That I may know Him and the power of His
resurrection, and the fellowship of His sufferings, being
conformed to His death."
(Philippians 3:10, NKJV)

God's voice often comes through my husband, and it's not always what I wanted to hear—but it was what I *needed* to hear.

Reading God's Word gives the Holy Spirit the opportunity to illuminate passages that astonishingly fit our situation, whether it's for correction or blessing. By studying His Word, we can begin to understand God's ways—how He does things; His mind—how He thinks. So, when a thought comes to us, we can discern it: "No, God wouldn't speak contrary to His word," or "Yes, it sounds like Him." Even so, we still have to step out in faith, listening.

"My sheep hear My voice...and they follow Me."
(John 10:27, NKJV)

Keith and I were praying about my eye infection that wasn't healing, even though I was faithfully using the prescribed eye drops. We waited in God's presence, listening...when I saw (in my mind) a picture of someone pouring liquid out of a container, I felt that God was saying I should stop using the medication. So, I did.

The next day it was worse. Now what? I could go back to the drops, try something else, thinking I had imagined the "picture." The conviction I had last night had long faded...I could decide I'm going to walk in faith and trust Him. That's what I did. I didn't feel a thing, but a funny thing happened the next day—it was better. And it kept on improving. I learned later I was allergic to the preservative in the drops, and God knew it. I had been healed by the medicine, but my eye was reacting to the allergy.

When you're learning to recognize God's voice, you can be assured He won't tell you to stop taking medication that might put your health in jeopardy or tell you to do bizarre things. If He does, it will be the exception, not the rule. God has always given me lessons that equal my growth while it stretches my faith.

Yesterday I heard God speak with a hint of humor after I reached for the Kleenex box and found it empty. I'll explain: between my sinus and Keith's lung problems, it was no surprise to find it empty. I don't usually say silly things to Jesus like I did yesterday: "Lord, I think someone comes in the middle of the night and takes our Kleenexes." Immediately, I heard, *"Not on My watch!"*

Things I have learned that help me hear His voice:

- Spending time in prayer and in His Word.
- Be willing to give up my own desires concerning the outcome.
- Waiting quietly before Him in faith, knowing His timing is perfect. (Never like mine!)
- If I don't hear anything, I will put it in His hands and leave it there.
- If I think I have heard from Him, I will take a step in faith, not being afraid of making mistakes. We all have, and that is a way we learn.

- I will never give up because I *know* God wants me to hear His voice.

> *"My sheep hear My voice, and I know them,*
> *and they follow Me."*
> (John 10:27, NKJV)

"Whatever things are true...noble...just...pure...lovely... whatever things are of good report, if there is any virtue and if there is anything praiseworthy—meditate on these things...these do, and the God of peace will be with you."
(Philippians 4:8–9, NKJV)

28. Look for the Good in People

I didn't want to work full-time when my kids were in school, so I subbed in special education in the school system for several years and loved working with the kids. When my kids were older, I decided to work full-time but couldn't find any openings there, so I decided to try a permanent job as a legal secretary/assistant. The results were disastrous. I was given the option to quit or be let go.

It turned out to be a blessing in disguise. The Lord led me back to school for a year studying floral design, a field that brought out my creative side. I loved it, except I still found some of the people and conditions at these jobs difficult to deal with.

I was on my third job as a floral designer and considering another move when the Lord started speaking to me about my attitudes at work. Finding another job wasn't the answer; He told me to start looking for the good in people whenever a negative thought came to mind, even if I felt they deserved it. It took a lot of practice and a whole lot of prayer, but the more I looked for the good—and told them so—the more I found it. Eventually, it changed my attitude and all the people around me!

One day, still in the process of learning, I was upset with a co-worker who I felt was mishandling a situation. I trampled down the basement steps to the restroom; each step downward increased my anger. I reached for a paper towel after washing my hands when my eye caught one of several phrases printed on the towel.

Seek out the good in people.

I had to laugh, thinking of Belshazzar and the handwriting on his wall (Daniel 5). God has His ways of reminding us, doesn't He? I quickly agreed, put the situation I was upset about in His hands, and while I wiped my hands with the "hallowed" towel, I prayed that He would change me and that I would always look for the good in everyone. I tore off another panel and put it in my pocket to remind me. I went back upstairs a different person.

When I started sowing His seeds of love at work, I could hardly believe the results: everyone was so nice; they went out of their way to help me. Some stopped swearing in front of me out of respect for my relationship with the Lord—and if they slipped, they apologized! It became a delight to come to work.

The principle of finding the good in people fits in our workplace and also in our church, neighborhood and families. It is a life lesson, something I continue to apply and occasionally have to relearn. Jesus was downright serious when He said:

> *"With the same measure that you use,*
> *it will be measured back to you."*
> (Luke 6:38, NKJV)

"Oh Lord, help," I said after I had read that verse. And help He did. It started at work, but it went beyond. There are times God leads us to confront others, depending on the circumstances, but God was teaching me a specific lesson—looking for the good in people—and it revolutionized my workdays.

"How was *your* day at work today?"

"It shall come to pass in the last days, says God, that I will pour out of My Spirit on all flesh; your sons and your daughters shall prophecy, your young men shall see visions, your old men shall dream dreams..."
(Acts 2:17, NKJV)

29. Dreams and Visions

If you look up the words "dream(s)" and "vision(s)" in a concordance, you will find that God spoke to His people through dreams and vision in the Old Testament around 125 times and in the New Testament about twenty-five times.

It would appear that God doesn't speak to His church through dreams and visions as much as He did in the Old Testament, yet it happens.

For our devotions, Keith and I were reading Charles Stanley's *How God Talks to Us*. We had been going through some rough times with our son, and I was hoping we would find some encouragement in our study that day. I opened the booklet and saw the next chapter title, "Dreams and Visions," and my heart sank a little. How could "Dreams and Visions" comfort us today?

Nevertheless, we started the lesson, and somewhere in the study, a dream I had many years ago surfaced; I had never told my husband about it, but I did then:

Keith and I and our two kids were driving towards my parent's home in the town we grew up in when the buildings on either side began to quake and fall, trees snapped in two, while sidewalks ripped apart. I looked in the back seat of our van to check on the kids, and our son was missing! Immediately I heard the Lord tell us to keep going toward my parent's house, and we would find him. A few blocks later, we were relieved to see him running towards us from a side street. We stopped the van, and as he jumped in, I saw my parents were in the back seat too. We continued on; about six blocks from their house, a huge tree fell across the street, preventing us from going any farther. The Lord told us to turn right. We turned, knowing it was a dead-end, yet my faith soared. I remember being amazed that it was so strong. We were near where the road ended, and the city ballpark began when I saw a shining gold city appear above the park with the road leading right into it. I woke up with my heart pounding and a verse racing through my mind: "A thousand may fall at your side, and ten thousand at your right hand; but it shall not come near you" (Psalm 91:7, NKJV).

The dream had been comforting in a couple of ways: God was assuring me He would take care of us and that my parents would give their hearts to the Lord—they are with Jesus today! But that morning, during our study, another aspect of that dream escalated. One I had never thought about: God was assuring us that our son, who had wandered off, would come back—and that's just what we needed to hear!

"There is hope in your future, says the Lord, that your children will come back to their own border."
(Jeremiah 31:17, NKJV)

Briefly, God was saying to us:
- Stay on the right road.
- Listen for His instructions.
- Believe God, live by faith, and
- Trust God to do the rest!

*"I will pour My Spirit on your descendants,
and My blessing on your offspring;"*
(Isaiah 44:3, NKJV)

Important update:

It took a while, but our son came home. Praise the Lord! If we do our part, God will surely do His!

"Two are better than one, because they have a good reward for their labor. For if they fall, one will lift up his companion. But woe to him who is alone when he falls, for he has no one to help him up."
(Ecclesiastes 4:9–10, NKJV)

30. To Everything There is a Season

My husband and I both committed our lives to the Lord within a few weeks of each other. From the beginning, I had an unquenchable thirst to know everything I could about this new life, while Keith seemed content with the way things were. In the process of running ahead of him, I neglected our relationship—instead of being closer, we became further apart.

Keith complained from time to time that I was too interested in spiritual things to the neglect of more practical matters. I couldn't imagine anyone being too interested in spiritual things and told him so.

I thought if Keith were more interested in spiritual things, we would have more in common, and an exciting marriage would ultimately follow. But no matter what I did to achieve that result, it fizzled. God was trying to get my attention, but I wasn't listening. Then one day, I ran across a verse that jarred my thinking and forced me to re-examine my convictions.

> *"The unmarried woman cares about the things of the Lord,*
> *that she may be holy both in body and in spirit. But she*
> *who is married cares about the things of the world—how*
> *she may please her husband."*
> (1 Corinthians 7:34, NKJV)

I read it again: *"But she who is married cares about the things of the world—how she may please her husband."* The Lord wasn't talking about "worldly" things that we should avoid but the practical things of the world that are important to a godly marriage. God says we will care for them if we have chosen the married life over the single.

I started praying for a better marriage when God told me to listen to my husband's complaints. I had totally ignored practical things, and marriage, I have learned, is terribly practical. As I began to change, I could see how unbalanced my life had become.

> *"A false balance is an abomination to the Lord."*
> (Proverbs 11:1, KJV)

About that time, Keith found himself in the middle of a difficult trial at work. He wasn't the most pleasant person to live with. In fact, at times, he was downright exasperating. "Lord, how can I live with someone like that?" His answer was simply amazing, something like:

"This trial is for you as well as him. When he's short with you, this is an opportunity to learn how to allow My love to come through you. He needs you to minister to him, although he doesn't know it. If you allow Me to come through you, he will grow in his love for you. He will listen because you will have the answers he needs as I give you wisdom. If you act defensively—like you often do—nothing will be accomplished. But as you put aside your fleshly reactions and reach out to him with My comfort and love, you will see him respond to you, and in time, he will respond to Me."

He cautioned me to give spiritual advice sparingly but to give love and comfort immeasurably. When Keith was short with me, God gave me ways to circumvent arguments: I would tell him he must have had a bad day and suggest giving him a back rub, pray for him, or suggest talking about what was bothering him, rather than taking it personally. There would be a time to be assertive (another devotional), but not now. The Lord said this was a time to "turn the other cheek."

The situation didn't go away overnight; it would take many weeks, while I learned to pray for God's wisdom, His words, and His love. He amazed me as He spoke through me, it sounded like me, but I knew it was Him! All God needs is a willing vessel, like you or me.

It was not without mistakes, no experience ever is, but in the end, it worked just the way the Lord said it would. Not only did my husband grow in his love for me, but he reached out to the Lord in a new and deeper way.

"This is the Lord's doing; it is marvelous in our eyes."
(Psalm 118:23, NKJV)

Who would think that something so practical would turn out so beautifully? He wasn't done with our marriage, no. He was just beginning. This was:

"A time to build up."
(Ecclesiastes 3:3, NKJV)

"To everything there is a season,
a time for every purpose under heaven:"
(Ecclesiastes 3:1, NKJV)

"The just shall live by faith."
(Hebrews 10:38, NKJV)

"According to your faith let it be to you..."
(Matthew 9:29, NKJV)

"Let him ask in faith, with no doubting..."
(James 1:6, NJKV)

31. That Elusive Faith

Faith! Why does it seem to be elusive most of the time and real only some of the time? Do you wish you had more faith but aren't sure how to get it? Yesterday you felt full of faith, and today, you wonder what happened to it. If you identified with any of the above statements, then you are among a huge army of Christians. The difference is—some will continue to seek after faith, while others will take a step or two and, if they don't see results, give up.

My father had a favorite aphorism for the latter group. He would say, "That's what separates the men from the boys."

It's the "men" who press on. Faith is found by those who refuse to give up.

Blind Bartimaeus was one of those. When he heard that Jesus was near, he cried out, "Jesus, Son of David, have mercy on me!" It would appear that Jesus kept walking because "many warned him to be quiet; but he cried out all the more..." Jesus commanded him to be called and said, "What do you want Me to do for you?" After Blind Bartimaeus told him, Jesus said, "Go your way; your faith has made you well" (from Mark 10:46–52).

Have you noticed when you refuse to give up and desperation forces you to press on, the answer comes? It is often in the pressing on that our faith comes alive.

> *"Therefore do not cast away your confidence,*
> *which has great reward. For you have need of endurance, so*
> *that after you have done the will of God, you may*
> *receive the promise."*
> (Hebrews 10:35–36, NKJV)

Faith has many facets. The one that I didn't understand in the beginning was having an overwhelming assurance that God was going to do something, and then it happened. It took little or no effort from me—the faith was just there.

We were at the Silver Dollar City in Branson, MO, with a group of friends waiting in line to see a southern gospel show, when over the loudspeaker came the announcement of a serious thunderstorm approaching. The sky was getting dark, and lines began forming at booths selling raingear.

God told me it wasn't going to rain. *I just knew it.* I told my husband I didn't want to buy rain gear because of what God had said. My friends kept asking me if I was going to buy one, and so I told them what God had said. I felt if I bought rain gear, the rain might come, and the show would be canceled. They didn't buy it—*what I said*—and that's okay. I probably wouldn't have either.

It didn't rain, the sky cleared up, everyone folded their rain gear into bags, and the show went on. It was a beautiful spirit-lifting show, the best I have seen there. God wanted it to go on; the enemy wanted it canceled. God won!

In the beginning, I mistakenly thought these rock-solid feelings were what real faith was—I was wrong. When I tried to figure out what I did to receive these rock-sure feelings and then replicate them, nothing happened. Eventually, I learned it was a gift of faith, and it didn't happen very often.

> *"There are diversities of gifts, but the same Spirit...*
> *for to one is given the word of wisdom through the Spirit,*
> *to another the word of knowledge through the same Spirit,*
> *to another faith by the same Spirit...distributing to each*
> *individually as He wills."*
> (1 Corinthians 12:4–11, NKJV)

But there's another kind of faith, it's the fruit of faith, and it's the kind we need every day; it grows as we use it:

> *"But the fruit of the Spirit is love, joy, peace...faithfulness..."*
> (Galatians 5:22, KJV)

I can hear you saying, "But my translation reads 'faithfulness not faith.'" When I read the word "faithfulness" in my NKJV, I felt grieved in my spirit. I looked in Strong's Dictionary, and the word was translated from the Greek word *pistis*, meaning "faith," whereas "faithfulness" is translated from the Greek word *pistos*. I have no background in this area, and I'm sure the translators have many letters behind their names; however, call it a gut-level feeling, I still believe it's "faith." If you feel it is important, I'd ask the Holy Spirit to teach you. That's His job as outlined in John 16:13, 1 John 2:27, and Proverbs 3:5–6.

Faith, as a fruit that comes to fruition (pun intended), is:

- A choice you make to have faith (believe) for something.
- Refusing to listen to doubts that come to your mind.

Granted, sometimes it's hard to tell the gift from the fruit, but don't get hung up trying to figure it out. It's important to know that you can believe (have faith), even when you don't have that infrequent overwhelming assurance.

Recall the Israelites when they walked on dry land through the Red Sea. Think of that as a gift. It took no effort on their part. But God wanted to teach them how to trust Him (have faith) when they found the waters of Marah bitter (Exodus 15:22–25). Instead of trusting Him to make the water sweet, they complained, and God showed them that He could change the situation. What He didn't understand was why they continued to complain trial after trial, year after year.

I think God gives us "gifts" in the beginning because He wants to show us what He can do, and then He withholds them so we can learn to live by faith. It's like weaning a child from a bottle; they put up a fuss because they want to keep the easier way. Growing up takes effort, so does growing in faith!

Sometime after I committed my life to the Lord, He withdrew His presence and presents; I remember thinking He deserted me when actually He was trying to teach me to walk by faith, even when I couldn't sense His presence. It took a while to learn; I made a lot of mistakes, but I refused to give up.

> "But recall the former days in which, after you were
> illuminated, you endured a great struggle..."
> (Hebrews 10:32, NKJV)

God loves perseverance. Eventually, I began to understand His ways by studying the Bible and taking His word to heart, praying,

> "Show me Your ways, O Lord; teach me Your paths. Lead
> me in Your truth and teach me, For You are the God of my
> salvation; on You I wait all the day."
> (Psalm 25:4–5, NKJV)

My husband and I were on a cruise in Alaska, where it rains more than the sun shines. Donning our rain gear, we left the ship with friends and walked briskly down the plank to catch the bus that would take us whale watching.

After we got off the bus, it was still raining, and someone suggested we pray, so there in front of God and everyone, we huddled together and asked the Lord to stop the rain. We had a little time to shop before boarding the whaling boat, so I walked alone throughout the store, repeating over and over, "Lord, I'm trusting You..." fully expecting the rain to have ceased when we left the shop—but it was raining *harder!*

Here comes the test of faith. It's not easy to kick out the doubts and tell Jesus, "I am trusting You," when the circumstances are saying the exact opposite. But if I want to see God work, if I don't want to end up like the Israelites, it's the only choice I have. I told Him, "Lord, I am trusting You," and I kept saying it. Just before we boarded the boat, the rain stopped, and the whales put on a fabulous show. That's our God!

As we neared the shore, we were met by a beautiful rainbow arching across the sky. I snapped a picture as we boarded the bus.

> "If faith is a decision I make and not a feeling I have to attain, then it's something I can do. Faith, which seemed so elusive before, becomes reachable."

A few days later, we prayed that the ferry would take our bus so we wouldn't have to wait over an hour for the next one—we waited! When my prayers are not answered, I often hear these words: "You're not in heaven yet," meaning not everything goes perfectly, and I have to accept it—that too takes faith!

When I was still in the learning process, the enemy would taunt me with "God didn't answer your prayer." I learned to resist him saying what Jesus said: "Get behind me, Satan! You are an offense to Me" (Matthew 16:23). Except I begin with "In the Name of Jesus…"

Have you said to someone, "I'll pray for you," and then forgotten? My daughter asked me to pray about something, and I totally forgot. When I thought of it, it was too late. But I thought of the verse:

*"Before they call I will answer; and while
they are still speaking, I will hear."*
(Isaiah 65:24, NKJV)

God answers before we speak; He sets things in motion. With Him, there is no time, so I prayed and believed He would answer the prayer I forgot—and He did.

"Is anything too hard for the Lord?"
(Genesis 18:14, NKJV)

"...God has chosen the weak things of the world to put to shame the things which are mighty...that no flesh should glory in His presence."
(1 Corinthians 1:27 and 29, NKJV)

32. The Deal of a Lifetime

I used to bemoan the fact that I had so many weaknesses: *if only I didn't have this...if that hadn't happened...or if I hadn't done...* until the Lord broke through my woe-is-me mindset:

> "If you didn't have those weaknesses,
> you wouldn't have needed Me."

I never thought of it that way. If everything had been the way I wanted, I may have gone through life and never had a need to know my Savior. "Oh God, truly all things work together for good" (from Romans 8:28). Then, He taught me little by little how to turn my weaknesses into His strengths.

"And He said to me, 'My grace is sufficient for you, for My strength is made perfect in weakness.'"
(2 Corinthians 12:9, NKJV)

The Apostle Paul's comeback:

"Therefore most gladly I will rather boast in my infirmities, that the power of Christ may rest upon me. Therefore I take pleasure in infirmities...For when I am weak, then am I strong."
(2 Corinthians 12:9–10, NKJV)

Think of it! When we are weak, we can exchange our weakness for His strength! Can you think of a better deal? In the ellipsis in the verse above, Paul lists situations from his life when he has exchanged his weaknesses for Christ's strength:

"Therefore I take pleasure in infirmities, in reproaches, in needs, in persecutions, in distresses, for Christ's sake. For when I am weak, then I am strong."
(2 Corinthians 12:10, NKJV)

Over and over, I read 2 Corinthians 12:9–10 until I owned those verses. Of course, they weren't really mine until I tested them. I stepped out in faith, with much trepidation, believing that the "power of Christ would rest upon me" because God said so. I didn't "feel" like it would, but faith isn't about feelings. I hung in there, knowing I could fall any moment if I looked at the circumstances instead of Jesus—like Peter, who started to sink when he took his eyes off Jesus and looked at the "boisterous wind" (from Matthew 14:27–31).

Doesn't it bless you to know that Jesus didn't let Peter sink when he cried out, "Lord, save me!" "Immediately, Jesus stretched out His hand and caught him." He has caught me a few times too.

But when I refused to listen to the enemy, when I refused to doubt God, when I kept telling Jesus I trusted Him, and repeated the verse: "My grace is sufficient for you..." I found that "the power of Christ rested upon me," just like Jesus said it would! It was a learning process; it took time, prayer, and repeating God's word to convince me.

I asked the Lord once, "Will I ever feel strong? I'm tired of feeling weak." The thought came to me: *if I felt strong, I wouldn't need Him, nor would my faith continue to grow stronger.*

If you feel weak or inadequate, here is good news—listen as He speaks:

> *"But God has chosen the foolish things of the world to put to shame the wise, and God has chosen the weak things of the world to put to shame the things which are mighty; and the base things of the world and the things which are despised God has chosen, and the things which are not, to bring to nothing the things that are..."*
> (1 Corinthians 1:27–28, NKJV)

We may identify with all or some of the above, but if we are strong or weak, we still have to rely totally on God,

> *"...that no flesh should glory in His presence...that, as it is written, 'He who glories, let him glory in the Lord.'"*
> (1 Corinthians 1:29 and 31, NKJV)

God said we have nothing to glory about because whatever good we do is because Jesus is in us. Before we were in

Christ, we had no wisdom, no righteousness, no sanctification or redemption. These are gifts from God. Gifts that have to be worked in us.

> *"But of Him you are in Christ Jesus, who became*
> *for us wisdom from God—and righteousness and*
> *sanctification and redemption—that, as it is written,*
> *'He who glories, let him glory in the Lord.'"*
> (1 Corinthians 1:30–31, NKJV)

There is a time to enjoy what God has done through us, and there is a time to give it back to Him. He paid an enormous price for us, so He deserves all the glory! Anything good in us comes from Christ alone, who is in us.

I recall a time when I tried to steal God's glory; I don't remember the details, but I recall asking forgiveness, picturing myself kneeling at His cross, and it was as though a drop of blood fell on me, and I heard, "I paid the price, I deserve the glory."

> *"...as it is written, 'He who glories,*
> *let him glory in the Lord.'"*
> (1 Corinthians 1:31, NKJV)

"And the peace of God, which surpasses all understanding,
will guard your hearts and minds through Christ Jesus."
(Philippians 4:7, NKJV)

33. Peace that Passes Understanding

Peace! Can you think of anything better? It can get us through the worst pain, the longest night, and the darkest trial. It is sought-after and highly prized by Christians everywhere. Peace is a by-product of faith; it comes when we are trusting God.

One evening, not long after I became a Christian, I decided to pray about the problems that had been weighing me down all day. The more I prayed about my unbudgeable situations, the more depressed I got. I stopped and contemplated what was happening—something wasn't right.

A *thought* came to me to praise the Lord for all the problems I had just poured out. So I did. After praying about each one, I thanked Him that they were in His hands. As I continued to pray, I felt surprisingly light in my spirit. Then God gave me a nugget of truth concerning His peace as I thanked Him and said,

"And besides, Lord, I don't want peace and
contentment by having all my problems gone.
Rather, Lord, I want to find peace and contentment
in You—right in the midst of them!"

As soon as I said that (I believe God inspired it), I knew I had found gold! I will always have problems in this life. But I can have peace anytime by doing what the word says:

"Casting all your care upon Him, for He cares for you."
(1 Peter 5:7, NKJV)

When we give our troubles to Him, we know that He takes them. But don't expect to always feel that He took them. That's where faith comes in. Faith and peace are synergistic; together, they help us reach our goals.

"Behold, I will extend peace to her like a river..."
(Isaiah 66:12, NKJV)

God may work out our problems without our help; He may give us wisdom to deal with them, or He may make us wait. But when we put our problems in His hands—they are *His* problems now. If we find that we are worrying about them, we can put them back in His hands—*as many times as it takes.*

Not my way but Yahweh!

"These things I have spoken to you, that in Me you may have peace. In the world you will have tribulation; but be of good cheer, I have overcome the world."
(John 16:33, NKJV)

*"Though He causes grief, yet He will show compassion
according to the multitude of His mercies. For He does not
afflict willingly, nor grieve the children of men."*
(Lamentations 3:32–33, NKJV)

34. Why Suffering?

When God causes grief, "He does not afflict willingly" (above verse). There are times when He has no choice, but in that suffering, He promises to "show compassion" because He is a merciful God. I've learned His words are true.

All of us experience suffering in one form or another. Most of us, sooner or later, will experience the death of a loved one. Penned in my Bible is "6/83 Dad" beside the above verses, four months before my father died of lung cancer. God used those verses mightily to comfort and assure me by parting the dark clouds just a little, so I could understand some of the "whys?"

One day as I was praying for my father, I saw a "picture" of him running (with his slight limp from polio) toward Jesus. I believed God was telling me he would be saved. A couple of months later, I had yet another picture, but this one was different: Jesus was carrying my father's lifeless body.

I drove home to spend a week with my parents in the sixth month of that very sad year. I witnessed God's compassion at work as He ministered to my father, choosing not to heal his body, but He touched his spirit, and because of that, my father is with Jesus today.

Each night before going to sleep that week, I spent about an hour, more or less praying for my dad, knowing too that I was riding on the updrafts of the prayers of family and friends. I wanted God to do a great work, so I felt I needed to be willing to give Him great amounts of my time.

> *"The effective, fervent prayer of a righteous man*
> *avails much."*
> (James 5:16, NKJV)

I wrote the above verse hesitantly because there were so many things in me back then that needed changing, but God reminds me that He sees me as righteous in Christ as long as I am willing to be changed when He points out things in my life He wants to deal with. I used to condemn myself until I read what Jesus said in John 12:47 (NKJV),

> *"I did not come to judge the world but to save the world."*

So, who am I to condemn what God calls holy as long as I walk in the light that He has given me at the time.

> *"Nevertheless, to the degree that we have already attained,*
> *let us walk by the same rule, let us be of the same mind."*
> (Philippians 3:16, NKJV)

Have you been through a time of suffering that has forced you to look to God? I've been there through a painful neck injury that brought me closer to Jesus than anything I have experienced. During that year and a half, I saw His hand more than any other time. God was allowing me to suffer to make me willing to be delivered from a stronghold. Yet, in the midst, He was showing me His love. Suffering is often God's way of getting our attention. He got my dad's attention the week I was there.

My dad was a wonderful husband, father, and friend. He held his family together with strong bonds of love. Growing up, we played endless games, spent countless hours talking, laughing, and learning. He told me, "Whatever I do, I try to do the best job I can do, not better than anyone else, but the best I can do." I learned more from how he lived his life than what he said. Everything he did turned out exceptionally well—until cancer struck.

The week I stayed there, he got the word that the radiation was no longer working. We were sitting at the kitchen table when my father, who was always the epitome of optimism, said, "Now there's no hope. I've always needed God, but now I need Him."

There it was—the key. He had always believed in God, but he did not have a personal relationship with Him; He simply never needed one until now. Towards the end of that week, he shared, "Every sermon I hear on TV, every article I read, tells me this is all working out for good."

He always said he would read the Bible when he retired. Although retired for some time, he hadn't gotten around to it. He began reading it that week and read it—or had someone read it to him—every day until He met the One who wrote it.

During one of our discussions, I quoted C. S. Lewis' remark from Charles Swindoll's booklet on why people suffer:

"God whispers in our pleasures
but shouts in our pain."

That remark piqued my dad's interest. I had brought the booklet along, and he read it avidly. There was an openness about him I had never seen before, even an eagerness to listen to what I had to say. God used a number of people to minister to him. Some talked about the Lord, some prayed with him and for him, but "God gave the increase" (1 Corinthians 3:6).

After I returned home, I kept in close contact by phone. Dad had no pain lying down, so he spent most of his time in bed. Mother said she and Dad would sit at the table for a while each day and pray until the pain went away so they could talk as they did throughout their married life.

On one of our weekend visits, my husband prayed the prayer of salvation with my Dad just to be sure. Afterward, he said to Keith, "Now you can have the same assurance I have."

Keith and I and our two kids visited him again the first weekend of October. Leaving for home 370 miles away was the hardest thing I've ever experienced, knowing it would be the last time I saw him on this earth. All of us were in tears as we hugged him many times, not wanting to leave.

The night before he left this earth, I talked to him on the phone. I told him, "I'll see you again, Dad." Because of the faithfulness of God, I know I will! He answered me with labored difficulty, but still the optimist, "I'm getting better; it's just taking a long time."

My sister, the nurse, took care of him and told me later that Dad tried to get out of bed that night, still connected to tubes, saying, "I've got to go." I think he knew it was time. He left us quietly the next morning, as pneumonia claimed his life, but not before he whispered somewhat inaudibly to my mother, *"I love you."*

When I got word from my sister that Dad was in God's arms, I told the Lord, *"You have to hold me; You have to take over..."* He did. He wrapped His arms of comfort around me! On our drive there, I was awed by the beauty of the fall season. The leaves had never looked more radiant or the colors more intense as God's presence accentuated my perception of the autumn season.

Although I have never hurt more, nor had I ever felt God's presence more up to that time—a strange mixture of joy and sorrow filled my heart, stayed with me for a month, lessening gradually, and then departed. There were many tears, yet even in the tears I sensed His comfort.

I witnessed to whoever would listen. What amazed me was the love I felt towards everyone and the fact that I couldn't even think a bad thought. I wondered afterward, *Why couldn't I live like that all the time?* Would I take it for granted, would I not grow in faith, or...?

> *"O Death, where is your sting?*
> *O Hades, where is your victory?"*
> (1 Corinthians 15:55, NKJV)

I stayed with my mother for a week and returned home. Yet a thought persisted in my mind: if I could just have one more hug, just *one*? Then one night, I had an unusual dream; it was ethereal and succinct. My father was standing there smiling like he always did, and I hugged him—one more time. I woke up feeling comforted. It was a dream; it wasn't real. The comfort I felt, however, was very real.

> *"Blessed are those who mourn, for they shall be comforted."*
> (Matthew 5:4, NKJV)

Do you need comfort? It's yours. God has promised to comfort us. Because we know we cannot handle situations without His comfort, we must believe He will give it to us. Let these verses soak into your heart:

> *"Blessed be God and Father of our Lord Jesus Christ, the*
> *Father of mercies and God of all comfort, who comforts us*
> *in all our tribulation, that we may be able to comfort those*
> *who are in any trouble, with the comfort with which we*
> *ourselves are comforted by God."*
> (2 Corinthians 1:3–4, NKJV)

> *"As one whom his mother comforts, so I will comfort you;"*
> (Isaiah 66:13, NKJV)

There is one condition that might prohibit God's comfort: a few days after my father went to be with the Lord, my mother shared that God had said to her, "Pour out your anger at My feet."

I understand that losing a husband, wife, and/or other family members goes much deeper than what I experienced above. We cannot change the situation, we still hurt, but God can help us through it. He longs to wrap His arms around us, giving us the comfort that Jesus promised.

> *"He (God) has sent Me to heal the brokenhearted...to comfort all who mourn...to give them beauty for ashes, the oil of joy for mourning, the garment of praise for the spirit of heaviness."*
> (Isaiah 61:1–3, NKJV)

Important update:

It has been many years since I wrote the above devotional. I lost the love of my life, Keith, three years and five months ago. In the beginning, I felt numb. I couldn't cry. Two days later, I experienced a panic attack; my son and daughter, who were staying with me, took me to the ER, where the doctor diagnosed it as "a broken-hearted widow's syndrome."

A week or so later, I had a dream that seemed *so* real. I saw my husband—he looked beautiful. He was smiling, took a few steps, and then disappeared. It comforted me.

I will never be totally over it, but with God's help, I have learned to live with it. God is closer to me than ever; I spend much time talking to Him and reading His Word. I am looking forward to seeing my husband again. But for now, my kids and my grandkids need me here.

"Our hope for you is steadfast, because we know that as you are partakers of the sufferings, so also you will partake of the consolation."
(2 Corinthians 1:7, NKJV)

35. The Rod and the Staff

It was a blessing in disguise—the mid-life crises that threatened to undo my husband. In the beginning, I wasn't sure if we would survive it until I understood that God allowed it for a reason.

When Keith expressed dissatisfaction in several areas of his life, my prayer was, "Lord, speak through me, help me to comfort and encourage him." As we talked endlessly, often late into the night, I was amazed at the practical wisdom coming from me. I knew it was God because Keith was listening to me.

Then all of a sudden, the tide turned. Whatever I said to Keith seemed to fall to the floor. "Lord, what am I doing wrong? Why aren't You speaking through me anymore?" I was in the car, turning a corner when a familiar phrase from the twenty-third Psalm popped into my mind:

"Your rod and Your staff, they comfort me."
(Psalm 23:4, NKJV)

I waited...then I thought, "How strange that the rod and staff comforts??" I had memorized the twenty-third Psalm in my childhood and never questioned its meaning. The rod is used to get the lamb's attention, whereas the staff goes around its neck to change its direction. Neither one sounded too pleasant and certainly not comforting. As I mused on this, the Lord spoke:

"You have to let him suffer."

When the Lord speaks, it's like a *Jesus moment*, perfectly framed in my mind. I could still see the surrounding area as I turned the corner. It reminds me of the Israelites picking up stones along the way to remind them what God had done for them.

I understood—it was God's turn. God had spoken to Keith through me. Now it had to be worked into his life. Suffering is necessary. I've seen the fruit of it in my own life. I don't like it. I'm not a martyr, I try to find an easier path, but God, in His faithfulness, won't let me bypass it—because in the long run—it's for my good. I need to listen to what He's saying.

"It is good for me that I have been afflicted,
that I may learn Your statutes."
(Psalm 119:71, NKJV)

Suffering can come in a multitude of ways: it can involve sicknesses, problems at work, marriage, family, finances, or any other way God chooses to get our attention. During one of those distressing times, a missionary (whose name is forgotten by me but not by God) prayed a succinct but meaningful prayer that has blessed me over and over.

"Lord, don't let me get through this until
You have what You want from me."

He won't because He loves us too much to let us settle for little when He wants to give us "exceedingly, abundantly above all that we ask or think accordingly to the power that works in us" (Ephesians 3:20).

We have His promise:

"May the God of all grace, who called us to His eternal glory by Christ Jesus, after you have suffered a while, perfect, establish, strengthen, and settle you."
(1 Peter 5:10, NKJV)

God faithfully brought Keith out of the crisis, teaching him to deal with the pressures and the people at work. And I learned that we have to put the people we are helping in God's hands and trust Him. We can't do it all, as we sometimes think. We have to know when to let go and let God.

One morning, several weeks later, as Keith left for work, he asked for prayer about a situation he would be encountering that day. After I prayed for him, he cupped his hands on my face and said, "You are my prism; I see the light of the Lord coming through you, giving me a beautiful rainbow."

I was speechless, overwhelmed! I had never heard such beautiful words coming from my husband. This crisis was bringing us closer to God and to each other, exemplifying God's great faithfulness.

> *"I know, O Lord, that Your judgments are right,*
> *and that in faithfulness You have afflicted me. Let,*
> *I pray, Your merciful kindness be for my comfort,*
> *according to Your word to Your servant."*
> (Psalm 119:75–76, NKJV)

God doesn't make mistakes. What He does and how He does it—*is perfect!* We need to look for His "faithfulness" in all our situations.

*"Your ears shall hear a word behind you, saying,
'This is the way, walk in it,' whenever you turn to the right
hand or when you turn to the left."*
(Isaiah 30:21, NKJV)

36. Present Help

I must have turned the wrong way. I could feel anxiety mounting as I drove along the unfamiliar streets. I made a U-turn and headed back towards the hospital, where I had gone for tests that morning, wishing I had paid more attention to the route taken from the Interstate.

"Lord, help me," I prayed, trying a different way...no, that wasn't it either. Several blocks later, I knew I was lost. "Lord," I said with all the courage I could muster. "Please show me where to go." Then I remembered that I had been in this place before. Not on these streets, but in the places of my life when I needed God to be my—

"...refuge and strength, a very present help in trouble."
(Psalm 46:1, NKJV)

Present help! Did you read that significant word? Did you grasp its meaning? Not tomorrow, not next week, not when I'm more spiritual, but *now!*

The word "present" jumped out at me when I was looking for guidance on a decision I had to make years ago. It gave me the faith I needed then and many times since. I thought of that verse as I pondered which way to go.

I don't have a good sense of direction. I have tried hard since that day to overcome that weakness by taking maps, checking the compass, and being more observant. (This was before smartphones.) When my husband ribs me about it, I tell him, "I'm glad Jesus is coming back for me because I'd never find the way myself...and for giving me a husband with a great sense of direction." Keith still amazes me when he finds his way around unfamiliar places—and I tell him so.

I took another turn that day, and nothing looked familiar. This is the fork in the road: I either waver in my faith, letting answers to prayer slip away, or I become determined to have an audience with the Almighty! Yes, even in something as simple as road directions.

Recall Elijah? He prayed and sent his servant seven times before he saw a cloud in the sky (1 Kings 18:41–45). He persevered and didn't give up until the answer came. So can we.

> "Lord, You are my *present* help.
> I'm trusting You to lead me..."

As I continued to pray boldly, I felt my anxiety lowering and my faith rising.

> *"Let us therefore come boldly to the throne of grace, that we*
> *may obtain mercy and find grace to help in time of need."*
> (Hebrews 4:16, NKJV)

Yes, Jesus cares enough to help us to find our way home. I listened...expecting to hear from Him as I continued to drive. Feeling an inclination to turn left, I did, and a block later, I recognized the street I had been on earlier. Breathing a sigh of relief, I praised the Lord and turned onto the street that would escort me to the Interstate.

This has happened more times than I care to count. Not long ago, I took my sister to a train station in another city. I had done my homework and had my directions planned out ahead of time, except the roads around the station were torn up, with several exits and entrance ramps closed. I made it to the station, but to be sure of getting back home, I asked the ticket agent for directions to the nearest open entrance ramp. He told me to look for a certain street. Thirty minutes later, I was still looking for it. I did all the right things, but I still needed God's help. (Have you been there?) I started singing and praising God, and within a few minutes—there it was—the street that the agent told me to look for.

Because I haven't got a good sense of direction, I get lost more than the average person. I like to think of it this way: my weakness is where I get to see God's hand. Paul seemed to feel the same way—

"Therefore most gladly I will rather boast in my infirmities, that the power of Christ may rest upon me. Therefore I take pleasure in infirmities...For when I am weak, then I am strong."
(2 Corinthians 12:9 –10, NKJV)

"Delight yourself also in the Lord, and He shall give you the desires of your heart. Commit your way to the Lord, trust also in Him and He shall bring it to pass."

(Psalm 37:4–5, NKJV)

37. True Grit

Have you ever wondered why things don't happen faster or easier for you? Especially after reading about how God did this or that for somebody else, it seemed like everything just fell into place for them, and you wonder, "How come God doesn't do that for me?"

Nothing ever comes easily for me. I am not technically minded. Getting my devotionals up and running on my website was a continuous trial. There were times I wanted to say, "God, what's the matter with You? Why aren't You helping me?" I didn't say it, but it took a while to grit my teeth and say, "Lord, I'm not going to give up; I am determined to overcome this present difficulty. But I need Your help to do it."

Then the thought came to me, *What if all these problems are coming because God doesn't want me to do this?* Have you heard that or something similar? Kick it out! Ninety-nine and nine times out of ten, it is from the enemy.

When my hairdresser moved out of state to open her own shop, she encountered manifold trials. Some of her friends questioned God's leading her there because of all the things that went wrong. Is that proof that God wasn't leading? It could be, but then why did God remind us—

"Many are the afflictions of the righteous,
but the Lord delivers him out of them all."
(Psalm 34:19, NKJV)

(But not before we have learned the lesson He wanted to teach us.)

"In Me you may have peace. In the world you shall have
tribulation; but be of good cheer, I have overcome the world."
(John 16:33, NKJV)

"We must through many tribulations enter the kingdom of God."
(Acts 14:22, NKJV)

"...that no one should be shaken by these afflictions;
for you yourselves know that we are appointed to this.
For, in fact, we told you before when we were with you that
we would suffer tribulation..."
(1 Thessalonians 3:3–4, NKJV)

Tribulation can show us our limitations and sometimes our own worst self, but in its highest hour, when we accept what God is saying and let Him change our hearts, our faith is released, and we see a portion of the prize.

"...forgetting those things which are behind and reaching forward to those things which are ahead, I press toward the goal for the prize of the upward call of God in Christ Jesus."
(Philippians 3:13–14, NKJV)

Paul may have had a loftier goal in mind when he penned those words, but God cares about the ordinary-everyday stuff too. In order to build endurance, I needed God to set up situations to help me grow in that area. I suspect I will have similar lessons coming in the future. One lesson rarely does it for me.

Blind Bartimaeus refused to give up. He was begging at the roadside when Jesus was coming his way. He cried out,

"Jesus, Son of David, have mercy on me! Then many warned him to be quiet; but he cried out all the more..."
(Mark 10:47–48, NKJV)

"So Jesus answered and said to him, 'What do you want Me to do for you?' The blind man said to Him, 'Rabboni, that I may receive my sight.' Then Jesus said to him, 'Go your way; your faith has made you well.'"
(Mark 10:51–52, NKJV)

I reread Jesus' question, "What do you want Me to do for you?" This time, I answered it.

"Lord, help me get this website up and running so You can use it for Your glory to encourage and

> strengthen Your people. Open their eyes so they will
> see You in all their circumstances and know what
> You are saying to them."

And me? I got my website up and running—to God be the Glory!

I was right. One lesson wasn't enough. The next one came when I purchased a new computer; it was almost like learning a new language. I can't tell you how many times I wanted to pitch it out on the front lawn—*right through the window!* I finally began making progress when I gave up my frustration and told the Lord again, "I am going to learn this if it kills me!" It did "kill" a little of the *old me*, and that's always good. No matter the project, when I finally put it in the Lord's hands, decide to trust Him, things begin to m-o-o-o-o-ve.

My husband says, "We have to go through the deep stuff to get to the good stuff." Keith's gone through a whole lot deeper stuff (health-wise) than I have and has shown a great deal of faith and fortitude. Overcoming my "technical" ineptitude may seem trivial in comparison, but God cares about that too.

It was faith that got my website up and running. Whether our request is major like Blind Bart or like mine, persevering and refusing to give up will cause the Master to say to us:

> *"What do you want Me to do for you?"*
> (Mark 10:51, NKJV)

"It's your turn now. Go ahead, *tell Him!*"

"...be swift to hear, slow to speak..."
(James 1:19, NKJV)

38. Learning to Listen

"You think you're an authority on everything," my husband hurled at me in response to a remark I made. This was a few years prior to our marital awakening, but I sensed he was right—because it alarmed me so.

I asked the Lord, "Do I really?" His answer didn't come back as a "yes" or "no," the Lord had a better way: the situation repeated itself until I finally got the message. It is possible to wander for years and not listen to what the Lord is saying—as did the Israelites in the wilderness—and it was during my own wilderness journey that we attended a Sunday school social with its theme: *marriage.*

On a humorous questionnaire, filled out by husband and wife separately, one of my questions was: "How well does your husband work around the house?" Jokingly, I put down, "Fine, if he does it my way."

The men had a similar question, like, "How well do you think you work around the house?" Ironically, my husband wrote: "Fine, if I do it her way." The chairman chose the more humorous answers to read, and of course, he read ours. Everyone laughed, including me. But it wasn't until God began working on our marriage that I began to see how critical I was—and I wasn't laughing anymore. Keith didn't need my so-called "knowledge" most of the time.

Being primarily of the melancholy temperament, plus a little choleric bossiness, and plagued with perfectionism, not under the Spirit's control, I demanded much more from others (and myself) than they or I could possibly deliver.

The trouble with being a "self-professed authority" is that no one listens even when you are right. So, at God's insistence, I began to pray: "Lord, help me to keep my mouth shut."

"To everything there is a season,
a time for every purpose under heaven."
(Ecclesiastes 3:1, NKJV)

"A time to keep silence, and a time to speak;"
(Ecclesiastes 3:7, NKJV)

One important lesson in communicating with Keith came while putting together a Christmas centerpiece. I was looking for pine branches to lie between candles and asked my husband to come along. We found huge roped pine bunches, but all I needed was a single spray. We continued to look around when I heard Keith call me. In his hands was a near-needleless bottom of a tree stump, and it was free. I walked away in a huff.

The next picture I have is Keith driving home—fast and fuming. God is never far from my consciousness, so it wasn't unusual to vent my feelings to Him inwardly. *Lord, I am so angry.* I got no further—I heard, "You didn't tell him what you wanted. How was he to know?" It was obvious He was taking Keith's side, so I figured I'd better listen. He continued, "Enough charades! Be specific; let him know precisely what you want."

Well, if he loved me, he'd just know. I answered Him. My spiritually-enlightened mind challenged me with *"What kind of logic is that?"* This had happened before: assuming Keith knew what I wanted without telling him. *Why hadn't I seen it?* I apologized on the spot and have since learned to speak up and tell him what I want or need, beginning with "I feel..." as opposed to an accusing "you don't..."

Listening to God is key. I was coming up the basement steps armed for battle; my husband was wrong, and I was going to confront him. As I hit the top step, a thought jarred me to a standstill: I had another option; I could forgive him. *Forgive him, Lord?* That wasn't what I had in mind, but I forced myself to say, "Jesus, help." I said it again; it was easier the second time, but I still wasn't convinced. Then,

> *In my mind's eye, I saw a huge weed being pulled from the ground as the soil stubbornly resisted efforts to uproot it— only the roots were lodged in my heart—but with a final tug from the Master Gardener, dirt clods exploded in the air as the earth yielded to the force of His pull.*

"Lord, help me to be as merciful with him as You are with me." I did bring it to him later that evening, but in the proper attitude—God's love, *agape* (a-GAH-pea)—and we worked it out together. God does not, nor will He accept sloppy *agape*!

The Lord said we needed to agree before we made decisions. One of our "disagreements" sat in the living room—the chair that only the cat laid on. That was the chair I wanted, and Keith didn't; I pushed until I got it. It was uncomfortable, too big for our living room, and much too expensive for a cat bed.

> *"Can two walk together, unless they are agreed?"*
> (Amos 3:3, NKJV)

And then there were two dogs I wanted that Keith didn't— the first turned out to be "the dog from Hades," the second one failed obedience school twice—but hey, he was a pedigree and free! I was learning the hard way. God was teaching me that if I didn't do things His way, I had to live with the consequences. After that, my motto was—no more dogs!

A year or so later, Keith and our son came home and told me about a puppy they had seen. Seeing my look of disapproval, my son said, "Mom, I think God wants us to have this dog." I said I would pray about it. I did, and the next day we went to look at the dog; we brought him home, and he turned out to be the best dog ever! This time we agreed!

> *"For it seemed good to the Holy Spirit, and to us..."*
> (Acts 15:28, NKJV)

We took that verse as God's motto, and it works for us. We continue to pray together about furniture, lawnmowers, trips, cars, doctors, and…Nothing is too small or incidental to ask for God's advice. As God said, "Do not be wise in your own eyes."

"Trust in the Lord with all your heart, and lean not on your
own understanding; in all your ways acknowledge Him, and
He shall direct our paths. Do not be wise in your own eyes."
(Proverbs 3:5–7, NKJV)

It seemed almost a way of life that we are close and gradually without realizing how or when that "separation syndrome" sets in. So many things enter our minds forcing us to think separately, and before we know it, that precious closeness is gone.

In the beginning, Keith did not understand when a separation existed between us. He seemed content with things the way they were. I wanted a close relationship with him, but "how, Lord, do I communicate in words describing the longing you've placed in my heart?" Probably the word I used to describe what I wanted during those days was "real."

After working through one of our episodes, our relationship would be "real," but in time, Keith's work and the pressures of it would overtake him, and his thoughts excluded me. We hadn't stopped talking or doing things together. It's just that we hadn't taken the time to share the deep places of our hearts. We need to know what the other is thinking regularly to keep the quality of oneness alive.

Instead of pouting, refusing to talk, accusing him of not caring, or other unproductive actions that would make the situation worse, I began praying about it. God said to tell him how I felt but in a God-like manner. And then, wonder of wonders— Keith called me from work and said, "We have to find time to be close again."

*"The heart of the wise teaches his mouth, and adds learn-
ing to his lips. Pleasant words are like a honeycomb, sweet-
ness to the soul and health to the bones."*
(Proverbs 16:23–24, NKJV)

Keith read about a way to communicate that worked for
us: he would tell me how he felt about something, and I would
listen without interruption. Then I would say, "This is what I
heard you say," and then repeat it. If it was correct, he would affirm it or explain further. By repeating our partner's thoughts
and/or requests, it helped us to understand how the other person thinks and also to remember to follow through in the days
ahead.

- Pray about everything.
- Together is better, but don't force it.
- Listen to God.
- I guarantee both of you will have to change.
- However, you can *only* change yourself by letting God
  change you.
- Let God do the rest!
- He will, I guarantee it.

"A man's heart plans his way, but the Lord directs his steps."
(Proverbs 16:9, NKJV)

39. Disappointments

A couple of weeks ago, I mentioned to a friend about a difficulty I was facing. "Oh, another devotional!" she quipped. I laughed.

Last week I wasn't laughing. My husband, a high-school teacher—ten years on the county board—lost his election through redistricting and was thrown into the ring with a thirty-year union supervisor. We knew the odds were slim, but I felt God was with us. "Look at David's odds with Goliath..." I encouraged Keith as we knocked on doors, praying over every doorstep.

Keith had prayed several times. "Lord, if this isn't what You have in mind for me..." In the beginning, he wasn't sure he should run again. He was the chairman of a very busy department that took a lot of his time after work and on weekends, and he felt the Lord might be saying he should spend more time with family.

In the next few days after the election, he received many phone calls and emails. One of his former students emailed, in part:

"Perhaps this is God's message to you to take more
time for yourself...go spoil your grandkids."

Accepting the loss was fairly easy for Keith. He simply believed God had shut a door. It always takes me longer. I was
disappointed. We had worked long and prayed hard. Thoughts
crept into my mind that God had let us down. We had seen His
hand during the campaign (at least I thought we did), so I assumed...forgetting the lesson I learned a few years ago about
"assuming."

> *"Now this is the confidence that we have in Him, that if we
> ask anything according to His will, He hears us. And if we
> know that He hears us, whatever we ask, we know that we
> have the petitions that we have asked of Him."*
> (1 John 5:14–15, NKJV)

"According *to His will.*" *All* the prayers in the world won't get
us something that isn't God's will—and that is our safeguard!
I'm learning to pray sooner, "Lord, help me to accept this,
work in me," when I am reluctant to accept situations. It never
fails to amaze me how He works in me the "want to" and changes my mind when I accept His will.

> *"For it is God who works in you both to will
> and to do for His good pleasure."*
> (Philippians 2:13, NKJV)

Somewhere I read: "Our disappointments are God's appointments." And as usual, the Lord confirmed in the days and weeks ahead—it would NOT have been a good plan to win the election for several reasons. I am so glad God intervened and used the *gerrymandering* for His perfect will.

> *"He who opens and no one shuts,*
> *and shuts and no one opens:"*
> (Revelations 3:7, NKJV)

Years ago, Martha Jacobson—a missionary—spoke in our church and shared how she wanted a husband to be with her on the mission field, but God didn't answer her prayer. It took a while to accept His denial, but she said, "Through experience, I have learned that...

> *"...no good thing will He withhold from those*
> *who walk uprightly."*
> (Psalm 84:11, NKJV)

She continued, "And when he withholds—what we think is a *good thing*—it only means He has something *better* for us." It was just what I needed to hear that night and many times since. I have shared that with others who were also blessed by it.

The missionary was blessed with many fruitful years in the field, and soon after she retired, God answered her prayer and blessed her with a husband who was also a retired missionary.

"But as for me, I trust in You, O Lord; I say, 'You are my God.' My times are in Your hand;"
(Psalm 31:14–15, NKJV)

Remind us, Lord, that our faith must be in You, not in the thing we want or hope for. We don't always know Your will, but we can trust You to close a door when you want to bless us with that *better thing*.

"Correct your son, and he will give you rest;
yes, he will give delight to your soul."
(Proverbs 29:17, NKJV)

40. Disciplining Kids in Love

My daughter and I were standing in line waiting to sign up for nursery school. At least *I* was standing in line; she was running around, unlike the other children standing close to their mothers. I hesitated, telling her to come over by me...what if she didn't listen, then what would I do?

As the day progressed, I couldn't shake that scene out of my mind. I confessed my feelings and frustrations to the Lord, expecting Him to chide me. Instead, I heard, "I understand how you feel, but you've allowed her to be that way."

I have? The realization hit: *Yes, I have allowed it.* "What do I do now, Lord?" I asked on my knees later that day. I had to admit I was inconsistent: some of the time, I disciplined correctly, sometimes in anger; other times, I let things go because it was easier than dealing with it. I disciplined much the way my mother did.

My daughter was born with a melancholy temperament. Most of the time, she was cooperative, but when her moody disposition took over, I didn't know how to handle her. But God did.

A couple of weeks later, a Christian magazine arrived with an extraordinary article on disciplining children. This was no accident—it was a Godsend! As I read it, I thought, *How simple.* I soon learned that doing it was *not* simple. God's counsel to me was:

> "You can discipline your children only to the extent that *you* are disciplined."

"Oh, help!" was my reply. And help, He did.

The steps of the article (in my own words) were:

1. Tell your child what you want them to do (or not do). Be specific and make sure they understand. Sit down and talk to them. Don't be timid, as if what you are saying is negotiable; don't end your request with an "Okay?" Speak *firmly*, letting them know you mean what you say, being careful not to appear angry.

2. If they do what you requested, be sure to praise them along with a hug and a smile.

3. Get up from whatever you are doing and deal with the needed situation *before* you get angry. There is nothing more important, not the housework, dinner, the TV program, or a phone call—*nothing!*

4. Letting the situation go will eventually make you angry. Yelling, even if it works occasionally, doesn't train the child. It only teaches them that *you* do not have self-

control, the very thing that you are trying to teach your child. If all you do is yell, you will have to keep doing that till they leave the house, and your kids will never learn self-discipline.

5. I've heard parents make threats that you know they aren't going to (and probably shouldn't) carry out. If you don't follow through, kids soon learn that you don't mean what you say and will test you repeatedly. Think before you speak.

6. If they do not cooperate, use consequences. Without consequences, there is little motivation to change. Do not choose consequences that will humiliate or harm the child.

7. Consequences are not punishment, and they shouldn't be; they are intended to help the child learn self-control, which is a necessity as the child grows up—the same way God corrects us because He loves us.

8. Choose to have time-outs on a chair where you can see the child—not in a corner, not with access to toys. Sending them to their room is hardly a timeout with all their "stuff" available. A timer is helpful. Make the time fit the age.

9. Revoking privileges works well, especially for older children. Again, makes sure you can carry it out and that it fits the situation. I've heard of kids being grounded for a month; if it takes that long for them to learn, then there is something wrong with the one setting the rules.

10. After you discipline them, hug them and tell them you love them; they probably won't respond, but they will re-

member you disciplined them in love. Then drop it! No more conversation and no condemnation. This is the way the Lord treats us; He doesn't harangue us. He chastens (disciplines) us for our good.

> *"For whom the Lord loves He chastens."*
> (Hebrews 12:6, NKJV)

Pray with and for your children. Ask God for strength and determination to continue day after day. Be patient. Results won't happen right away, depending on the age and how you have disciplined up until now. But if you persevere, God will change both you and your children.

> *"Let us not grow weary while doing good, for in due season*
> *we shall reap if we do not lose heart."*
> (Galatians 6:9, NKJV)

I learned right along with my children. The first thing the Lord told me was to stop watching late TV. I needed to be wide awake early in the morning when my kids were getting ready for school. He also told me to get the kids to bed at a reasonable hour.

On a day that I wasn't doing well, God reminded me what He told me a month or so earlier:

> "The greatest "calling" I have given you
> is a wife and mother."

A year or so later, He tackled our marriage, but for now, my kids needed a mother who was willing to be taught by God.

Whenever I was overwhelmed, God reminded me, "You and I can handle this." I was learning to rely on *His* strength because mine gave out too soon.

When I didn't handle things right, I took responsibility and apologized to my kids. I was learning to deal with every situation *every* time. Kids get confused about mixed signals. Consistent and loving discipline gives them a sense of security, helping them to mature emotionally, but remember they will never be perfect because you and I aren't!

The more I invested in the ten steps, the more my daughter's disposition improved. Within weeks she was a happier child; she wanted to please me—and that is a key.

My kids—somewhere around five and seven—and I were going to play a game with cards. The problem was that both of them wanted to use *their* cards, and they started arguing about it. I told them,

> "The one who is the most mature
> will stop arguing first."

They looked at each other and then almost simultaneously said that they would use the other's cards. I used that phrase whenever they argued, and it worked well.

Kids need boundaries. They need to know how far they can go. It makes them feel secure. Yes, they may complain, but you don't have to argue the point. It may seem easier to give in to kids at the moment, but you will pay the price later on.

Eli, the priest at Shiloh, paid the price because he refused to correct his sons, among other things. God, through a prophet, asked Eli,

"Why do you...honor your sons more than Me?"
(1 Samuel 2:29, NKJV)

My husband and I led an adult Sunday school class on parenting. The teacher (on DVD) shared a truism regarding discipline; we have learned from it and shared it with others:

"If you are trying to keep your kids happy all the
time, you aren't doing your job."

My son, as a teenager, wanted to do something I didn't agree with. I let him have his say, to which I responded, thinking I had sewn up the situation. But he came back with another point. This went on back and forth. Finally, my husband walked into the kitchen and pointed his finger at me (as though I were the child), and said matter-of-factly, "You-do-not-have-to-argue-with-him!"

He was right. I need to listen to my kids' opinions and tell them if I don't agree, and with wisdom, know when to respond "the matter is closed," and walk away.

A young mother asked me how to get her children to stop arguing—one of the biggest complaints of parents. I had observed that the only consequence for their behavior was telling them to stop several times until it escalated into yelling. The kids stopped for a while but resumed it later. Yelling doesn't work, neither does inconsistent disciplining.

I shared some of the steps outlined above with her, emphasizing that kids without consequences (never physically) will not be motivated to learn how to discipline themselves. If they know there will be consequences, in time, they will think twice before repeating the offense and will be more likely to learn to listen when you tell them to stop.

My daughter used the "1–2–3 method" when her kids were young. Whenever they would do something that wasn't acceptable, she would start counting, "One...two..." If she ever got to three, there would be a time-out. To my knowledge, the kids always responded before she hit three. She had an advantage: the kids wanted to please her because she spent lots of time loving on them.

Discipline and love should be perfectly balanced. Disciplining without loving is almost as bad as loving without disciplining. Kids need both. Without one or both, they do not feel secure, loved, or confident. Depending on their temperament, they will react accordingly.

It is important to spend lots of time having fun with your kids by talking with them, playing games, taking walks/hikes, reading books, singing, working on projects, cooking with them, and watching their favorite TV programs with them. The more time you spend with them, the more they will want to please you. Watching "The Brady Bunch" and "Scooby-Doo" and other favorite (not mine) shows with my kids and "Sponge-Bob Squarepants" a couple of decades later with my grandson wasn't all that enjoyable, but I watched them because they liked them.

We were visiting our family in Arizona when I walked past my granddaughter's bedroom and saw her and my daughter on the floor playing Barbies. After a while, my daughter came into the kitchen and exclaimed, "I can't stand playing Barbies." Knowing she spends a lot of time with her daughter, I laughed and said, "I felt the same way when I played Barbie with you. But the important thing is, you're playing it because she likes it."

A mother told me she had tried to read to her kids, but they didn't listen. I told her to get involved with the story. Have the kids "taste" the porridge; knock on the door (table) of the little pig's homes, or pretend to pound nails into the ark. My grandson watched with eyes wide open as I plopped on the bed after being hit by David's well-aimed stone. Reading to kids when they are young will increase their attention span. My daughter's family read to their kids *before* they were born as well as after. They're teenagers now and still love to read.

I was reading (and acting out) a book with my four-year-old granddaughter:

"Jesus said to the little girl, 'my child, I say to you arise,' as He took her by the hand, raised her up, and she danced around the room."

As I read the book to her, I took her hand and lifted her off the couch. Then we danced around the room. What little girl doesn't love to dance? We acted out parts of the book whenever it deemed possible.

Do you remember the *Gingerbread Boy?* My second grandson and I were on our hands and knees, crossing the "river" from the living room into the kitchen. He was the fox, and I had the gingerbread boy (a stuffed animal) on his back as I retold him the story. (We had read the book many times.) In the middle of the "river," he turned to me and said, "Grandma, are your jeans getting wet?" *He was really into it!*

Get out the play-do and help your children form the Three Bears and Goldilocks or Beauty and the Beast or whatever story the kids are into today. You don't have to be talented; kids have a lot of imagination. You just have to make it come alive.

I know my limitations, and I can't draw, period. But I can copy. So, I ran off several pictures of cartoon characters from the internet. Then we drew them on pumpkins with non-permanent pens and then painted them with acrylic paint. The grandkids loved it. Reading, making projects, decorating ornaments, and playing games inside and out (even the ones you don't like) are all memory builders. We loved taking the kids sightseeing, swimming, zoos, mini-golf, parks, and more.

God has given Keith and me five beautiful gifts—two kids and three grandkids—and we are blessed!

One last thought: just because I told you what to do with your children doesn't mean that I did everything right. I didn't. I wish I could go back and do things differently, but I can't. I wished I would've learned the lessons sooner, but I didn't. I had to change in many ways. None of us do everything right. In prayer, ask God for help. He was my biggest Helper!

"Watch and pray, lest you enter into temptation.
The spirit indeed is willing, but the flesh is weak."
(Matthew 26:41, NKJV)

41. The Secret Place of Prayer

Ever have one of those days you just don't feel like praying? I have. "Lord, will I ever get to the place where I won't have to force myself to pray?" Immediately, I thought of the above verse with the emphasis on "the flesh is weak." The flesh is and always will be weak. There will always be that dichotomy to remind me of my weakness and how much I need God's strength. On the days when I "faith it," by starting to pray even when I don't feel like it, those times often turn into special times of closeness with the Lord.

"Pray to your Father who is in the secret place; and your
Father who sees in secret will reward you openly."
(Matthew 6:6, NKJV)

Did you catch that promise? God said He would "...reward you openly" if you meet with Him in secret. When we "watch and pray" regularly, the enemy will be less likely to get a foothold.

Too often in years past, I found myself wandering in the wide chasm between procrastination and discipline. Talk is cheap. Each day I tried to find time to pray, but there was always something I had to do *first*, and at the end of the day, there was only poverty.

"In all labor there is profit;
but idle chatter leads only to poverty."
(Proverbs 14:23, NKJV)

Years ago, Keith and I started a Bible class; in the beginning, we prayed together diligently. But after several weeks, our *diligence* turned into *pray-quickly-on-the-way-to-class*. We began leaning on ourselves instead of God. The same thing happened when I began praying diligently first thing in the morning. Stuff comes up, and before I knew it, "diligently" becomes a word sitting in the Bible. It wasn't as though I didn't talk to Jesus throughout the day, I did, but He deserved more from me.

God said that the hardest thing I would do each day was to *start* praying. There are still days I don't feel like it, but I know that once I take that step of faith and start, God will meet me in that secret place.

"My voice You shall hear in the morning, O Lord; in the
morning I will direct it to You. And I will look up."
(Psalm 5:3, NKJV)

On the other hand, if you miss some days, don't fall into condemnation. Our God is a very patient God when we are learning His ways. Start praying again, and keep on "keeping on."

"...He is a rewarder of those who diligently seek Him,"
(Hebrews 11:6, NKJV)

I read somewhere that less than twenty percent of Christians have regular prayer time with God. Imagine the power available if even half the believers prayed regularly, or, what would church be like if we all prayed before *going* to church? It would rock it!

"Nevertheless, when the Son of Man comes,
will He really find faith on the earth?"
(Luke 18:8, NKJV)

If the world continues to deteriorate the way it is now, we may be forced to meet with Jesus in order to survive. The Apostle Paul reminded his followers that "Satan himself transforms himself into an angel of light," therefore, we must learn to discern what is said, what we read, what we see...by meeting with Jesus, studying His Word, and becoming more like Him. How much easier it will be if we get a head start now.

"If you faint in the day of adversity, your strength is small."
(Proverbs 24:10, NKJV)

Have you noticed how many times God warns us of false prophets in the end times?

*"For false christs and false prophets will rise and show great
signs and wonders to deceive, if possible, even the elect."*
(Mathew 24:24, NKJV)

*"Beloved, do not believe every spirit, but test the spirits,
whether they are of God; because many false prophets have
gone out into the world."*
(1 John 4:1, NKJV)

I have read some prophetic things that were supposed to
happen and didn't. I also have read some so-called prophets
who take a verse and make it a book. That might be alright, except the few I read didn't make any sense. I get the feeling that
some of the so-called "prophets" get a big head because God
showed them something that no one else knew.

I have also seen Christians who allow prophecy to become
their first love. It's okay to study it but *never* put it first! Jesus
had John write to the church of Ephesus, who had put "works"
ahead of Jesus,

*"I know your works, your labor, your patience, and that you
cannot bear those who are evil."*
(Revelations 2:2, NKJV)

*Nevertheless I have this against you, that you have left
your first love. Remember therefore from where you have
fallen; repent and do the first works..."*
(Revelations 2:4–5, NKJV)

"Strengthen us, Lord, to keep us from fainting. Work in us to be ready and full of faith and power when adversity comes, beginning today, to "watch and pray" by consuming Your Word and be filled with Your Spirit so we can discern Your voice, Your will, and Your way. We want to love You, Lord, "with all our hearts, with all our souls, with all our minds, and with all our strength" (Mark 12:30), and not let anything or anyone come before our Lord and Savior Jesus Christ!"

*"For it is God who works in you both
to will and to do for His good pleasure."*
(Philippians 2:13, NKJV)

42. God's Part and Mine

The above verse is one of my "cornerstone" verses. God will work in me—not only to make me want to do His will but to do it. Of course, there is pragmatics involved. When God began teaching me this principle, He started with love, the first fruit listed. Notice that "love" is a fruit of the Spirit, not of us.

*"The fruit of the Spirit is love, joy, peace, longsuffering,
kindness, goodness, faithfulness, gentleness, self-control.
Against such there is no law."*
(Galatians 5:22–23, NKJV)

God will bring a variety of people across our paths we cannot love in order to teach us how to let Him love through us. They may come from our family, down the street, on the job, or in our church. There was a time I thought I loved everyone...until God brought *Impossible-to-love #1* into my life, and I wrestled with Jesus' words:

"This is My commandment, that you love one another
as I have loved you."
(John 15:12, NKJV)

There was no way I could love this person. Then to justify myself, I questioned God: "How can I possibly love like You?" Back then, I had no idea how to let God love through me.

Although I had "received the Spirit...by the hearing of faith" (Galatians 3:2), I was like the foolish Galatians with one foot in grace and the other in the law. The Apostle Paul admonished them:

"Are you so foolish? Having begun in the Spirit, are you
now being made perfect by the flesh?"
(Galatians 3:3, NKJV)

Early in my Christian life, I heard a sermon titled "Righteousness by Faith." The minister quoted Paul as he preached on the following verse:

"I have suffered the loss of all things, and count them
as rubbish, that I may gain Christ and be found in Him,
not having my own righteousness, which is from the law,
but that which is through faith in Christ, the righteousness
which is from God by faith;"
(Philippians 3:8–9, NKJV)

I marked it in my Bible because it made such an impression on me. I understood "faith" for salvation, but "faith" for righteousness? It sounded great, and I hoped it was true because I wasn't making much progress on my own. But it seemed too easy. I didn't understand it, so I packed it away and went back to believing basically what I was taught at the time: we were saved by faith, and now we pray, ask for help, try hard to obey—and sometimes it works.

As I studied the Scriptures over the years, the truth was revealed—righteousness is by faith. Not just faith for salvation but faith for living the life every day.

> *"...the life which I now live in the flesh I live*
> *by faith in the Son of God..."*
> (Galatians 2:20, NKJV)

> *"'...And their righteousness is from Me,' says the Lord."*
> (Isaiah 54:17, NKJV)

> *"...that I may gain Christ and be found in Him, not having*
> *my own righteousness, which is from the law, but that*
> *which is through faith in Christ, the righteousness*
> *which is from God by faith."*
> (Philippians 3:8–9, NKJV)

Remember I said there is pragmatics involved? God was teaching me His ways, one of which was: I don't have to love this person on my own. God wants to love through me (His part). My part is to be willing to:

- *"Do good to those who hate you..."* Give them flowers, a compliment, food. In the beginning, I did it only because He said I should, not because I wanted to.

- *"Bless them that curse you..."* I asked God to bless them—reluctantly.
- *"Pray for those who spitefully use you."* I start praying for them by faith, not because I felt like it.
- *Apologize for my part if I need to,* but don't expect a reciprocal apology.
- *Accept people where they are at.* The way Jesus accepts us.

You might ask God, "What if they don't deserve it?" God says to love them anyway. Isn't that what He did for us? Did we deserve it?

When I started to do the above by faith—it wasn't easy—but as I prayed for *Impossible to Love #1,* the ungodly feelings I had for this person slowly diminished. I cannot explain it, but I know it was the Holy Spirit in me. It felt like me, but I know it was Him. The Apostle Paul describes it perfectly:

> *"I have been crucified with Christ; it is no longer I who live,*
> *but Christ lives in me; and the life which I now live in the*
> *flesh I live by faith in the Son of God, who loved me and*
> *gave Himself for me."*
> (Galatians 2:20, NKJV)

The only prerequisite is that I am willing to let God work through me—and if I'm not, He will work in me until I am.

There were other things God said I had to do. He won't do my part, and I can't do His:

- *Kick out the scenarios.* The scenarios of what they did pounded on the door of my mind. I learned if I didn't kick those thoughts out (my part) and give them to Jesus, darkness would come to my soul.

- *Stop talking about the scenarios to others.* I recall the thought that came to me just before I started to tell someone—it was the Holy Spirit telling me not to say anything, but I didn't listen. It felt good to tell it, but it wasn't worth the days of darkness I felt after I grieved the Holy Spirit.
- *Do what God impresses us to do.* By doing that, we are allowing the Lord to make us willing so that he may love through us.

> *"For Your sake we are killed all day long;*
> *we are accounted as sheep for the slaughter."*
> (Romans 8:36, NKJV)

I love the explanation in the next verse.

> *"Yet in all these things we are more than conquerors*
> *through Him who loved us."*
> (Romans 8:37, NKJV)

Do you get it? If we let Christ crucify us, we win. I recall telling Jesus years ago, "It hurts to die..."

His reply, "It hurts more not to." I've learned that is true.

When I started to let God love through me, I realized I didn't really love people like I thought I did. Looking back, I can see many situations, even after I was a Christian, where I didn't act in love. Our own love is never enough, and everything we'll ever need is in the Holy Spirit, who is in us. He will...

*"...make you complete in every good work to do His will,
working in you what is well pleasing in His sight, through
Jesus Christ, to whom be glory forever and ever. Amen."*
(Hebrews 13:21, NKJV)

Not long ago, we attended a church out of town, and the pastor shared how he had walked through the sanctuary Saturday night praying for those who would be attending Sunday morning when God spoke to him, saying, "It grieves Me that My children rely on their strength, instead of *Mine*."

That's one of the lessons God has been teaching me over the years, and it is not an easy lesson to learn. It takes faith, but the outcome is God's power in the situation vs. my meaningful effort. It's trying vs. trusting. "Trying" never got me anywhere. If it's not in the Spirit, it won't make a difference.

"Without faith it is impossible to please Him..."
(Hebrews 11:6, NKJV)

Just recently, in the middle of what I felt was an impossible situation, I cried out, *"Lord, I can't handle this!"*

God responded, "Carole, you can't, *but I can!*"

Immediately I knew I was trying when I should have been trusting, "Lord, I'm trusting You to handle this, I'm putting it in Your hands..." As I prayed, He calmed my anxiety and took over. Sometimes feeling our weakness is good because we realize how much we need Jesus to do what we can't. We need to let Him work through us because we have entered His rest and have ceased from our works like God did from His!

"There remains therefore a rest for the people of God. For he who has entered His rest has himself also ceased from his works as God did from His."
(Hebrews 4:9–10, NKJV)

When I do my part, God will do His part (things only He can do). I am able to work out (through the Spirit) what He is working in me—and He gets all the glory where it belongs.

Recall what I said about "righteousness by faith" sounding too easy? I have learned that it's not always easy to let God "crucify the flesh" in order to let Him come through me. But when I follow His lead and do what He says (my part), the Holy Spirit comes through me (His part), and to my delight, the end result of letting God have His way feels s-o-o-o-o-o good!

Not my way, but Yahweh!

"I sought the Lord, and He heard me,
and delivered me from all my fears."
(Psalm 34:4, NKJV)

43. The Spirit of Fear

For as long as I can remember, fears have been my unwelcome adversaries. I didn't grow out of them; they increased as I got older. I could never understand why I was wired with so much susceptibility? And why did some experiences affect me so deeply, whereas others could brush them off easily?

After I became a Christian, I read how Jesus miraculously delivered people from a variety of infirmities; surely, He could deliver me from my fears as He did for David (Psalm 34:4 above). When I read that (above verse), I thought, *This promise is for me too.* I prayed, fasted, and trusted the Lord to deliver me, but the fears were still there. *What does it take?* I questioned the Lord impatiently. I didn't hear a thing—you probably guessed that.

I searched my Bible, thinking, *Surely the answer must be in here, somewhere.* I looked up every verse in my concordance containing the word "fear" and wrote on a tablet the verses that caught my attention. One was:

> *"God has not given us the spirit of fear, but of power and of*
> *love and of a sound mind."*
> (2 Timothy 1:7, NKJV)

God said He did *not* give us a spirit of fear, so it must come from another source—our own mind and/or the enemy. The enemy knows our weaknesses and exploits them in order to render us useless. God reminds us,

> *"Be sober, be vigilant; because your adversary the devil*
> *walks about like a roaring lion, seeking whom he may*
> *devour. Resist him, steadfast in the faith..."*
> (1 Peter 5:8–9, NKJV)

I read 1 Samuel 16 in order to find out how God delivered David from all his fears. I discovered it took more than one prayer to bring deliverance. David *"sought"* the Lord, implying he prayed fervently. Even so, God sent him on a long and difficult road to the throne. On the way, Saul tried to kill him; when that didn't work, he sent him into battle, hoping the enemy would kill him. When that failed, Saul sent others to kill him, but none of his plans were successful. Actually,

> *"Now Saul was afraid of David, because the Lord was with*
> *him, but had departed from Saul."*
> (1 Samuel 18:12, NKJV)

Did you know that our enemy is afraid of us too? Afraid that we will believe God's promise that He has given us authority over the devil, and, that he is afraid we will learn how to use that authority. Jesus said:

> *"Behold, I give you the authority...over all the power of the*
> *enemy, and nothing shall by any means hurt you."*
> (Luke 10:19, NKJV)

Samuel had anointed David to be King of Israel, and yet David was running from place to place in order to stay ahead of Saul. He hid in caves, strongholds, forests, and deserts. It's hard to imagine why David was afraid of Saul since he had killed lions and bears when they tried to steal his sheep; he struck the giant Goliath with a sling and a stone; slew his "ten-thousands" of enemies at war, yet it appears that he didn't have enough faith to believe God would keep him safe from Saul.

Just imagine if David would have said to Saul: "I am not afraid of you because God is with me; thus far, He has kept me safe, and He's not about to let me go. He has anointed me to be King of Israel, and His plan is to give me 'a future and a hope' (Jeremiah 29:11, KJV). You have no power over me whatsoever." Sounds good, huh? But David, the giant killer, wasn't there yet.

Neither was I—in a much lesser sense. No one was trying to kill me, but my "road to freedom from fears" dealt with is-sues God was bringing to the surface: passivity, insecurity, and indecisiveness were a few of my enemies. He was changing me from a people-pleaser to a God-pleaser and teaching me to have faith, to believe what He said in His Word. This is the verse He gave me:

"And He said to me, 'My grace is sufficient for you, for My strength is made perfect in weakness.' Therefore most gladly I will rather boast in my infirmities, that the power of Christ may rest upon me. Therefore I take pleasure in infirmities, in reproaches, in needs, in persecutions, in distresses, for Christ's sake. For when I am weak, then I am strong."
(2 Corinthians 12:9–10, NKJV)

I believed it—in my head—but head belief has no power over fears. It took a serious amount of time, prayer, and determination to sink that promise from my head into my heart, making it mine. God was working in me through the difficult circumstances He was bringing into my life.

I repeated the above verse over and over, and when I finally had the faith to believe it and act on it—then my enemy no longer had any power over me. Oh yes, he tried. There were times I weakened, but I didn't give up. I leaned more and more on Christ—and the more I leaned, the more I overcame some of my fears.

Meanwhile, Saul continued to chase David, and God continued to keep him safe in a variety of ways:

- "The prophet Gad said to David, 'Do not stay in the stronghold; depart, and go to the land of Judah'" (1 Samuel 22:5). He went.
- David prayed and asked God if the men of Keilah would deliver him into Saul's hand if he went there. "And the Lord said, 'They will deliver you'" (from 1 Samuel 23:11–12). David didn't go.

- "Jonathan, Saul's son, arose and went to David in the woods and strengthened his hand in God. And he said to him, 'Do not fear, for the hand of Saul my father shall not find you...'" (1 Samuel 23:16–17).

- David was on one side of the mountain, and Saul and his men were on the other, about to capture David and his men, when God stepped in: "A messenger came to Saul, saying, 'Hurry and come, for the Philistines have invaded the land!'" (1 Samuel 23: 27) Saul and his men left, and God spared David again.

- Saul stopped in a cave, not knowing that David and his men were in the recesses of the same cave. It was there that David called out to Saul, "My Lord the King!" and "David stooped with his face to the earth, and bowed down" (1 Samuel 24: 8). As he bowed down, he was putting himself in a perilous position. I believe he was trusting God and finally overcoming his fear of Saul.

- Abishai volunteered to kill Saul, and David refused, saying, "As the Lord lives, the Lord shall strike him, or his day shall come to die, or he shall go out to battle and perish" (from 1 Samuel 26:8–10).

- David was trusting God, and the latter is exactly what happened: Saul perished in battle.

David was learning that God was in control. It wasn't chance or coincidence that many situations were working in his favor, and his road to the kingdom was getting shorter.

Our fears begin to dissipate when we trust God's love for us when we see His hand in our circumstances, and our faith begins to overcome our weaknesses as we are tested and come out stronger.

> *"Behold, I have refined you, but not as silver; I have tested*
> *you in the furnace of affliction."*
> (Isaiah 48:10, NKJV)

Just a warning from experience. If we begin to relax and not find times to meet with the Lord, our faith can weaken, causing our fears to overtake us. Living in victory is only possible when we stay close to Jesus; He is the only one who can deliver us.

> *"Watch and pray, lest you enter into temptation. The spirit*
> *indeed is willing, but the flesh is weak."*
> (Matthew 26:41, NKJV)

The flesh is and always will be weak. It does not become strong. Don't be tempted to think it will. What makes us strong is our faith, and faith comes when we "watch and pray," believing,

> *"...that the power of Christ may rest upon me...for when I*
> *am weak, then I am strong."*
> (2 Corinthians 12:9–10, NKJV)

It took me a long time to understand what Jesus meant when He said,

"There is no fear in love; but perfect love casts out fear,
because fear involves torment. But he who fears has not
been made perfect in love."
(1 John 4:18, NKJV)

"Perfect in love" is when we have the faith to believe that God is in total control of our lives and that He will come through for us every time. I'm not totally there yet, but I am not giving up. I know I will go through situations that try my tenacity because that's how faith increases. My goal is to live by faith, not fear!

"Strengthen the weak hands, and make firm the feeble knees. Say to those who are fearful-hearted, 'Be strong, do not fear! Behold, your God shall come with vengeance, with the recompense of God; He will come and save you.'"
(Isaiah 35:3–4, NKJV)

44. The Spirit of Fear—Pt. II

Of all the fears I had, the most difficult one to conquer was my fear of violence. It started in grade school when my friend and I were on the playground and saw a bully unmercifully picking on a kid who was a little "different." My friend, a sanguine (happy-go-lucky), probably forgot it by the next day. I, primarily a melancholic (deep thinker), couldn't. It got worse. If I was near a group of people and heard any kind of disruption, I froze, and fear overwhelmed me to the point of physical pain. Whenever I encountered violence on TV, I changed the channel.

I had been a Christian for several years, learning to know and love God before He began delivering me from that fear. I recall the night that Keith and I were walking through a darkened parking lot after a Festival when fear started rising with-

in. I started shouting—not out loud—but in my mind, something like:

"Jesus, I am trusting you! I refuse to be afraid. You are my
savior, my lord, my helper, my redeemer. You promised you
would never leave me nor forsake me. I know you are with us,
that you love us; I believe you are keeping us under your wing,
close to your heart."

1. The physical benefit: talking out loud if I am alone or
    shouting inwardly when others are present blocks a
    good share of the adrenalin rush, which feeds fear.
2. The Spiritual benefit: by talking to Jesus—whether in-
    wardly or out loud—fears and doubts are blocked from
    entering my mind. I am forced to center on Christ and
    trust Him to deliver me from what I think might happen.

Yes, it is a choice I have to make: do I listen to the enemy/my
own mind, or do I believe Jesus when He told his disciples that
His Father would send us the Holy Spirit, saying,

"Peace I leave with you, My peace I give to you; not as the
world gives do I give to you. Let not your heart be troubled,
neither let it be afraid."
(John 14:27, NKJV)

"But Lord," I asked Him, "How do I not let my heart be
afraid?" In the beginning, I expected Him to deliver me on the
spot. Now He was saying when I do my part, He will do His.
Some things I do or say:

- Searching scripture to find a verse(s) that I can repeat until it settles down in my heart, then I believe it, and can repeat it when I need it—such as:

"Whenever I am afraid, I will trust in You. In God, I will praise His word, In God I will put my trust; I will not fear. What can flesh do to me?"
(Psalm 56:3–4, NKJV)

- Staying close to Jesus through prayer and the Word—that's where the power originates.
- Controlling my mind by *kicking out* fears, whether they are from my mind or the enemy, repeating what Jesus said with authority, "Get behind Me, Satan, you are an offense to Me..."(Matthew 16:23). Then tell Jesus: "I am trusting You! I believe You are keeping me close to Your heart, and You will fight this battle for me..."

"Resist the devil and he will flee from you. Draw near to God and He will draw near to you."
(James 4:7–8, NKJV)

- Believing that Jesus gave us authority over the enemy because He said so.

"Behold, I give you authority...over all the power of the enemy, and nothing shall by any means hurt you."
(Luke 10:19, NKJV)

- Telling Jesus, "Lord, I can't handle this, but I know You can. I have faith that You will deliver me from this fear."

Recently I encountered another type of fear: post-traumatic stress disorder (PTSD), which happens primarily to military men and women who have served in action. It can also occur after a traumatic experience such as major surgery.

My husband was suffering from flashbacks after a botched-up surgery. The flashbacks weren't always related directly to the surgery. They included situations that happened years ago and would rapidly strike as Keith started falling asleep. Prayers and pills didn't halt the problem. I had seen Jesus do some awesome things by His promise of "binding" and "loosing" in Matthew 18:18, and so Keith and I read and prayed over what Jesus said,

"Assuredly, I say to you, whatever you bind on earth
will be bound in heaven, and whatever you loose on earth
will be loosed in heaven."
(Matthew 18:18, NKJV)

I bound the flashbacks and loosed "the peace of God" for Keith, and the flashbacks stopped. A few weeks later, the flashbacks returned, and Keith resisted them in the name of Jesus, thanking God and praising Him for His faithfulness.

A few months later, they returned briefly. We resisted the enemy, bound the flashbacks, loosed God's peace, and they retreated. It has been several months since then. God's Word works!

"The word of God is living and powerful,
and sharper than any two-edged sword..."
(Hebrews 4:12, NKJV)

The fears I have written about—here and in different devotionals—all have different sources, so our teacher, the Holy Spirit, will teach us how to deal with each one. Deliverance is a promise, but it rarely happens overnight. It can, because God can do anything He chooses, but going the distance, at least for me, has its rewards:

I am learning to exercise faith,

Understand His ways.

Believe what He says in the Holy Bible, repeating it until it becomes mine.

"For I, the Lord your God, will hold your right hand, saying
to you, 'Fear not, I will help you.'"
(Isaiah 41:13, NKJV)

Our God is a God of His word!

"And he who does not take his cross and follow after Me is not worthy of Me. He who finds his life will lose it, and he who loses his life for My sake will find it."
(Matthew 10:38–39, NKJV)

45. Taking up Our Cross

Years ago, I heard people describe "their cross" as having a physical handicap, living with an irritable person, or being in a burdensome situation that would never change. What Jesus was describing in the above verse is that and so much more. He brought a new perspective to it when He started convicting me to pick up my cross on a *daily* basis.

When my husband reminded me again that I had forgotten to turn the light out when I left a room, I was tempted to tell him that I had turned a light out earlier that day that he had forgotten, but instead, I prayed, "Lord, help me remember to turn out lights..."

I have heard "Carole, you left the refrigerator door open..." many times from my husband. Tonight, my grandson said, "Grandma, you left the refrigerator door open."

"Lord, please help me to remember!"

During communion one Sunday in church, a person on the other side of the near-empty pew was handed the plate but didn't get up to pass it. I had started walking, thinking she would meet me halfway, but she didn't move. I went to get it. I was grumbling on the way back when I heard, "Would you have walked over there and picked it up for Me?"

Yes, Lord, yes! I picked out a piece of "bread" from the communion plate and handed the plate to my husband when a verse dropped into my mind:

> *"Inasmuch as you did it to one of the least of these My brethren, you did it to Me."*
> (Matthew 25:40, NKJV)

I tell you, when the next plate came, I jumped up and went to get it—smiling!

I was trying to fix something that wasn't working. I kept trying until my patience wore thin, and I contemplated throwing it in the corner. I had a choice. I can give into my impatience, or I can stop and say: "Lord, I need Your help with this..."

Years ago, my husband poked his head into the kitchen and said, "You need to shut those cupboard doors. Someone will get hurt."

I replied, "I always close them; I just forgot tonight." I closed the doors and said, "Don't I, Lord?" I noticed in the days to follow, I left the doors open a lot. I was praying about it when God said, "You need to see things from your husband's perspective." He wasn't talking just about cupboard doors but about many other things as well. Listening to my husband is a way of giving up my pride and picking up my cross.

When I choose to let Christ crucify the flesh, the Holy Spirit takes over, and He changes my attitude. It is amazing! It's an inner miracle!

"I have been crucified with Christ; it is no longer I who live, but Christ lives in me; and the life which I now live in the flesh I live by faith in the Son of God, who loved me and gave Himself for me."
(Galatians 2:20, NKJV)

Sometimes it's not that easy. It depends on the circumstances and the people involved. Let me tell you a few of the many times I chose the wrong response.

I had just lost my job—it was quit or be let go—the job was way over my head, but I didn't want to admit it. It was so stressful I broke out in huge blotches everywhere except on my hands and face. I had to quit. God was saying, "Accept it." But I didn't want to. When I was tired of being miserable, I accepted it, and eventually, God turned it into good.

"I will give you the treasures of darkness..."
(Isaiah 45:3, NKJV)

I was telling my sister in great detail how a person we knew had mistreated me. I had a feeling that I shouldn't be dredging this up again, but I wanted to tell it—and I ignored that still small voice. The next few days felt like I had been stranded on a desert island, and all my efforts to pray came back like sand in my face. I missed God's presence. I could never live without it, and because of that, I picked up my cross and started to pray daily for that person. It took some time, but God eventually changed my heart.

> *"But I say to you, love your enemies...and pray for those*
> *who spitefully use you and persecute you."*
> (Matthew 5:44, NKJV)

Everything that happens to us works together for good. I learned that is true as long as I accept what's happening and look for God in it. His purpose is that we become more like Him.

> *"And we know that all things work together for good to*
> *those who love God, to those who are the called according to*
> *His purpose. For whom He foreknew, He also predestined*
> *to be conformed to the image of His Son..."*
> (Romans 8:28–29, NKJV)

God has ordained that everything that happens to us can work together for good if we accept it. He lists tribulation, distress, persecution, famine, nakedness, peril, or sword. All these situations are opportunities for us to die to ourselves and take on Christ's likeness. Every day we have opportunities to pick up our cross and follow Him.

> *"For Your sake we are killed all day long; we are accounted*
> *as sheep for the slaughter. Yet in all these things we are*
> *more than conquerors through Him who loved us."*
> (Romans 8:36–37, NKJV)

When we pick up the cross and die to ourselves, we become conquerors through Him! Becoming conquerors means we become more like Him.

Aren't the Lord's ways mind-boggling? Unfathomable? God said,

> *"'For My thoughts are not your thoughts, nor are your ways*
> *My ways,' says the Lord."*
> (Isaiah 55:8, NKJV)

Just a few months ago, I became aware of two people that I had been critical of for years. I prayed about it, and then I began praying *for* them. It's amazing how God can change my thoughts; I really like them now, and I can't imagine why I was critical of them. I have learned that it's hard to dislike anyone I am praying for. By praying for them, we are crucifying the flesh and allowing the Holy Spirit to take over. John the Baptist put it this way:

> *"He must increase, but I must decrease."*
> (John 3:30, NKJV)

Many of God's promises come with a "if you do...the Lord will." That means we have to give up something in order to get what we are asking God for. For instance: I was praying for a fantastic marriage like my parents had, but nothing was working. I thought if my husband would be more spiritual, our marriage would be great until I heard God say, "If you allow Me to change you first, I'll change your marriage." I was contemplating what that meant when He continued, "Listen to your husband's complaints." *Ouch!*

Change is never easy, but it worked just like God said it would. Eventually, Keith began changing as well, and the joy that came afterward was worth far more than what it cost me by allowing God to change me.

We win when we lose! Aren't God's ways awesome?

King David poignantly set an example when he was looking for a place to sacrifice to the Lord. The prophet Gad directed David to go to Araunah's, who offered David whatever he needed without cost, but David refused, saying:

"I will surely buy it from you for a price; nor will I offer
burnt offerings to the Lord my God with that which costs
me nothing."
(2 Samuel 24:24, NKJV)

Jesus paved the way as our supreme example of taking up the cross:

"For the joy that is set before Him, endured the cross,
despising the shame and has sat down at the right hand of
the throne of God."
(Hebrews 12:2, NKJV)

"And a little child shall lead them."
(Isaiah 11:6, NKJV)

46. Letting Go of Questions

It was Christmas in Arizona, and I was determined not to let the same thing happen again this year. Last year my husband and I cut our vacation short and flew home after I spent three days in the hospital along with numerous tests that failed to explain my symptoms.

And now, a year later, I could feel the same burning in my chest. "Lord, I don't understand. Why is this happening?" The usual holiday stress was no stranger to me, but I had prayed and planned very carefully to make sure this year was different. "Why aren't You answering my prayers?" I questioned God.

I wasn't sleeping well. Our granddaughter woke up at least twice each night for a bottle; I tossed and turned, trying to fall back asleep as my ears picked up the subtlest sighs from her crib across the room while my back rebelled against the hard mattress.

"Grandma, will you watch 'Joseph' with me, just the two of us?" asked my three-and-a-half-year-old grandson. He had gotten the movie *Joseph: Kings of Dreams* for Christmas, and we had watched it at least three times.

My daughter, knowing I hadn't been sleeping well, said, "I think Grandma is tired and would like to take a nap this afternoon."

"I'm talking to Grandma!" he responded.

"Yes, I will," I answered him.

The guys were watching football, so we watched "Joseph" in one of the bedrooms. As we sat on the bed, I noticed that whatever I did, he mimicked. When I pulled my legs up and wrapped my arms around them, so did he. I stretched my legs out and leaned back on the pillows, so did he. I put my arm around him, and he looked up at me and gave me one of those melt-your-heart-grandma smiles before becoming entranced again with the movie.

Joseph was his father's favorite, and that made his brothers jealous. When Joseph began sharing his prophetic dreams with his brothers, they decided to do away with him by throwing him in a well.

However, God had his own plan. When a group of Ishmaelites stopped at the well on their way to Egypt, Judah, one of the brothers, convinced the others to sell Joseph to them. The Ishmaelites took him to Egypt, and he was bought by Potiphar, an officer of Pharaoh.

> "And his master saw that the Lord was with him and that
> the Lord made all he did to prosper in his hand..."
> (Genesis 39:3, NKJV)

In time Joseph was given authority over all of the Master's house, and he prospered in all that he did—until his master's wife unjustly accused him of assaulting her, and Joseph was thrown in prison.

A year or so later, and still in prison, Joseph interprets two dreams for Pharaoh's butler and baker who had been tossed in prison. He tells the butler to remember him to Pharaoh when he gets out, but the butler forgets.

Two years later and still in prison, Joseph questions God (in the movie only) as to why this is happening to him and what has he done to deserve this. And then the pinnacle point of the movie comes when Joseph decides to trust God and let go of his questions, even though he still doesn't understand.

Tears rolled down my cheeks as I let go of my questions. God had used my grandson to soften my heart so I could hear God. Letting go of questions when we don't understand is called faith, and faith is what God loves to hear from His children. It is what He responds to. I didn't need to know "why" because I knew Someone who did, and I decided to trust Him.

The rest of the vacation went smoothly. Keith and I moved to the sofa bed in the living room, slept well, my heartburn subsided, and we watched Joseph with our grandson two or three more times.

We don't want to leave Joseph in prison nor miss the lesson we can learn from him:

Pharaoh had a dream that no one could interpret. The butler remembered Joseph, who was in prison and had interpreted his dream. Pharaoh sent for Joseph and he interpreted Pharaoh's dream, that there would be seven years of prosperity and seven years of famine. After that, Pharoah placed Joseph in charge over all the land to execute his plan to store grain.

Pharaoh made Joseph second in command over the land of Egypt, gave him a wife, and Joseph named his firstborn son Manasseh, meaning:

> *"For God has made me forget all my toil and all my father's house. And the name of the second child he called Ephraim, meaning: 'For God has caused me to be fruitful in the land of my affliction.'"*
> (Genesis 41:51–52, NKJV)

During the famine, his brothers came to buy grain. They didn't recognize Joseph until he revealed himself to them.

> *"I am Joseph your brother, whom you sold into Egypt. But now, do not therefore be grieved or angry with yourselves because you sold me here; for God sent me before you to preserve life."*
> (Genesis 45:4–5, NKJV)

His brothers brought Jacob, their father, to Joseph, and Pharaoh gave them the best land in Egypt to live. After Jacob died, the brothers were afraid Joseph would repay them for the evil they did to him, and they fell down before him. Joseph responded:

> *"'Do not be afraid, for am I in the place of God? But as for you, you meant evil against me; but God meant it for good,*

> *in order to bring it about as it is this day, to save many*
> *people alive. Now therefore, do not be afraid; I will provide*
> *for you and your little ones.' And he comforted them and*
> *spoke kindly to them."*
> (Genesis 50:19–21, NKJV)

What a beautiful lesson in forgiveness. He saw God's blessing in it, not his brothers' egregious act. Have you discerned God's hand in your deepest valleys? Do you see God in the unpleasant things that happen? Notice how Joseph comforted his brothers:

> *"Then he fell on his brother Benjamin's neck and wept...*
> *Moreover he kissed all his brothers and wept over them..."*
> (Genesis 45:14–15, NKJV)

God had a plan for Joseph, but he had to be refined—tested in the furnace of affliction. Joseph saw God's hand in it, not right away, but he was trusting God long before He was freed from prison.

God recorded Joseph's affliction in the Psalms:

> *"He sent a man before them—Joseph—who was sold as a*
> *slave. They hurt his feet with fetters, he was laid in irons.*
> *Until the time that his word came to pass, the word of the*
> *Lord tested him."*
> (Psalm 105:17–19, NKJV)

And Joseph passed the test admirably!

*"I know, O Lord, that Your judgments are right, and that in
Your faithfulness You have afflicted me."*
(Psalm 119:75, NKJV)

47. Afflictions, Who Needs Them?

It started at the beginning of the year—a neck injury with multiple visits to doctors, various meds, a couple of ER trips, shots in the neck, acupuncture, chiropractic, and physical therapy—all bringing no resolve. My husband cooked, cleaned, washed clothes, etc., while I did a few jobs on the good days.

I knew God was in it, but it was difficult seeing Him in the dark hours of the night when the pain was at its height and fears were manifold.

*"I rise before the dawning of the morning, and cry for help;
I hope in Your word."*
(Psalm 119:147, NKJV)

In time, those night sessions with God became my mainstay as I prayed fervently, fought doubts, and repeated His word over and over. "God, You said, 'I will never leave you, nor forsake you...'" "Fear not, for I am with you..." "When you walk through the fire, you shall not be burned. Nor shall the flame scorch you. For I am the Lord your God…" He was stretching my faith while dealing with some things in me that needed changing.

> *"My eyes are awake through the night watches, that I may meditate on Your word."*
> (Psalm 119:148, NKJV)

It's hard to say "no" with His foot on my neck, but it was the perfect motivation to want to change. God was stretching me to the point that I thought I might break.

> *"Many are the afflictions of the righteous, but the Lord delivers him out of them all."*
> (Psalm 34:19, NKJV)

But not right away! Not until we've learned what the Lord is saying. Not before we learn how to "wait on the Lord," as He works in us "both to will and to do of His good pleasure" (Philippians 2:13).

David wrote a lot about waiting in Psalm 39:7–8 (NKJV),

> *"And now, Lord, what do I wait for? My hope is in You. Deliver me from all my transgressions; do not make me the reproach of the foolish."*

Psalm 40:1–3 (NKJV) changes tone as David continues,

> *"I waited patiently for the Lord; and He inclined to me, and heard my cry. He also brought me up out of a horrible*

*pit, out of the miry clay, and set my feet upon a rock, and
established my steps."*

Not only will God bring us out of our afflictions and take us to a higher level, He will use those times as a testimony to the greatness of God. Joyce Meyer said, "He takes our mess and makes it our message."

*"It is good for me that I have been afflicted, that I may
learn Your statutes."*
(Psalm 119:71, NKJV)

I had told the Lord I would accept the neck injury if it brought Him glory. That night my granddaughter (around three years old) called, with her mom's help, "Grandma, are you feeling all right?" She told me she had prayed for me. "Grandma, are you coming over tonight?" She was 2,400 miles away. Because of my neck injury, we had to cancel our flight at the end of that week. "I love you, Grandma," she said as tears filled my eyes, then she gave the phone to my daughter.

"Lord, if I don't get well, I can't travel to see my grandkids— the apples of my eye."

*"Before I was afflicted I went astray.
But now I keep Your word."*
(Psalm 119:67, NKJV)

I believe this kind of training will go on until I see Him. For a time, all is well. Then, the Lord gets my attention again—there is something He wants to perfect in me, sometimes through affliction or lesser circumstances. I have told Him, "Don't let me go until You have what You want from me." He hasn't.

Most of us want to know Him in the "power of His resurrection" but don't understand the other half, "the fellowship of His sufferings." You can't have one without the other.

> *"That I may know Him and the power of His resurrection, and the fellowship of His sufferings, being conformed to His death."*
> (Philippians 3:10, NKJV)

But afterward...it is s-o-o-o-o-o worth it! Is there anything better? Afflictions—who needs them? I do!

"The secret things belong to the Lord our God,
but those things which are revealed belong to us
and to our children forever..."
(Deuteronomy 29:29, NKJV)

48. God's Answer to Cancer

The inspiration and conviction to write about cancer came in a dream. It was succinct and to the point. I saw a page with a dedication to my father on it. I woke up, still seeing the page, knowing I needed to write what God had been showing me. Although my dad lost a valiant battle against cancer, in the process, he found eternal life with Jesus Christ.

Back in the mid-seventies, when our children were young, I became concerned about the rising tide of cancer. I wanted to know what I could do to protect my family from that dreadful disease. "Lord, show me," I prayed over and over. "Teach me what I do not know."

An article in the newspaper started out:

"Not long ago, the defeat of cancer seemed inevitable. Decades of research would soon pay off with a completely fresh approach..."

But it didn't turn out the way the experts had hoped. There have been some advances over the years, but just maybe there's something we haven't considered. Maybe the answer isn't as elusive as we once thought.

What God showed me may be considered by some too simplistic. But the longer I walk with the Lord, the simpler His ways become. Even the story of salvation is so simple people stumble all over it.

> *"Behold, I lay in Zion a stumbling stone and rock of offense,*
> *and whoever believes on Him will not be put to shame."*
> (Romans 9:33, NKJV)

I'm asking you to open your mind and prayerfully listen for confirmation as I relate what I believe God has revealed to me.

> *"Trust in the Lord with all our heart, and lean not to your*
> *own understanding; in all your ways acknowledge Him, and*
> *He will direct your paths. Do not be wise in your own eyes;"*
> (Proverbs 3:5–7, NKJV)

The first thing God dropped into my mind was to read labels. I was shocked! I read cryptic words like guar gum, propyl gallate, monoglycerides, diglycerides, nitrites, amylase, ammonium caseinate, malic acid, and red #2, blue #1, and dozens more additives that are in cakes, cookies, cereals, bread, sodas, snacks, canned food, frozen goods and...*Were we really eating all that?*

At about time, an interest in nutrition began developing in the media. I went to the library several times, coming home with an armload of books on cancer, nutrition, and food additives. I cut out mega articles on cancer from newspapers and magazines.

As I read, praying for the mind of Christ, a deep conviction settled over me that the chemicals we were putting in our bodies were not as innocuous as we were being told. But was it all or some—and which ones? God taught me a little at a time. The first chemicals that He impressed me to avoid were the preservatives BHT and BHA.

Do you have any idea how many breakfast cereals contained one or the other? While grocery shopping, I heard my son say to his little sister after reading the ingredients, "Mom won't let us have this one either," as he stuffed it back on the shelf.

I tried various brands of granola with no additives, but I couldn't find one that tasted good or was nutritious, so I developed my own. After numerous attempts, I finally balanced the right ingredients, the right temperature, and the right taste with nutritious ingredients: whole-grained oats, flaxseed, wheat germ, honey, olive oil, walnuts, pecans, pepitas, sunflower seeds, spices with optional raisins or fruit.

While opening a loaf of bread labeled "Our Daily Bread" at my mother's house, the Lord said, "Don't believe it." The label was a misnomer; when I came to 'sodium benzoate,' I knew that it was something I shouldn't consume. There are now numerous other preservatives out there to stay away from.

As I continued reading labels, I decided to change our eating habits—our meals became simpler but healthier. I made most meals from scratch. Fortunately, I didn't work full-time; I either subbed or worked short-term.

Colors were the next thing on the Lord's hit list. Adding colors is a cover-up used for aesthetic purposes. If you read labels, you will usually find one that doesn't contain coloring, and it probably tastes better. Eliminating colors produced more complaints from the little cereal eaters. In their vernacular that left "just a few crummy cereals." I hung in there and cooked hot cereals with fruit or made blueberry pancakes, keeping the "crummy" cereals around just in case.

> *"Bless the Lord, O my soul, and forget not all His benefits…*
> *Who satisfies your mouth with good things, so that your*
> *youth is renewed like the eagle's."*
> (Psalm 103:2 and 5, NKJV)

That's a promise from God!

Besides food, I uncolored my soap, shampoo, toothpaste, lotions, deodorant, etc., and they all work just as well—and in the long run, even better! I searched for a lower percentage of aluminum zirconium tetrachlorohydrex in deodorants, lowering it from nineteen to sixteen percent, and no talc—both have been linked to cancer. Lipstick? That's a difficult one. Before eating, I wipe my lipstick off dainty-like; it's either that or eat it.

Nitrites joined the pack. You will find them in hams, bacon, cold meats, hot dogs, pork, and sausages, with few exceptions. Most of them had contained nitrates which were known carcinogens and were replaced with nitrites with often-added vitamin C to neutralize the nitrites—but do they?

How do I know these additives were verboten? I was listening for God's voice, praying diligently, and the knowledge I received was "out of the ordinary." But for you, that is not enough; you need to perceive if this is from God.

> *"When He, the Spirit of truth, has come, He will*
> *guide you into all truth; for He will not speak on His own*
> *authority, but whatever He hears He will speak;*
> *and He will tell you things to come."*
> (John 16:13, NKJV)

I am reminded of my son-in-law, who was trying to introduce his son to a new concept but wasn't getting anywhere. He paused...and then quoted, "A mind is like a parachute; it only works when it is open." I would add: "...*open* to God."

In all my early reading, I came across only one reference connecting cancer and the immune system: when various organs are transplanted into the body, certain chemicals were given to weaken the immune system to prevent it from attacking the transplant—in doing so, it sometimes caused leukemia.

If our immune system is being weakened through the chemicals God was showing me to stay away from, that would be a factor in acquiring cancer, as well as how strong our immune system is, to begin with.

Did you know our immune system attacks anything that is foreign? What if our immune system couldn't keep up with all the additives swirling around in our bodies?

Lately, I have been reading about immunotherapy, i.e., increasing the ability of the immune system to combat certain cancers. That's great news for those who have cancer if it's caught in time. But for those who don't have cancer—an old adage rings true:

"An ounce of protection is worth a pound of cure."

According to the American Cancer Society's website, it is estimated that in 2020 there will be 1.8 million new cancer cases in the U.S., and 609,520 people will die from it.

I have shared with others what I believe God has revealed to me, and the responses are mixed. Some agree, some remark unceremoniously, "*Everything* causes cancer," some laugh it off, saying, "We all have to die of something." Believe me; it is *not* funny when you see someone you love suffer and die long before you are ready to let them go.

My father and mother both smoked, and both had cancer. My mother survived breast cancer. My father exchanged cigarettes for a pipe. He contracted lung cancer, causing him to leave us much too soon.

My brother's wife died of liver cancer, and my niece of breast and lung cancer which metastasized to her brain. Neither one of them smoked. Even though I know they are all with Jesus, I learned firsthand what a loathsome disease cancer is and how it can take those you love away much too soon!

My grandfather used DDT extensively in his lot-sized garden. He died from prostate cancer in 1946; my grandmother (his wife) died from complications of breast cancer surgery six years later.

Rachel Carson, a marine biologist, questioned the safety of chemical pesticides in her book *Silent Spring*.[1] She reported on several insecticides, weed killers, and herbicides and how they

---

1 Rachel Carson, *Silent Spring*, Fawcett World Library, New York, 1962.

affected rivers, streams, and soil. The fish, birds, and frogs were examined a year later and found that their bodies *still* contained DDD." (DDD is a close relative to DDT.)

After her book became a best seller in 1962, President John Kennedy ordered a study on the effects of pesticides in 1963. The Environmental Protection Agency (EPA) was proposed by President Nixon in 1970, and in 1972 the EPA outlawed DDT and several other pesticides.

David Rueben MD, in his book *The Save Your Life Diet*,[2] maintains that a lack of fiber in our diet is killing us. His extensive research—prodded by losing his father to colon cancer—revealed that people on a low-fiber diet allowed the remnants of their digested food to stay within their colon for several days at a time, which he equated to harboring a time bomb.

A high fiber diet will help empty the colon sooner—and that's good—but why take the risk and allow chemicals to enter your body at all? Every part of the body can be affected by the chemicals we eat, not just the colon.

Eileen Renders MD, wrote in *Food Additives, Nutrients & Supplements A–Z*,[3] that many substances if consumed in large concentrations have been proven or suspected of being carcinogens. Their effects long-term in addition to the mix of substances has yet to be adequately considered and studied.

The FDA investigates all additives and pesticides, setting tolerance levels, and giving those found safe, a rating of "Generally Recognized as Safe" (GRAS). When red #2 was discovered to be carcinogenic after a long time listed as "safe" (1976), the

2 David Reuben MD, *The Save Your Life Diet*, Random House, Inc., New York. 1975.
3 Eileen Renders MD, *Food Additives, Nutrients & Supplements A–Z*, Clear Light Publishers, Santa Fe, NM. 1999.

FDA removed it from the GRAS list. Also removed were orange #1, 2, yellow #1, 2, 3, 4, and violet #1.

Until the 1960s, food colors were derived from coal tar—a known carcinogen. I have read recently that colors no longer come from coal tar but from petroleum, crude oil, or bugs. Yes, bugs! Do you find these components comforting?

Additives are not the only cause of cancer. Other causes of cancer include asbestos, aspartame, formaldehyde, pesticides, radon, tobacco, talc, working in coal mines, working with certain chemicals—to name a few. But the combination of these, plus the additives we eat every day, are even more frightening.

Why did God reveal this to me? Because I asked Him. I gave Him my time, I listened, I prayed, I wanted His mind—not mine. At the time, I was concerned about keeping my family safe. I feel the need to share this with those who are willing to take the time to listen to God. George Washington Carver listened to God. I learned about him in school, when God could still be talked about, and how he developed over 300 products from the peanut, soybean, and sweet potato. I admired his humility, his commitment, and how he and God communed in his lab. In his book, he says he comes into his laboratory as a servant of God. He defines himself as a vessel through which God chooses to speak through and reveal things to when he puts his trust in Him.[4]

"Teach me Your way, O Lord; I will walk in Your truth."
(Psalm 86:11, NKJV)

---

4 *George Washington Carver*, Doubleday & Co. Inc., Garden City, NY 1943.

God designed a complex immune system to keep us healthy. Perhaps you've run across words like lymphocytes, macrophages, B-cells, T-cells, and antibodies, to name a few.

Years ago, I saw the movie *Fantastic Voyage*. The story was a fabrication with some truth in it. The crew and ship were miniaturized to the size of a microbe, put in a saline solution, and injected into the arterial system of a scientist who had been shot but held valuable information our country needed.

The team's mission was to save his life by breaking up a blood clot on his brain with a laser before being attacked by his body's immune system. With the intrigue of a hair-raising chase, split-second timing of accomplishing their goal, and overcoming a saboteur on their team—the movie kept you on the edge of your seat. As the final minutes tick away, the crew uses a laser to unblock the scientist's blood clot, narrowly escaping the deadly attack of the antibodies and being extracted from the body in the nick of time.

The movie is fantasy and fiction, but what happens in the body's defense system is real and significantly more complex than the movie portrays. Our immune system is part of God's "fearfully and wonderfully made" body described by David:

> *"You formed my inward parts...I will praise You,*
> *for I am fearfully and wonderfully made; marvelous are*
> *Your works..."*
> (Psalm 139:13–14, NKJV)

Marvelous indeed! Most of us are not aware of the intricacy of the immune system and what it does to keep us alive. God's powerful army battles intruders, night and day, unceasingly. The white blood cells called lymphocytes play an important part as they travel from the bone marrow to the thymus gland, where they become T-cells—major defenders of the body—remembering *every* enemy they have ever encountered. When these same enemies try to re-enter the body, they are pre-programmed to fight immediately.

Other lymphocytes called B-cells go to another spot where they learn to cope with germs and other enemies. They are alerted to join the T-cells and produce the needed A.B. protein to help the T-cells demolish the enemy. Next, they assemble themselves at various posts in the lymph system, patrolling while the T-cells come and go from the lymph system into the bloodstream to surround and destroy any possible invader.

The B-cells that stay in the lymph system release special proteins called antibodies that enter the bloodstream to help the T-cells. Joining the T-cells and the antibodies are the macrophages, and if that's not enough, enforcements come in from proteins called "complement." Macrophages catch some of the organisms and, after bringing them to the B-cells, devour whatever the B-cells leave. And so it goes, minute after minute, hour after hour; God's powerful army is keeping us safe by attacking anything that is foreign.

But I wonder, *Did God design our bodies to deal with all the chemicals we are consuming? What if our immune system couldn't keep up with all the additives swirling around in our bodies?*

God confirmed again that I must share what He has been teaching me. During a trip in Washington DC with our family and extended family, we viewed American treasures, felt patriotic pride touring the buildings, were awed by the monuments—seeing things we'd only seen in books. By the end of the day, we were exhausted, looking for a place to rest, when a sign revealed that the statue of Albert Einstein was a couple of blocks away. I had to see it; one of my nieces joined me. Graven in stone was a quote that spoke clearly:

"The right to search for truth implies also a duty,
one must not conceal any part of what one has
recognized to be true."

This devotional is dedicated to my extraordinary father, who was loved and admired by everyone who knew him!

"Blessed is he who is not offended because of Me."
(Matthew 11:6, NKJV)

49. Cancer! In My Home

The doctor was on the phone informing my husband of the results of his biopsy. I was on the other extension listening when I heard the word "malignant," inwardly, I shouted, *Not in my husband; not in my home!*

I was devastated—not with Keith's report, it wasn't life-threatening—but with the God whom I had thoroughly believed and had given me many confirmations on how to prevent cancer in my house. If that wasn't true, how would I know if I had *ever* heard His voice?

I fell into a deep depression. I didn't want to go anywhere or talk to anyone. My husband seemed more concerned about me than his own dilemma; I felt guilty that I couldn't comfort him.

A week or so later, I was walking down our hallway and distinctly heard, "Check out _____," (the statin Keith was taking). I had no idea why. I looked up JAMA (Journal of American Medical Association) on the internet and found a journal stating there seemed to be a connection between statins and cancer.

"Blessed is he who is not offended because of Me."
(Matthew 11:6, NKJV)

I let go of my depression, confessed my lack of faith in God, and began encouraging my husband. Throughout the chemo and radiation, Keith soared with Jesus. We prayed, read the Bible, and every day, he would sing or say, "One day at a time, Sweet Jesus." He was leaning on Jesus, and life was good.

Years ago, Keith's doctor had told him that the statin he was taking leached the Co-enzyme Q-10 from his body, but his doctor questioned if taking the enzyme would make any difference. I have since read that statins reduce CoQ-10, which could link the body to heart disease, diabetes, brain disorders, and cancer.

Keith had acid reflux. His doctor ordered an endoscopy—the results were good. He also told him to stop eating after eight p.m., lose weight, exercise, and take omeprazole to reduce the acid—he took the meds.

Four years later, Keith had another endoscopy. This time he was diagnosed with esophageal cancer. *This was serious!* Only nine to eleven percent live past the first year due to side effects from the surgery. He almost didn't make it through the first month and ended up in the hospital. I was driving home from the hospital, and I felt the Lord say, "If there are no changes, things will continue the same." I knew what He meant.

"Blessed is he who is not offended because of Me."
(Matthew 11:6, NKJV)

Keith made it through five years, taking the co-enzyme Q-10, cutting the statin dosage in half, losing weight, exercising, and not eating after eight p.m. He didn't want to walk down the same path, so he made the changes—praise God!

And through it all, Keith and I were closer to God and each other. We look for God in all our circumstances because we know—

"All things work together for good for those who love God."
(Romans 8:28, NKJV)

God can take even our mistakes and turn them into good. A favorite song that fills our car and often brings tears is "Sometimes it Takes a Mountain." It took a mountain for us, and we are glad the *three* of us climbed it together.

"God has blessed me..." Keith tells whoever will listen, "by living over five years past esophageal cancer surgery." He shares with others not to snack after eight p.m. if they have acid reflux, hoping they will learn to do what he didn't.

Losing weight, exercising, and not eating late may seem impossible at first, but going through chemo and radiation and chancing the side effects of surgery is simply not worth it—not at all!

But we can't do it in our strength. Our strength may work sometimes, but God's strength works *all the time!*

"The spirit indeed is willing, but the flesh is weak."
(Mathew 26:41, NKJV)

He has promised to work in us to do His will. He knows we can't do it, and He has the perfect solution. Why does it take us so long to learn that? God says to us,

"My grace is sufficient for you, for My strength is made perfect in weakness." Therefore most gladly I will rather boast in my infirmities, that the power of Christ may rest upon me...For when I am weak, then I am strong."
(2 Corinthians 12:9–10, NKJV)

And we need to believe it!

"Let each one of you...so love his own wife as himself, and let the wife see that she respects her husband."
(Ephesians 5:33, NKJV)

50. Football and Our Fiftieth

My husband and I were on the committee of the "Hilltoppers," a young senior's fellowship group at our church; we volunteered to give the devotional at the fall "Packer's Party" during the half. We had to compete with a buffet, so we didn't have a lot of time. Keith suggested combining our fiftieth wedding anniversary with football for our talk.

"Football?" I said. "You're kidding." He wasn't. We prayed, wrote our own responses, and Keith named it:

"The Game of Life"
(recorded)

KT: Carole and I celebrated our fiftieth wedding anniversary at the end of August. It's inevitable that we who reach this level of marriage be asked, "What is your secret of success?" And I would say to make it succeed requires:
- a lot of hard work,

- a determination to tackle the problems,
- forgive the fumbles,
- and score a lot of touchdowns.

CT: That was our "goal" (pun intended), and eventually, we reached it, but it took some radical changes on both our parts. When we were first married, we got along great...

KT interrupted: "Yeah, but then we left the wedding reception..." (laughter)

CT: Several years passed before I started praying for our marriage. I had it all figured out. If Keith changed, everything would be fine. God didn't agree with me, however. He told me, "Listen to your husband's complaints."

KT: The first years weren't easy. They required a lot of learning before we started reaping the rewards. Robert Browning wrote, "Grow old along with me! The best is yet to be, the last of life for which the first was made." Carole and I have grown older and wiser for many reasons. We learned that our marriage would survive if we were willing to listen to God and make changes. Now, that took some effort on my part. Too often, we guys have all the answers and are not willing to just "listen" to our wives. First Peter 3:7 says:

"Husbands... dwell with them with understanding, giving honor to the wife, as to the weaker vessel..."

Did you catch that "with understanding?" Listening without interrupting and giving advice was the most difficult concept for me to learn and accept. When I did start listening, our relationship changed, and I began to understand Carole's needs.

CT: I like what you said about listening. I needed to listen to you, too, because all of us have "blind spots," and you could see things in me that I couldn't. God told me there were times I needed to see things from your perspective. That wasn't easy for me because I was defensive.

KT: Ogden Nash wrote, "To keep a marriage brimming with love in the loving cup, whenever you're wrong, admit it, and when you are right, shut up!"

CT: It works! I have scars on my tongue to prove it. But seriously, being right isn't where it's at! God told me it was more important to "get it right" than to "be right." If two people are trying to be right—no one wins. If we both try to get it right, we both win!

KT: Another secret is knowing each other in little ways. I recall a game we played with several couples at a New Year's Eve party. Someone read a list of questions, like, "What is your wife's favorite color; her favorite food, etc.

CT interrupted: I remember that game; one of the questions was, "What is your wife's favorite flower?" And you leaned over and whispered, "It's Pillsbury, isn't it?" (laughter)

KT: But you know, hon, that game really bothered me. I had very few correct answers. I was determined to be more observant of you and not take you for granted.

CT: When I was growing up, I frequently boasted to my friends, "My parents have the perfect marriage." I remember lots of hugs and kisses, how much they enjoyed each other. I wanted to grow up and marry a man just like my father and live happily...

KT interrupted: What changed your mind?

CT: Ahhhh...I met you?

KT: Don't forget we tend to choose a partner with about the same maturity level as ourselves.

CT: That's true, and with God on our side, we helped each other grow up. Pop Psychology would describe it as "unpacking our baggage." It wasn't easy, change is hard, and it took a lot of prayers, a lot of tears, forgiveness, determination, and a whole lot of changing!

KT: We talked about some of the work. Let's talk about some of the blessings we've experienced in the "last of life for which the first was made."

CT: I love the way you call me your bride; how you tell me I'm beautiful (beauty is in the eye of the beholder, every wife should be beautiful to her husband). I appreciate the way you encourage me, your willingness to listen, pray for me, grab my hand when we walk, and always take care of me, and so much more. And I have learned to reciprocate in similar ways. Through the lessons and the learning, we have grown closer to each other and to God.

KT: We couldn't do it without God's intervention. The Bible says,

"Unless the Lord builds the house,
they labor in vain who build it;
(Psalm 127:1, NKJV)

We need His help unequivocally. The building never stops; we're still learning, we still make mistakes, but we are determined to finish strong—together!

While we were shopping one day, I found a pillow embroidered with this saying, "I want to be as good a person as my dog thinks I am." That was profound. But more profound is the fact has through all the situations we've gone through, Carole and I have learned how important God is in our lives and what He thinks of us. Proverbs 3:5–6 (NKJV) says it all:

"Trust in the Lord with all your heart, and lean not on your own understanding. In all your ways acknowledge Him and He shall direct your paths."

CT: While we were putting together our fiftieth celebration, we ran across another pillow that spoke to us: "A good marriage is falling in love many times—with the same person." Each time our love is deeper. Like our relationship with God—It's bottomless.

KT: I'm sure all of you have a story to tell, and we thank you for listening to ours…

And the Packer's game was on…

*"Let the little children come to Me, and do not forbid them...
And He took them up in His arms, laid His hands on them,
and blessed them."*
(Mark 10:14 and 16, NKJV)

51. "Let the Little Children Come to Me"

I don't remember a single Sunday school teacher except for my very first one. I adored her. I was around four or five; I can still see her sitting at our table, and right above her hung a picture of Jesus. I fell in love with Jesus because of her. Her name was Pearl—it fit her. Of course, we called her Miss Anderson. She never married because she wouldn't give up her religion to marry a man from a different denomination.

Next to our house was a lot filled with trees. I remember climbing up one of the taller trees because I wanted to be closer to God. The sun was shining, and I felt that God was smiling as I recited the twenty-third Psalm to Him.

I collected pictures of Jesus and taped them on my bedroom wall. One Sunday morning, in the newspaper, I saw a picture of Jesus that covered the "Parade," and I asked my mother to frame it. She hung it in my bedroom, and it stayed there all through my growing-up years when I was close to Jesus and even through the years that I chased after other gods.

I remember asking my mother a lot of questions about God, like—"How can there be no end to space? How can it keep going on and on?" I don't remember her answer if she had one, but I still wondered about it. One day I thought I had the answer. I ran to my mother and told her, "There is a big wall all around us." After I said it, I realized that there had to be space beyond the wall. Decades later, I still don't know the answer, but that's a good reason to know there has to be a God!

Another question I asked her was, "Will God allow the Russians to bomb us?" She said, "I don't think so." I still don't know that answer, but I do know that whatever happens, God is still in control.

I was twelve when the Gideons came to our school and passed out small New Testaments; I filled out the "Decision to Receive Christ as My Savior" on the last page. My mother saved it and gave it to me after I recommitted my life to Jesus.

Around fourteen, I went to catechism and church; it was required in our house. During that time, I watched my former Sunday school teacher, nearly blind and ill, being carried into the church and laid on the back pew. Her faithfulness impressed me.

After I was fifteen, confirmed, and no longer required to attend church, I forgot my first love—but He *never* forgot me. However, during those rebellious years, some of the songs I liked were religious songs, such as: "He's got the whole world in His hands; You saw me crying in the chapel, the tears I shed were tears of joy; Put your hand in the hand of the Man who calmed the waters."

At twenty-seven, Jesus revisited me in a way that changed my life forever. I told my family about this awesome Savior I had met. Being the youngest, I remember my mother saying, "And a little child shall lead them" (Isaiah 11:6).

Today my picture of Jesus hangs in our bedroom. It reminds me to never underestimate the power of God as we teach young children about Jesus and the faithfulness of our Good Shepherd, who will chase us down until He catches us—no matter how far we've strayed.

"Jesus loves me, this I know,
For the Bible tells me so.
Little ones to Him belong;
They are weak, but He is strong.
Yes, Jesus loves me..."
Anna B. Warner, a poem, 1860
William Bradbury, music & chorus, 1861

"Thank you, Miss Anderson."

"Have faith in God."
(Mark 11:22, NKJV)

52. Trusting in Circumstances or in God

I was singing along with Chris Tomlin's "Arriving/Amazing Grace CD on my way up to the hospital to see my husband, Keith. The songs had blessed me before, but today the words were *powerful!* God's presence refreshed me as I praised Him throughout my forty-minute trip.

God had given me amazing peace while watching Keith undergo chemo, radiation, two operations, and countless tests, plus several trips to the ER with subsequent hospital stays to mop up the aftereffects of surgery.

Praising God was just what I needed after the past three days of Keith's setbacks. I could feel God's strength surrounding me. Somewhere in the midst of praising, I started to pray for Keith, and a verse penetrated my mind like a well-aimed arrow:

"For assuredly, I say to you, whoever says to this mountain,
'Be removed and be cast into the sea,' and does not doubt
in his heart, but believes that those things he says will be
done, he will have whatever he says."
(Mark 11:23, NKJV)

"Enough!" I said as I faced the mountain of setbacks. "Be removed and be cast into the sea. Lord, You said if I believed it would be done—*and I believe!*" I continued to praise God, thoroughly convinced that Keith would start moving forward instead of backward.

Keith looked hopeful when I shared with him about the "mountain being removed..." I shared it later that day with our son and daughter.

The next day Keith's condition worsened. He broke down and said he didn't know if he could take anymore; I began to wonder if he would recover at all. Around ten percent make it through the side effects from this surgery. I talked to three people by phone that day and related the negative things that had happened. Not once did I communicate my faith.

Instead of looking at Jesus, I looked at the circumstances much like the disciples did when "a great windstorm arose, and the waves beat into the boat so that it was already filling" (Mark 4:37). They woke up Jesus, asleep in the stern, and said, "Teacher, do You not care that we are perishing?" (Mark 4:38) He rebuked the wind and the sea, and then He turned to His disciples and asked:

"Why are you so fearful? How is it that you have no faith?"
(Mark 4:40, NKJV)

On my way home that night, the weight of what I had done fell on me. I felt horrible. I repented all the way home. *Why was I so fearful? Why did I look at the circumstances and lose my faith?* Not only that, but when I delivered the negative news to my three friends, I found myself bathing in their sympathy.

I had just gone through some pretty scary circumstances, trusted God, and witnessed an unparalleled miracle—then, three days later, I fell flat on my face.

I had often wondered how Elijah, who had "called down the fire of God" (1 Kings 18:38), among other miracles, could have been so fearful of Jezebel's threats on his life? (1 Kings 19:1–4) Or John the Baptist, seeing the dove land on Jesus' head and hearing God say, "This is my beloved Son..." then, being in prison, sent the question via his disciples to Jesus: "Are You the Coming One, or should we look for another?" (Luke 7:19–23)

If the ones who saw great miracles are capable of doubting, I can get back up and "press toward the goal for the prize of the upward call of God in Christ Jesus" (Philippians 3:14), a little bruised, a lot humbled, and more *determined than ever* to trust God instead of unreliable circumstances.

The next day when I went to visit Keith, the tide had turned—he felt much better. Isn't that just like our God? It's our decision: we either trust in circumstances or in what God says. I've trusted in circumstances, and nothing good happens. But when I decide to believe what God says, regardless of what I see or feel, God responds in His time to my faith.

It's easy to have faith when we "get a word or the inspiration," but when time passes, the feelings are gone, and the circumstances stay the same or get worse, it's then we prove—

> *"...that the genuineness of your faith, being much more*
> *precious than gold that perishes, though it is tested by fire,*
> *may be found to praise, honor, and glory at the revelation of*
> *Jesus Christ..."*
> (1 Peter 1:7, NKJV)

That's the kind of faith I want to have *every* time!

Since Keith came home, there have been a few "hills" but no mountains. Just last night, we had what I would facetiously call a "foothill." Keith woke me up in the middle of the night and said he was stressed about his feet—they were swollen and not responding to treatment.

I am no stranger to the overblown night-time fears that loom like giants. I fought off the urge to sleep and prayed silently, "Lord, speak through me; I'm trusting You..." He did, and Keith went back to sleep a short time later. I am always amazed that when we ask Him to speak through us, He does—just like He promised—in simple, ordinary, everyday words, but just the right ones that bring reason and peace to the situation.

> *"The preparations of the heart belong to man, but the an-*
> *swer of the tongue is from the Lord."*
> (Proverbs 16:1, NKJV)

"Thank you, Lord! I am so grateful for your love, compassion, and forgiveness. Help me, Jesus, to trust You, not just when things are going well but even when everything is falling apart."

"When He (Holy Spirit) has come, He will convict the world of sin, and of righteousness, and of judgment."
(John 16:8, NKJV)

53. Helping God Out

"Lord, she isn't listening to what I'm saying," I said with frustration as I walked down the hallway. I had been talking to my niece about the Lord every day for a week, and she still didn't understand.

"I do believe in God," she protested as I explained it was more than just believing. "I believe I am going to heaven," she responded.

A few months earlier, I was praying for her when I felt a deep heaviness in my heart; I continued to pray until it lifted. The next time we traveled to our home town she wanted to tell me about a book she had been reading on horoscopes. It promised wonderful things, the answer to all her problems, she said. As she reviewed the entire book chapter by chapter, I felt the Lord telling me not to say anything, just listen. I was praying for the right words, and when she finished, I said, "It sounds good but does it work?"

She thought for a moment and then responded succinctly, "No." She seemed surprised by her own answer. Then I told her

I had found something that *did* work, and I shared what Jesus was doing in my life. She didn't seem too interested, but she listened.

The next time we were in town, she told me about a dream she had that alarmed her. In her dream, she was dying. But what bothered her was that she was dying without a purpose. Her life, she felt, was "meaningless." (I believed the dream came from God.) I told her I had similar feelings about my life before I turned it over to the Lord. We talked; this time, she was more interested in what I had to say.

Something she said reminded me of Paul's dilemma at the end of Romans 7. I read it to her, and she said, "That's me!" I invited her to stay with us for a couple of weeks so we could talk. She came, she listened, but she resisted.

By the way, the Lord responded to my frustration in the hallway. When I complained, she wasn't listening to me,

> "Because you are trying to do My job. Just tell her about Me and let Me take care of the rest."

So, I did. We continued to talk. I didn't try to make her understand; I let God do that. We talked about a lot of things pertaining to life, and when I could, I told her about Jesus.

> *"And when He (the Holy Spirit) has come, He will convict the world of sin, and of righteousness and of judgment:"*
> (John 16:8, NKJV)

A couple of days later, we were sitting at the kitchen table when it hit me—she was no longer resisting what I was saying.

As we continued to talk, I felt as though I was seeing a rosebud unfold before my eyes. I said to her, "_____ (her name), you are different!"

"You're right," she said, first realizing it herself. "I *am* different!" God did His part when I ceased trying to do His. His presence fell upon her in the most unique way.

It was a lovely lesson but not well-learned because a few days later, I was helping God out again. My niece had brought along what I considered "worldly music," and I decided she should listen to Christian music. I went out and bought what I thought young people would like and played it for her—she called it "bubble-gum music." Feeling dejected, I went to the Lord for solace. His answer:

"You're trying to do my job again. Let me decide
what to do in her life; keep telling her about Me."

She went home and told her sister about Jesus, took her to a meeting, and her sister gave her heart to Jesus. In time the rest of her family became committed Christians as well.

A postscript on the music. Years later, my niece graduated magna cum laude with a degree in Music Composition and is presently working on an opera for her master's degree from the *Book of Daniel*.

And unless God tells me otherwise, I am telling others about Jesus, what He has done for me, what He can do for them, but I am letting Him convict and raise His own children, and He does so superbly.

"The steps of a good man are ordered by the Lord, and He delights in his way."
(Psalm 37:23, NKJV)

54. My Times are in His Hands

My thirteen-year-old grandson and I were driving along while he was munching on pizza and talking about a myriad of things when something he said reminded me of an accident that never happened, and I related it to him—

"Grandpa and I were driving on the Interstate in the right lane, which curved sharply to the left; we had started to turn when a small car full of college-age kids in the left lane suddenly turned right in front of us towards the exit ramp on our right. I yelled, "Jesus!" and braced myself for the collision.

Grandpa jerked the wheel to the right, rocking us back and forth, forcing us onto the exit ramp where we pitched along half on the road and half off, traveling side-by-side with the little car. At the end of the ramp, we stopped, shaken and overwhelmed by what had happened—or not happened— and the little car kept going."

We thanked God over and over for his intervention. We wondered if the other car knew that God had spared their lives that day too. For running along the curve we were heading into was a short railing that guarded *a forty-foot plunge!*

I remember seeing the little car in front of us, and I recall rocking back and forth, but I didn't see anything else until I saw the car next to us traveling on the exit ramp. How we got there, only God knows. Our times are truly in His hands!

"Grandma, you and Grandpa could have been killed!" my grandson said, wide-eyed and alarmed.

"We could have, but God says, 'The steps of a good man are ordered by the Lord.' He certainly proved it to us that day." After talking it over, my grandson summed it up with an out-of-the-mouth teenage observation: "Getting out of that situation would have been a giant leap for man, but for God, it was just one small step!"

"Amen!" I heartily agreed.

Scriptures are replete with promises that God is always with us, but sometimes He allows situations to develop—not to scare us—but to push the knowledge that often sits in our heads down into our hearts. Because we have experienced it, we don't just know it; we *know* it! And our faith grows.

"He shall give His angels charge over you,
to keep you in all your ways."
(Psalm 91:11, NKJV)

"As the mountains surround Jerusalem, so the Lord sur-
rounds His people from this time forth and forever."
(Psalm 125:2, NKJV)

"I will never leave you nor forsake you.
So we may boldly say: 'The Lord is my helper;
I will not fear. What can man do to me?'"
(Hebrews 13:5–6, NKJV)

And yet, what about the times when God doesn't prevent the accident or doesn't cure the disease? Most of us can point to a friend or relative who wasn't spared; how do we explain that? We can't! We simply don't have the knowledge—only God does. Sometimes God reveals it to us; most of the time, He doesn't.

There were times I didn't understand what God was doing in my life until weeks or months later, and then I understood: even though some of the situations were difficult and trying, it was exactly what I needed.

"The secret things belong to the Lord our God, but those
things which are revealed belong to us..."
(Deuteronomy 29:29, NKJV)

Someday, we will understand when we stand before Him, but then it probably won't make much difference.

*"Now faith is the substance of things hoped for,
the evidence of things not seen."*
(Hebrews 11:1, NKJV)

55. Seeking the Lost

After reading the great faith chapter in Hebrews 11, God challenged my thinking about a roll of lost wedding pictures. As I reread those verses, I thought, *I believe the lab will find my daughter's pictures.* "Lord," I said out loud, "I believe You will find them for us." My daughter's photographer-friend had taken her wedding pictures, and a camera shop had developed them— one roll was lost.

I called the lab again. She told me they still hadn't found it. Now what? A thought came to me, and I vocalized it, "Will you look in the front of the store? Perhaps one envelope was misfiled."

"Just a minute." I'm learning to step out on my thoughts; it could be the Holy Spirit speaking. If it isn't Him, whatever I say will "die on the vine," and no harm will be done. In this case, the consequences were non-existent. I waited..."Yes! I found them," she said.

"Yes! Lord. Yes!"

Jesus is a master at finding lost things. I have a long list of things He has found for us, some important, some not so.

I recall the horror I felt many years ago when I looked at my engagement ring and saw a barren space where my diamond should have been. I panicked, and then I prayed and looked everywhere.

Sometimes we have to get "fervent" in our prayers to release our faith, and sometimes we have to get "quiet" so our minds are free to hear God. Somewhere after the fervent and during the quiet, I "saw" in my mind's eye the driver's seat in our car—the area by the floor. I ran outside, opened the car door, and saw my diamond lodged in the carpet fuzz. Glory to God! (This was long before automatic seats; it must have rubbed out as I pulled on the side lever.)

> *"And when she found it, she calls her friends and*
> *neighbors together, saying 'Rejoice with me, for I have*
> *found the piece which I lost!'"*
> (Luke 15:9, NKJV)

A few years later, it happened again. My husband and I prayed, and later that day, I saw a glint in the rug I was vacuuming. We decided not to test the Lord again and reset my diamond in Keith's grandmother's engagement ring—with six prongs instead of four. Both the rings were set high, which causes the prongs to wear down quickly.

My husband called me at work not long ago to tell me he couldn't find his checkbook and had looked all over. I said, "Let's pray," and we did. He called back to tell me he walked back into the computer room and felt God was telling him to look in one of the drawers, and it was there.

"I never keep it in that drawer," Keith said, but God sees. Think of the last time you asked someone, "Did you see my _____?" If they had, they would tell you. Right? Why wouldn't God do the same? He sees what we cannot see, and I believe He delights in showing us where our lost items are.

> *"What man is there among you who, if his son asks for bread, will give him a stone? Or if he asks for a fish, will he give him a serpent? If you then, being evil, know how to give good gifts to your children, how much more will your Father who is in heaven give good things to those who ask Him!"*
> (Matthew 7:9–11, NKJV)

Let's decide to trust Him! The next time you misplace or lose things, ask Him. He will love you for it.

> *"Faith is the substance of things hoped for, the evidence of things not seen."*
> (Hebrews 11:1, NKJV)

When I take the time to ask God to help me find the "things not seen," I can circumvent frustration, anger, or lost time looking. If I don't find it, I need to stop, quiet my spirit and listen. That is especially hard—when I'm in a hurry—but not impossible. There is no guarantee when God will answer, but we can refuse to listen to doubts, tell Jesus you are trusting Him, and thank Him in advance—that's faith.

> *"...in everything by prayer and supplication, with thanks-*
> *giving, let your request be made known to God;"*
> (Philippians 4:6, NKJV)

I looked at my watch while shopping one day, and I saw a bare arm. I had tried several articles of clothing on, so I went back to the dressing room, praying all the way—it wasn't there. I felt anxiety starting to rise. "Lord, I'm trusting You to help me find it," I told Him as I looked under the racks I had visited. Nothing. I continued to kick out anxious thoughts with positive thoughts like, "Lord, I refuse to panic; I know You know where it is, and I am praising You for helping me find it." When I persevere, the unrest I feel begins to settle down, allowing faith to rise to the surface.

When we choose to trust God, He honors it. There are no feelings involved, simply the decision not to worry. Then I went to the customer service desk nearby and asked if anyone had found a watch. I described it. "Yes, she said, someone found it in the dressing room."

"Thank You, Lord!" As I walked away, putting on my watch, I asked the Lord to bless the one who returned it because He who is faithful said:

> *"I will bless those who bless you..."*
> (Genesis 12:3, NKJV)

Then there was the time I couldn't find my keys, and as I prayed, I "saw" them behind the love seat. One of the kids probably put them there.

Sometimes the answer doesn't come right away: I lost an amethyst earring I had bought at Niagara Falls, and it took several months before I found it 2,400 miles away! We were visiting our daughter, and she and I were playing with my granddaughter on the floor when my daughter spotted my earring under a dresser.

Recently, I lost my diamond again. We prayed and searched—nothing! After a month or so, I quoted the verse, "The Lord giveth, and the Lord taketh away; blessed be the name of the Lord" (Job 1:21). I told Him I would accept it.

Weeks later, I was at Care Net,[5] straightening up a bulletin board because my client had not come that hour. I was throwing outdated information away when I saw a note reading: *"Is this yours?"* I didn't find anything near it and assumed someone had taken the item. I was about to crunch the note when I saw something scotch-taped to the paper; I looked closer. *"Is that my diamond?"* I said incredulously. *It was!* "Thank you, Jesus!" I still find the circumstances hard to believe, nor have I found who put it there. But God knows! "Bless them, Lord, really bless them!"

Misplacing items often increases as we get older, but even our weaknesses can turn into a blessing. I had hidden the keys to the safe deposit box—too well. I prayed and looked *everywhere* for weeks; then, I put it in the Lord's hands and waited. This morning I woke up and "a place" came to mind—the keys were

---

5 Care Net Family Resource Center: An international Christian organization for women who are pregnant and/or have children under two, providing classes with dozens of teaching DVD's, peer counseling and spiritual encouragement for mothers; clothing and material items for children. For a center near you: www.care-net. org.

there! If I hadn't found them, it would have cost over $200.00 to break the box open.

So what is it you are looking for? Ask "The-God-Who-Sees," El Roi is His name: God sees, and He cares! (Genesis 16:13)

"You have heard that it was said, 'An eye for an eye and a tooth for a tooth.' But I tell you not to resist an evil person. But whoever slaps you on your right cheek, turn the other to him also."

(Matthew 5:38–39, NKJV)

56. Passive/Aggressive: Finding the Balance

Is Jesus advocating passivity in the above verse? That we should let people walk all over us? Is assertiveness merely a modern-day fad?

When Jesus' actions were questioned by the Pharisees and Scribes, He stood up to them, calling them "hypocrites," "blind guides," "whitewashed tombs," "serpents," and "brood of vipers" (from Matthew 23). That sounds like assertiveness to me, but when Pilate asked Jesus to defend Himself against the accusations of the chief priests and elders, "He answered him not one word..." (Matthew 27:14). He resisted, knowing it was God's will to endure the cross.

Judge for yourself, but I believe He is warning us not to retaliate in like manner, "eye for an eye, tooth for a tooth." If someone hits us, we are not to strike back; if someone insults us, we are not to do likewise. God says He will stand up for us if we refrain from wrath.

> *"Beloved, do not avenge yourselves, but rather give place*
> *to wrath; for it is written, 'Vengeance is Mine; I will repay,'*
> *says the Lord."*
> (Romans 12:19, NKJV)

There may be times Jesus will tell us to keep quiet and embrace persecution. But to allow someone to put us down doesn't make us more righteous; it makes us withdraw into ourselves.

I used to be a passive person—a real wimp! When an aggressive person put me down, I wouldn't say anything. I might mumble something no one could hear, complain to a co-worker or friend, and think of what I should have said later at home, where my husband would hear about it several times. Then I would repress the incident and go on. But it never really went away—until God came on the scene.

After I read several books on assertiveness, I made a conscious decision to speak up. I prayed and asked the Lord to help me. I took a few steps in faith even though my two adversaries, "fear" and "trembling," stuck tenaciously to my side. It took a lot of prayer and patience to change my behavior of many years because passive persons tend to suffer from low self-esteem.

Just because others disagree with what we say doesn't mean they are putting us down. Condescending remarks sound like the other person is lifting themselves up as the authority while putting us down. For instance, a friend and I disagreed on a biblical principle. It was a friendly discussion until she said,

"When you grow in the Lord, you will learn..." I didn't say anything, we dropped the subject, but it felt like a putdown. I wondered, "Lord, is this me? Do I take things too personally?" Then I began hearing similar comments about her from others, to which I didn't respond, but I took it as a confirmation from God. He impressed me with the thought,

"When you allow someone to put you down, you are
allowing them to put Me down."

He and I are one. That's how much He identifies with His children.

So, what should we do when a person puts us down in a condescending manner, or when they say something they think is funny but, to us, it's hurtful? There isn't a simple answer. Every situation is different; that's why we have the Holy Spirit to lead us. Ecclesiastes reminds us there is,

"A time to keep silence, and a time to speak;"
(Ecclesiastes 3:7, NKJV)

If we do speak up, we need to stay "in the Spirit." I pray inwardly, "Lord, help my words be Your words." If nothing comes to me, I wait. Every situation is different. Who says that after you get home and have some prayer time, you can't call the person and discuss the situation, telling them what you think in an assertive way? They might say, "I'm sorry, I didn't mean to offend you." Or they might say, "I didn't realize you were so sensitive," which is another putdown!

After a quick *"Lord help,"* you might say something like: "No, I'm *not* being sensitive; I believe every person should be able to express themselves, wouldn't you agree?"

You spoke up in an assertive manner, and now you can end the conversation—your goal is not to get the person to agree with you; your goal is to speak up—period! Then put it in God's hands and *leave it there!* If it comes back to your mind, resist it and give it back to God.

So, what if your knees are knocking and your voice is a little shaky? You're in good company: Paul had similar feelings when he spoke to the Corinthians:

> *"I was with you in weakness, in fear,*
> *and in much trembling."*
> (1 Corinthians 2:3, NKJV)

The circumstances may be different, but God will honor our faith in stepping out. We may get an apology, and maybe not, but as long as we stay "in the Spirit," God will work on our behalf. He cares how other people treat us. We can't stop people from being condescending, but we can speak up by being assertive, and that is what God wants us to do.

> *"For he who touches you touches the apple of His eye."*
> (Zechariah 2:8, NKJV)

When God started working on our marriage, He encouraged me to be assertive with my husband. Instead of kicking the cupboard door shut and all the other immature ways I used to express myself, I had to tell him how I felt about things. Being honest about my feelings made me vulnerable. Because my self-esteem was low, it was difficult to crawl out from under my old-thinking patterns. In my crippled reasoning, I thought the root cause of every problem might be my fault. What if I am wrong?

God said, "Do it anyway!"

I did. I learned to say to myself, "If I am wrong, I can learn from it," and there were times I did just that. I learned that being wrong is okay as long as I admit it and deal with it.

In the beginning, my husband's response was not always what I wanted to hear; I prayed inwardly, "Lord, help me to stay in the Spirit, let my words be Your words." I resisted the temptation to argue—or the extreme—withdraw and pout. Rather, I put the situation in Jesus' very capable hands, trusting Him to work things out for me just like He promised. I didn't learn without failures; when I took things in my hands, nothing good came out of it. When I put things in God's hands and left them there, He worked it out.

The balance of being passive and
aggressive is being assertive.

It might be easier to be quiet and say nothing, but it does nothing for your self-esteem. It takes backbone to express your feelings or your opinion without feeling you have to justify yourself. Has anyone responded to your complaint by saying, "No one else has ever complained about it?" I've been there! I don't remember exactly what I said. But a good response might be: "Perhaps no one has had the courage to give their opinion before, but it offended me," or something similar. Know when to stop, don't argue, instead put it in God's hands and leave it there.

Has anyone gotten into line ahead of you? I've learned to say, "Excuse me, I was next in line," and smile.

The workplace was no different. I had trouble with aggressive people. No matter how hard I tried to find the perfect work environment, there was always someone waiting to take advantage of my passivity. I was praying for the "perfect place" to work and wondering why God wasn't answering my prayers until I *finally* got it!

"Now I see it, God. Now I understand what You've been trying to tell me. If I had found that perfect place, I wouldn't have been forced to change."

Being passive never felt good. It made me feel like a little child. When I allowed people to treat me badly, my self-esteem plummeted. But to my delight, when I started acting assertive, I felt better about myself. And when God began to change me, people around me changed as well. Absolutely amazing! But not so amazing when you think that others treat us the way we *allow* them to. God wants to change that!

The non-Christian books I read on assertiveness were enlightening and helpful, except I needed more. I needed "a mighty, awesome One" (Jeremiah 20:11) to give me guidance, strength, courage, and power! Through prayer, reading His Word, and stepping out in faith, I found—

"The Lord is with me as a mighty, awesome One. Therefore
my persecutors will stumble, and will not prevail."
(Jeremiah 20:11, NKJV)

What a beautiful verse that fits our situation perfectly!

When I step out in faith, I rarely *feel* faith; I quote scripture
in telling God:

- I am trusting You, Lord; I believe You will "never leave
  me nor forsake me" (Hebrews 13:5).
- "Your grace is sufficient for me; Your strength is made
  perfect in my weakness" (2 Corinthians 12:9).
- "Whenever I am afraid, I will trust in You" (Psalm 56:3).
- "Under Your wings, I will take refuge" (Psalm 91:4).
- "I refuse to look at the "wind" the "waves" or the "storm;" I
  am going to look at You, Jesus!" (from Matthew 14:26–32)

There are dozens of verses. As I walk through various circumstances, my faith grows stronger. I am finding God's balance between passivity and aggressiveness; I am feeling comfortable being assertive under God's control.

Is it easy? No, but not impossible. Do I still need Him when
I speak up? Yes! Do I still occasionally feel inadequate? Yes! But
when that thought comes to me, I kick it out. I refuse to accept
those thoughts. They do not come from God. I cannot rely on
my own strength; I rely totally on His strength—*by faith.*

"But God has chosen the foolish things of the world to put to shame the wise, and God has chosen the weak things of the world to put to shame the things which are mighty..."
(1 Corinthians 1:27, NKJV)

Read that verse again. "God has chosen the weak things..." That's me, one of the reasons He chose me is because I am weak. I asked Him once, "Why did I have so many weaknesses?"

His answer: "If you had no weaknesses, you wouldn't have needed Me."

"And He (Jesus) said to me, 'My grace is sufficient for you, for My strength is made perfect in weakness.'"

"Therefore most gladly I will boast in my infirmities, that the power of Christ may rest upon me. Therefore I take pleasure in infirmities, in reproaches, in needs, in persecutions, in distresses, for Christ's sake. For when I am weak, then I am strong."
(2 Corinthians 12:9–10, NKJV)

"Lord, I don't want to be strong in myself; I want to be strong in You because your strength *far exceeds* my abilities."

"Let us hold fast the confession of our hope without wavering, for He who promised is faithful."
(Hebrews 10:23, NKJV)

57. Holding On

It seemed like it should be morning; I felt as though I had slept a long, long time. As I opened my eyes, the darkness of the room proved me wrong. I could feel my faith wavering in the wee hours of the morning as the darkness surrounded me, intensifying my fears.

As parents, we were going through one of those heart-wrenching ordeals that sap the strength right out of you. We knew that leaning on the Lord was the answer, but we hadn't quite gotten to that point—we were still reeling from the latest happening.

I got up and picked up Charles Stanley's booklet of verses, *God's Power through Prayer*.[6] It opened with the verses on "Praying in Faith." *Faith*, I thought, *that's what I need*. (God has used Stanley's booklet multiple times to speak to me.) As I read the verses, I noted that the promises were accessible *only* by faith.

---

6 Charles Stanley, *God's Power through Prayer*, J. Countryman Publishers, Houston TX.

"Now faith is the substance of things hoped for,
the evidence of things not seen."
(Hebrews 11:1, NKJV)

"By faith Noah...moved with godly fear, prepared
an ark for the saving of his household..."
(Hebrews 11:7, NKJV)

"By faith Sarah...received strength to conceive seed,
and she bore a child...because she judged Him faithful
who had promised."
(Hebrews 11:11, NKJV)

"By faith Abraham, when he was tested, offered up Isaac...
concluding that God was able to raise him up,
even from the dead..."
(Hebrews 11:17–18, NKJV)

"By faith they passed through the Red Sea as
by dry land, whereas the Egyptians, attempting
to do so, were drowned."
(Hebrews 11:29, NKJV)

"By faith the walls of Jericho fell down..."
(Hebrews 11:30, NKJV)

On and on I read, until the last one:

"Let us hold fast the confession of our hope without waver-
ing, for He who promised is faithful."
(Hebrews 10:23, NKJV)

That did it! I told the Lord, in part, "Father, You know what my feelings are right now, but feelings aren't facts. These are the facts, Lord:

- You love me; I am Your child.
- You promised never to leave me nor forsake me. You said You would be with me until the end of the world.
- You are faithful to Your promises.
- I am laying the problem at Your feet; I believe You have taken it.
- I trust You. I believe You; I have faith in You."

As I continued to declare the "facts" (there were more), my voice grew more confident. Something was happening inside me: faith was replacing fear, confusion was giving way to peace, and the situation was no longer in my hands but in God's very capable, loving hands.

The above steps are the very essence of faith. When you refuse to doubt, when you affirm your faith "without wavering," the light will come and chase the darkness away because Jesus is the light.

"The entrance of Your words gives light; it gives
understanding to the simple."
(Psalm 119:130, NKJV)

The situation itself may not change, but *we* change as God gives us the peace and the patience that comes from trusting God for "He who promised *is* faithful" (Hebrew 10:23).

"I will pour My Spirit on your descendants,
and My blessing on your offspring;"
(Isaiah 44:3, NKJV)

58. Standing on His Word

We were the typical parents of a child who had laid aside their Christian beliefs and started following the ways of the world. We wondered where we had gone wrong, feeling guilty for some of the things we had done—or not done—and wishing we had done some things differently. We were confused, searching for answers, living with a mixed bag of disappointment, hurt, and little hope.

My husband was in a deacon's meeting when one of the other deacons shared a verse that God had given him the night before—he felt it was for one of the men present.

"Train up a child in the way he should go, and when he is
old he will not depart from it."
(Proverbs 22:6, NKJV)

The night before the deacon's meeting, Keith and I had been discussing our child's situation when I began to verbalize my true feelings. Between tears and anger, I quoted that very verse, "Train up a child in the way..." questioning God's faithfulness and telling Him His words could not be trusted. Keith tried to console me, but I was beyond consolation.

Then God sent His word through another, and it comforted me like a mother's cool hand on a child's warm head. I repented of the accusations, grateful that God in His love had met me in my anger. God will sometimes overlook our lack of faith—like He did with the children of Israel when they first came out of Egypt—but there comes a time when we have to grow up and trust the Lord regardless of what happens. The Israelites that were delivered from Egypt never learned to trust Him, so God did not allow that generation to enter the Promised Land.

A few years later, the prodigal child was even further from home. I was discouraged, but instead of doubting, I asked the Lord for a word of encouragement. We were in church, and I was praying fervently when I heard this verse coming from the pulpit:

"Train up a child in the way he should go..."
(Proverbs 22:6, NKJV)

I looked up, and the youth pastor was announcing a young people's meeting. I don't remember what he said next, but I will never forget what God said:

"Feelings change, circumstances change,
but My word *never* changes."

It has been years since that night. We are still waiting, still trusting. Many things have happened to show us God's hand is on the Prodigal. It's just a matter of time. We have put our trust in the One who spoke those words: "My word never changes."

"The grass withers, the flower fades,
but the word of our God stands forever."
(Isaiah 40:8, NKJV)

"Because you did not do it the first time,
the Lord our God broke out against us, because
we did not consult Him about the proper order."
(1 Chronicles 15:13, NKJV)

59. Pray First!

Doing the right thing in the wrong way was David's experience when he attempted to bring the Ark of God back to the City of David.

"David consulted with captains of thousands and hundreds, and with every leader. And David said to the assembly of Israel, 'If it seems good to you, and if it is of the Lord our God, let us send out to our brethren everywhere...and let us bring the ark of the Lord our God back to us...'"
(1 Chronicles 13:1–3, NKJV)

The plan sounded great, everyone agreed, except it doesn't say that David inquired of God, nor did the people, only that it—

"...was right in the eyes of all the people."
(1 Chronicles 13:4, NKJV)

So David and all of Israel reclaimed the Ark of God. On their way back, they sang and played music with all their might, when suddenly the oxen stumbled, Uzza reached up to steady the Ark, and the Lord struck him dead. David became angry with God and left the Ark at the house of Obed-Edom for three months. He drops his Ark project and establishes himself as King over Israel.

The Philistines made a raid on the Valley of Rephaim; this time, David inquires of God himself,

> *"'Shall I go up against the Philistines? Will you deliver*
> *them into my hand?' The Lord said, 'Go up, for I will deliver*
> *them into your hand.'"*
> (1 Chronicles 14:10, NKJV)

And God delivered them just as He said He would. Then the Philistines made another raid. Instead of reverting to what God said last time, David inquires again, and God says,

> *"You shall not go up after them; circle around them,*
> *and come upon them in front of the mulberry trees.*
> *And it shall be, when you hear a sound of marching...*
> *then you shall go out to battle..."*
> (1 Chronicles 14:14–15, NKJV)

God had a plan, and David drove the Philistine army back for the second time. I believe those two battles were strategically placed in David's life to teach him to ask God for instruction each time.

> *"The fame of David went out into all lands, and the Lord*
> *brought the fear of him upon all nations."*
> (1 Chronicles 14:17, NKJV)

I suppose all of us have neglected to pray first at times. My husband and I started praying about everything we purchased because we were tired of buying lemons! Making lemonade won't suffice—prayers do!

We don't limit our prayers to things. We pray about everything because God says to do it. We have a saying in our house: *"Everything goes better with prayer,"* and it does! This morning I prayed about a disagreement my husband and I had last night. I ended with, "Lord, if I'm wrong, show me," because I have had blind spots, things my husband could see and I couldn't, and God has told us it is more important to get it right than to be right. This afternoon Keith came home with a dozen roses and an apology.

Back to the Bible. In the meantime, David prepared a place for the Ark of God, pitched a tent for it, and said,

> *"No one may carry the ark of God but the Levites, for the*
> *Lord has chosen them to carry the ark of God..."*
> (1 Chronicles 15:2, NKJV)

> *"For because you did not do it the first time, the Lord our*
> *God broke out against us, because we did not consult Him*
> *about the proper order."*
> (1 Chronicles 15:13, NKJV)

So the Levites carried the ark of God on their shoulders, by its poles, as Moses had commanded, and the ark of the Lord was set in the midst of the tabernacle that David had erected for it. This time David did everything right, and God honored it.

It behooves us to study the Old Testament as well as the new, for it holds many practical examples we can learn from. The Apostle Paul says,

"All these things happened to them as examples, and they were written for our admonition, upon whom the ends of the ages have come."
(1 Corinthians 10:11, NKJV)

Nehemiah, the cupbearer to the king in the Persian palace, told the king that he was sad because the walls in Jerusalem were broken down, and the gates were burned with fire. The king asked him, "What do you request?" Nehemiah "prayed to the God of heaven" and said to the king what he needed, and the king granted all his requests (from Nehemiah 2:1–8).

Have you done that? Prayed inwardly, "Lord, help..." or "Give me the words..." then said what you had in mind.

But what if we forget to pray first?

I had been wrestling with a serious situation and had no answers to my questions. I had made a decision without praying. I was plagued with the question, *Why didn't I ask God about it? Why?*

I searched the Bible for answers, prayed, and listened but heard nothing. This went on for some time until I had to put it in His hands—it was getting too heavy for me to carry.

"Casting all your care upon Him, for He cares for you."
(1 Peter 5:7, NKJV)

I told the Lord I was trusting Him to give me answers, and then I put it into His hands and left it there. Questions crept into my mind several times, but I refused to listen, determined not to take them back, still trusting Him for answers.

A few days later, I woke up with thoughts flooding through my mind. I was looking at the situation from a whole new perspective—God's. I understood why it happened the way it did. I couldn't have changed it; it was God's will—and all my questions fell at His feet.

"When evening had come, they brought to Him many who were demon-possessed. And He cast out the spirits with a word, and healed all who were sick, that it might be fulfilled which was spoken by Isaiah the prophet, saying: 'He Himself took our infirmities and bore our sicknesses.'"
(Matthew 8:16–17, NKJV)

"Surely He has borne our griefs and carried our sorrows; yet we esteemed Him stricken, smitten by God, and afflicted."
(Isaiah 53:4–5, NKJV)

60. Yahweh Rapha: The God Who Heals

Healing—what a vast subject! It is so complex that every situation demands a fresh batch of God's wisdom. I believe healing is part of God's plan; Isaiah's prophecy (above) substantiates that. Also, it is one of His names, and He cannot deny Himself—His Rx is unique, personal, and sometimes beyond comprehension.

My first experience with healing came in the dead of night when I stubbed my toe on a chair leg and spent the rest of the night awake and in pain. In the morning, my toe was swollen, black, with a red band around it, and the pain was shooting into my calf.

My husband was on the phone trying to locate a doctor when a thought came to me that God wanted to heal me. In my mind, I heard very clearly: *"Put your foot on the floor."* I stood up, stepped on my foot, and immediately, the pain and swelling left; I began jumping around the floor while a Christian radio station was playing "I Believe in Miracles." Keith was still on the phone, mouth open, staring at me incredulously.

From time to time, I tried to replicate that miracle, but it didn't work. As a new Christian, I didn't know much about healing, but I wondered why the faith that I experienced that morning was so real, and from then on, it was so elusive. I prayed for healing off and on, but nothing happened. I read a book on the subject, looked up some scriptures, and decided I didn't understand it, so I placed it on a shelf and left it there.

When our daughter hurt her back in diving class, we were concerned that she was missing too much school. I was lying in bed praying for her, thinking about the song we sing in church that went something like: "I'm Yours, Lord, everything I am, try me now and see, see if I can be completely Yours." I remember singing, "She's Yours, Lord, everything she is..." and I put her in God's hands and went to sleep. The next morning she woke us up as she jumped in bed between us, saying her back was fine, and she was going to school.

Several months later, our daughter reinjured her back, we prayed, and nothing happened. I sang the same song as I did before, to no avail. The next Sunday, our church had a guest speaker who had a "prayer ministry." My daughter was near the front of the church with friends when the speaker asked if anyone wanted prayer to come forward. I was praying that she would go, but she didn't move. I prayed harder—nothing happened. Then I put her in God's hands, and *immediately*, she stood up and went forward for prayer. "God touched my back, and the pain left," she told us later.

Sometimes we have to put the situation in God's hands and leave it there because He does things *His* way, in *His* time—not ours!

Years later, we were in Arizona, and our grandson was recovering from an eight to ten day flu, our daughter was sick in bed with a high fever, and a day or so later, it spread to our granddaughter. Keith and I were praying that God would keep us well so we could take care of everyone.

It was close to bedtime a few days later when I felt flu-like symptoms coming on: my head was stuffy and sore, my temp was a little over a hundred degrees, and I was thinking how good it would feel to lie down and sleep. I started my usual night-time praying—with what I felt would be short—when a thought came to me that I should start praising the Lord. I did, and then I quietly began singing praise songs and then hymns until I fell asleep. In the morning, I woke up refreshed and ready to meet the day.

Another time we were in Arizona when our grandson had a very high fever that wouldn't break despite praying for him, giving him medicine, removing some of his clothes, and wiping him down with cool cloths. When someone suggested taking him to the ER, I decided to pray one more time, and as I walked into his room, I thought of Jesus and how he rebuked the fever in Peter's mother-in-law. So, I quietly rebuked the fever in the name of Jesus and then touched my grandson's head; he was still very hot, and so were his arms and legs. Then I touched his feet—they were cooler. I touched his legs—they were cool too. "It" traveled up to his head, and then the fever broke. Unlike Peter's mother-in-law, who got up and served dinner (in Luke 4:38–39), it took our grandson a couple of days before he was up and running around.

The only similarity between the healing of the fever, back, and the toe was the "thoughts" that came to me. I attributed them to the Holy Spirit. I can't make the thoughts come, but I want to be receptive when they do come—whether it's healing or anything else.

Most Christians pray for healing, but not all are willing to invest the time it takes to develop a deeper relationship with Jesus when a deeper relationship could be God's pathway to healing.

From my own experience, God uses sicknesses to bring me closer to Him. I pray for healing, but more often than not, it doesn't come, so I grab my Bible, a Christian book, put on Christian music or sermons, and use the downtime to draw closer to the Lord.

For months I prayed for the healing of a neck injury. The healing came, but it took over a year and a half. I went to a variety of doctors, took different meds, all to no avail—when I gave up what I thought I needed and let God change my heart, the right meds were found.

Early in my Christian life, I was praying for God to fill me with His Spirit. He did. And for one month, my psoriasis was totally gone. Then it returned. "Why, God?" I have come to believe it is stress-related because a year or so after we were married, we were dealing with a lot of baggage, my stress level was high, and my psoriasis was out of control. It subsided as we worked on our problems. And later on, when I learned to be "anxious for nothing" and began "resting in God," the condition healed itself totally.

Faith is an important component of healing, but it isn't always the faith of the one being healed that has it. Consider the paralytic healed in Capernaum. The four who carried him couldn't get into the house to see Jesus, so they broke through the roof. When Jesus saw their faith, He said to the paralytic, "Son, your sins are forgiven you," then He healed him (Mark 2:1–5).

Jesus said to the woman, who touched the hem of his garment, believing she would be healed,

"Be of good cheer, daughter; your faith has made you well."
(Matthew 9:22, NKJV)

When the two blind men cried out to Jesus, "Son of David, have mercy on us!" Jesus asked if they believed that He could do this. They said, "Yes, Lord," and Jesus replied:

"According to your faith let it be to you."
(Matthew 9:29, NKJV)

The above is just a sampling of the times Jesus healed those who came to Him. His methods were seldom the same. He knew exactly what each person needed. The only common denominator was faith.

When Jesus went to Nazareth, where He grew up, He met a stone wall of unbelief. He taught in their synagogue, astonished them with His wisdom, but they were offended by Him, and consequently,

> *"He did not do many mighty works there*
> *because of their unbelief."*
> (Matthew 13:58, NKJV)

When cancer struck my husband for the second time, I prayed for wisdom, looked up every verse on healing in the Bible, and wrote them down. We both felt we had faith, and we were trusting God to heal him. We were in the doctor's office when he told us the test came back positive.

After the doctor left the room, the nurse said, "I guess you'll have to go through the fire," in response to something I had said about praying. Her remark resonated with me. God often speaks through people, and I *knew* I had heard from Him. It was God's plan to go through the fire and not be healed immediately. But on the positive side, we would see God work in us in ways that a healing couldn't accomplish. As the Master told Peter,

> *"What I am doing you do not understand now,*
> *but you will know after this."*
> (John 13:7, NKJV)

We went through the fire, but we were not alone. Over and over, I have found that going the distance causes us to be closer to the Lord, and my husband would agree.

Every morning Keith would sing or say, "One day at a time, sweet Jesus..." We would read the Bible and pray. We both felt closer to God. Keith would share what he was going through, even with strangers, telling them how good God was.

Then there was the heart surgery. Keith developed fibrillation right after the surgery, and it went on for days. I recalled my mother telling us how she prayed all night for my dad when he was delirious from the influenza epidemic in 1943. Because of the perseverance and faith of my mother, my dad woke up the next morning feeling much better.

Thinking about that, I decided to stay at the hospital and pray all night. About four o'clock in the morning, the one who monitored the machines came into our room and said the fibrillation had stopped. Praise God!

When God doesn't heal, He may be allowing the sickness to bring us closer to Him; He might want to change something in us or get our attention if we are going in the wrong direction. Whatever the reason(s), we need to spend time in His presence, in His Word, and listening for His voice.

"Fear not, for I have redeemed you; I have called you by your name; you are Mine...When you walk through the fire, you shall not be burned. Nor shall the flames scorch you. For I am the Lord your God, the Holy One of Israel, your Savior;"
(Isaiah 43:1–3, NKJV)

"And we know that all things work together for good to those who love God...For whom He foreknew, He also predestinated to be conformed to the image of His Son..."
(Romans 8:28–29, NKJV)

61. Looking for an Apology

We were on vacation, playing a board game with our family and another family we knew fairly well. The game consists of a list of clues that are read one at a time until someone guesses the answer. We were on the fourth or fifth clue, and I had forgotten the country revealed in the first clue and guessed a city in a different country. One person commented on it, which brought a few chuckles. A little later, a similar question came up, and person number two reminded me that it wasn't in that country—more laughter.

A little later in the game, and for no reason, a third person brought it up again (more laughter), to which I said facetiously, "That was so nice of you to bring that up again..." letting him know I didn't think it was funny.

A while later, the fourth person read the first clue and said loudly with emphasis, "And this is *not* in _____! (The country I had mistakenly guessed)," and the "four" of them literally

roared. I did not think it was funny. I said, "This is too much."
Silence. I said it again.

No one said anything; no one apologized. I let it go, pretending I wasn't upset, but I was—very much so!

The next day someone asked if anything was wrong because I was so quiet. I expressed my feelings. A family member said, "You're a Christian; you should just let it go." *Don't you just love that?* My husband was concerned that it would affect the relationship with the family and wanted me to forget it. I was upset with him because he put others before me. God seemed unusually quiet, and I needed time to decipher what He was thinking.

That night our family went out for dinner. My granddaughter was telling us something she had done to her hair, and we started kidding her. I joined in at the end, and she retorted by referring to the country I had mistakenly said the night before—and the subject was quickly changed.

The next day I decided to take a long walk; I needed time to think. I walked for about three miles, praying off and on. I sat on a bench and prayed, wondering if I was overreacting? The hurt was beginning to turn into anger. "God, why aren't you saying something?" I said on the way home.

I was nearing the house when I heard, "Apologize to your granddaughter." I went into her room and asked her if I had hurt her feelings at the restaurant. She said, "Yes." I said I was very sorry; she said she was sorry for what she said, and we hugged.

Later that day, I recalled how I caused someone to feel inferior during that "game" a few nights ago. I didn't do it intentionally, but I did it. I was looking for an apology, but God was looking to teach me to be more sensitive to other people's feelings. Funny, I always thought I was—but I learned that day I had more to learn.

I had just read Patsy Clairmont's *Under His Wings*,[7] where she talks about humor and how it can hurt, saying that a good rule for use of humor is that if it hurts someone, it isn't funny and shouldn't be said.

If I had let it go, I wouldn't have learned what God wanted to teach me. After He showed me what He wanted me to learn, the hurt and anger melted away. Learning to be like Jesus is seldom easy—

> *"...but painful; nevertheless, afterward it yields the peaceable fruit of righteousness to those who have been trained by it."*
> (Hebrews 12:11, NKJV)

---

7 Patsy Clairmont, Under His Wings, Focus on the Family Publishing, Colorado Springs, CO 80995, 1994.

"And my God shall supply all your need according to His riches in glory by Christ Jesus."
(Philippians 4:19, NKJV)

62. Great is His Faithfulness

Job said, "The thing I greatly feared has come upon me. And what I dreaded has happened to me" (Job 3:25). There was a time I could identify with that statement: I was battling chronic pain from a neck injury, and my fear was having the pain so intense—even with pain pills—that I couldn't handle it. Two weeks during the summer of 2006 answered that fear.

When the pain was at its zenith, the presence of the Lord was so strong that I said to my husband, "I don't know if I ever want the pain to go away because I know His Presence will go also." Keith was aghast. He couldn't understand. The pain did lessen, and so did the overwhelming presence.

After that experience, I felt everything would go well forever. It did until my husband and I were driving home after visiting relatives. While there, I tripped on their cement patio and broke a bone in my foot.

"If you had watched where you were going..." my husband snapped. I couldn't believe the words coming from the one who

had spent the last year and a half praying, comforting, and caring for me.

I told Keith I wasn't going to accept it as carelessness. It was
an accident, even though I had tripped over the patio twice before on other visits.

We drove home in silence. But the enemy was anything but
silent. My hurt feelings escalated into feeling sorry for myself.
It was bad enough with a neck injury. How would I manage
with a broken foot? I started agreeing with the enemy. "Maybe
I was at fault; maybe I was careless and clumsy."

"Above all, taking the shield of faith with which you will be
able to quench all the fiery darts of the wicked one."
(Ephesians 6:16, NKJV)

I had let the "shield of faith" down, and the fiery dart had hit
its mark.

I couldn't use crutches; they put too much pressure on my
neck, so Keith set up a bed on our bedroom floor with a TV set.
When I had to get up, I crawled around the house like a dog.

We were eating lunch the next day, and I said to Keith in
tears, "God said all things work together for good. How can any
good come from this?"

Keith said, "I don't know, but I can tell you something good
God is doing in me. When you broke your foot, I selfishly
thought of myself that I would have to keep cooking and clean-
ing, but I don't want to be selfish. I'm asking God to give me
more love so I can take care of you..." And then he told me he,
too, had tripped on the patio while we were there.

"Two are better than one, because they have a good reward
for their labor. For if they fall, one will
lift up his companion."
(Ecclesiastes 4:9–10, NKJV)

Sometimes our trials aren't just for us. It's been over a month, and I have seen my husband's love and devotion expressed in a hundred ways. I have had to fight my way back to communion with God, not in the surreal way that it was for the two weeks, but for the "peace that passes understanding" we can have any time we decide to trust Him and walk in faith.

I no longer fear *the thing*, for it has come upon me, and God has proven Himself more than enough. I have often wondered about the fate of John the Baptist, Stephen, and other martyrs. Weren't God's promises for them too? The experience I had (although it was in no way martyr-like) changed my way of thinking. When Stephen accused the rebel Israelites of murdering "the Just One," they gnashed at him. "But he, being full of the Holy Spirit, gazed into heaven and said,"

"Look! I see the heavens opened and the Son of Man stand-
ing at the right hand of God!"
(Acts 7:56, NKJV)

Then they cast him out of the city and stoned him as he was calling on God, saying, "Lord Jesus, receive my spirit." Then he knelt down and asked the Lord to forgive them, and he died. I have to believe he felt God's presence more than he felt the pain.

*"Through the Lord's mercies we are not consumed, because
His compassions fail not. They are new every morning;
great is Your faithfulness."*
(Lamentations 3:22–23, NKJV)

"Assuredly, I say to you, if you have faith as a mustard seed, you will say to this mountain, 'Move from here to there,' and it will move; and nothing will be impossible for you."
(Matthew 17:20, NKJV)

63. Mustard Seed Faith

My husband was in surgery, and I was in the waiting room reading E. M. Bounds' *Classic Collection on Prayer*. I read for a while and then prayed—back and forth. At one point, I prayed, "Lord, don't let the surgery go longer than three and one-half hours."

The nurse, who had taken Keith to surgery at seven a.m., said it could last up to five hours. Because the risks increase with time, I didn't want him under anesthesia that long.

So when the doctor walked in *exactly* at ten-thirty and said he believed he had gotten all cancer, I was elated for the good news and also for the precise answer to prayer. I took it as a sign believing God was saying, "I have everything in My hands." I praised His faithfulness and shared His answer and good news with family and friends.

The next afternoon Keith came home, tired but feeling well. Later that night, he developed a high fever, could not lie down because of intense pain, and the urine in his bag had turned a bright red. He took pain pills and finally fell asleep; I went into the spare bedroom, got down on my knees, and prayed for some time.

God reminded me of the "ten-thirty promise." I believed Him then. Would I believe Him now? I knew I had to make a decision. My next thought was,

> *Faith is easy to have when everything is going well, but when things aren't going well, and you still believe, then your faith is real.*

I believed it was from God. I took a step of faith and said, "Lord, I trust You," I said it over and over. Then I prayed some scriptures to bolster my faith. I reminded myself of His faithfulness, His marvelous love, His power—by then, my face was on the floor. I opened my eyes, and a glint of gold got my attention from under the desk drawers. I reached under and pulled out a gold chain link bracelet, and hanging from it was a mustard seed encased in glass. A verse came to mind:

> *"If you have faith as a mustard seed, you will say to this mountain, "Move from here to there,' and it will move; and nothing will be impossible for you."*
> (Matthew 17:20, NKJV)

I praised Him through tears of joy. I didn't know how or when the bracelet got there or whose it was, but at that moment, it was God's gift to me. I went to bed praising the Lord.

The next morning Keith's fever was gone, so was the pain, and the urine was a light pink becoming clear by midday—proving once again the faithfulness of God, the power of faith, and the unreliability of looking at circumstances.

When I told my daughter about the bracelet, she said it was hers but hadn't seen it in years. "But now, Mom, it's yours."

When adverse circumstances arise, we have a decision to make. We either decide to trust (have faith in) God, or we decide to trust in what we see around us. Think of it. Wouldn't you rather trust in Almighty God than the fallibility of the situation? I've been in that situation, and I have failed. God never condemns us when we fail, but He wants us to learn. He wants us to trust Him.

"Let us hold fast the confessions of our hope without waver-ing, for He who promised is faithful."
(Hebrews 10:23, NKJV)

God means what He says. If we hold on and do not waver, He will honor that trust just like He promised—for He is faithful who promised!

*"And Hannah prayed and said: 'My heart rejoices
in the Lord; my horn is exalted in the Lord. I smile at my
enemies, because I rejoice in Your salvation. No one is holy
like the Lord, for there is none besides You, nor is there any
rock like our God.'"*
(1 Samuel 2:1–2, NKJV)

64. Pour Out Your Bitterness

"Oh Lord, what a difference this journey to Shiloh is than the last time. My heart is bursting with praise; then it was clenched in bitterness—bitterness for my husband Elkanah, who didn't understand my longing for a child, and bitterness for Peninnah, who was never without a child."[8]

Elkanah and his family went to Shiloh yearly to worship and sacrifice to the Lord. Elkanah was married to Hannah; he was also married to Peninnah, Hannah's rival who...

*"...provoked her (Hannah) severely, to make her miserable
because the Lord had closed her womb. So it was, year by
year, when she (Hannah) went up to the house of the Lord,*

---

8 Dialogue is author's perception of Hannah taken from 1 Samuel Chapters 1–4.

that she (Peninnah) provoked her; therefore she (Hannah)
wept and did not eat."
(1 Samuel 1:6–7, NKJV)

"How I hated her when she made fun of me. I thought my feelings were justified; You, Lord, showed me I was wrong. I didn't realize Peninnah was jealous of me because Elkanah loved me. I was too bitter to appreciate his love."[9]

"Whenever the time came for Elkanah to make an offering,
he would give portions to Peninnah his wife...but to Han-
nah he would give a double portion, for he loved Hannah,
although the Lord had closed her womb."
(1 Samuel 1:4–5 NKJV)

"Elkanah tried to comfort me in his own way, Lord, but I wanted him to understand how I felt, not just try to make it better."[10]

"Hannah, why do you weep? Why do you not eat? And why
is your heart grieved? Am I not better to you than ten sons?"
(1 Samuel 1:8, NKJV)

"And You, my Lord, I was angry at You—the Giver of Life. I thought You were making fun of me, too, for I was the only woman I knew who couldn't bear children. I felt so alone in my

---

9 Dialogue is author's perception of Hannah taken from 1 Samuel Chapters 1–4.
10 Ibid.

suffering when I started praying to You in the Tabernacle in Shiloh."[11]

> *"And she was in bitterness of soul, and prayed to the Lord*
> *and wept in anguish. Then she made a vow and said, 'O*
> *Lord of hosts. If You will indeed look on the affliction of*
> *Your maidservant and remember me, and not forget Your*
> *maidservant, but will give Your maidservant a male child,*
> *then I will give him to the Lord all the days of his life, and*
> *no razor shall come upon his head."*
> (1 Samuel 1:10–11, NKJV)

Eli, the priest, watched as Hannah prayed. Thinking she was drunk, he said to her,

> *"How long will you be drunk? Put your wine away from you!"*
> (1 Samuel 1:14, NKJV)

Hannah defended herself and answered,

> *"No, my lord, I am a woman of sorrowful spirit. I have*
> *drunk neither wine nor intoxicating drink, but have poured*
> *out my soul before the Lord...for out of the abundance of my*
> *complaint and grief I have spoken until now."*
> (1 Samuel 1:15–16, NKJV)

"Until now," said Hannah. Before she knew her prayer had been answered, she was no longer complaining, nor was she

---

11 Ibid.

grieving. Hannah's heart was changed as she poured out her soul to God.

> *"Then Eli answered and said, 'Go in peace, and the God of*
> *Israel grant your petition which you have asked of Him.'*
> *And she said, 'Let your maidservant find favor in your*
> *sight.' So the woman went her way and ate, and her face*
> *was no longer sad."*
> (1 Samuel 1:17–18, NKJV)

And God remembered Hannah; she bore a son and named him Samuel, meaning *Heard by God.*

"How grateful I am, Lord, that You opened my heart to hear You when I emptied my soul of the poison I kept bottled up inside me. When I willingly gave up what I wanted more than I wanted You, Lord, You met me! And now I understand, Lord, why You allowed those circumstances that made me desperate enough to seek You with my whole heart. Since I gave up my bitterness, I am able to love my husband, and he respects me by not questionings my vow to give our beloved Samuel to You Lord."[12]

> *"So Elkanah her husband said to her, 'Do what seems best*
> *to you; wait until you have weaned him. Only let the Lord*
> *establish (confirm) His word.'"*
> (1 Samuel 1:23, NKJV)

"How could I have trained my beloved Samuel for what lies ahead if You had given me a child before You changed my heart.

---

12 Dialogue is author's perception of Hannah taken from 1 Samuel Chapters 1–4.

And now, Lord, I am not only giving him to You, I am trusting You take care of Him, and that He will follow you all the days of His life."[13]

> *"For this child I prayed, and the Lord has granted me my petition...as long as he lives he shall be lent to the Lord."*
> (1 Samuel 1:27–28, NKJV)

After Samuel was weaned, Hannah and Elkanah brought him to Eli, the priest in the house of the Lord in Shiloh.

Perhaps you are thinking if Elkanah had been a better husband, he would have demanded Peninnah to quit provoking Hannah; or perhaps Hannah should have been more assertive and stood up to her rival. But God had another plan: to use the imperfections in others to persuade Hannah to "pour out her soul before the Lord." And when she did, God met her.

Can you identify with that? I can. God had used the imperfections in others to change me before He dealt with them. I find it interesting to note that Peninnah is not mentioned again. If she did say anything to her, I believe Hannah would have just smiled at her.

Hannah's statement, "I smile at my enemies because I rejoice in Your salvation" (1 Samuel 2:1), tells me, from experience, that it wasn't just the answer to prayer that made her smile at her enemies. It was a change of heart. I could "smile" at my rivals only because God used them to change me from the inside out.

Hannah's desire for a child consumed her. Sometimes we want something so much that it becomes a *stronghold* in our

---
13 Ibid.

lives. If God gave us our request, we would find leanness in our souls. So He sends affliction—sometimes from others—so that we are forced to seek Him, to pour out our hearts before Him, so He can wrench the thing that hinders us out of our hearts. Depending on what the thing is—and if it is His will—when He knows we can handle it, He will give us the desire of our hearts. And if it isn't His will, we can accept the fact that the thing we wanted isn't good for us—either way, we can say, like Hannah,

"My heart rejoices in the Lord...I smile at my enemies, because I rejoice in Your salvation. No one is holy like the Lord. For there is none besides You, nor is there any rock like our God."
(1 Samuel 2:1–2, NKJV)

> *"For God has not given us a spirit of fear, but of power and of love and of a sound mind."*
> (2 Timothy 1:7, NKJV)

65. Fears and Phobias

Claustrophobia runs in my husband's family. The only time it manifested itself in Keith was in places like the crowded elevator in the Sears Tower and the Arch in St. Louis, but it didn't interrupt his lifestyle until a record snowstorm hit the Midwest one New Year's Eve.

Keith was unusually quiet that night, absorbed in reading the Bible, while the kids and I tried to get him in a celebrating mood. He seemed overly concerned that he couldn't get out of the driveway if he had to. Later that night, after the kids were sleeping, the anxiety escalated to the point where he called the Rescue Squad.

Several things were transpiring in his life: he was in midlife, experiencing difficulties after transferring to a different job, and our relationship was changing. God was working in all three areas. Only Keith didn't know it at the time.

He came home from the hospital early the next morning and spent most of the next three days in the bedroom, reading the Bible and praying. It was Christmas break, and as a teacher, he had a few days to relax before venturing back into the working world.

But his re-entry didn't go smoothly. Claustrophobic feelings would overtake him in closed-in places at work, in malls, and even driving in the fog. He fought back by praising the Lord out loud until his fears subsided. He said he didn't care if others heard him, although he tried to praise quietly—it was the only way he could get free.

> *"Whenever I am afraid, I will trust in You. In God I will praise His word, in God I have put my trust; I will not fear."*
> (Psalm 56:3–4, NKJV)

Sometimes God has to tear things down before He begins to build according to His specifications. He will do whatever it takes to get our attention, make us willing to see our weaknesses, and then teach us how to overcome them.

> *"Unless the Lord builds the house, they labor in vain who build it;"*
> (Psalm 127:1, NKJV)

We talked and talked, sometimes far into the night, while I prayed fervently that God would speak through me. I was amazed at the things that were coming out of my mouth and that Keith was listening to what I had to say. We drew closer as we sifted through his difficulties at work, his expectations in life, and the changes in our relationship.

Claustrophobics do not relish flying. When our daughter moved to the Southwest, we flew there, but only if we sat in the bulkhead seats in the front, assigned on the day of the flight. God stretched Keith's faith as he fought fear until the day of the flight when God provided those seats every time! After a while, those seats were no longer available, and we began sitting a little farther back. Keith wasn't sure he could do it, but God knew he could. He knows when to push us forward (or, in this case, backward). Once, we had seats assigned halfway back, and Keith was more than a little apprehensive when an attendant came from behind the desk and asked Keith if he wanted seats closer to the front. Keith accepted them gratefully. It was one of many times God assured us we were "under His wings."

> *"He shall cover you with His feathers, and under*
> *His wings you shall take refuge; His truth shall*
> *be your shield and buckler."*
> (Psalm 91:4, NKJV)

Most of us pray that our problems be removed immediately and miraculously. But God's ways are not our ways because most of the time, He removes them "little by little" as we grow in the Lord and learn to trust Him. God wants to bring us into our own "promised land," in the same way He wanted to bring the children of Israel to the "land flowing with milk and honey" when He told them:

> *"I will not drive them (their enemies) out from before you*
> *in one year, lest the land become desolate and the beasts of*
> *the field become too numerous for you. Little by little I will*

drive them out...until you have increased and you inherit
the land."
(Exodus 23:29–30, NKJV)

We were on vacation, standing outside the bus that would take us to our cruise ship, searching bags, pockets, and my purse for our tickets. When we finally found them, the bus was filled except for a few seats in the back. Keith leaned over to me and whispered, "I can't go back there," and a couple who were in the front seat stood up and said, "We want to go to the back; you can have these seats." We were amazed—God can do anything!

It happened again. We were late boarding another nearly-filled bus and saw a "Reserved" sign on the front seat. The driver removed the sign and said, "You can sit here." I leaned over to Keith and said, "God reserved these just for you."

"Fear not, for I am with you;...I will strengthen you,
yes, I will help you..."
(Isaiah 41:10, NKJV)

And help He did. The phobia didn't disappear, but it subsided considerably as Keith continued to praise the Lord and see God's hand in difficult places.

Keith and I were in an office several stories high, admiring the beautiful scenery, when he mentioned his vertigo—not being able to look down. The person we had come to see gave Keith some practical advice that worked:

1. Fix your gaze straight ahead, and slowly move your head to the left; pause.

2. Then pass the center and go all the way to the left, moving your gaze down *just a little*, and continue slowly back and forth until you get to the ground.

Many years passed, and still, the "height" problem lingered. Then we planned a trip to New York City, and everyone knows NYC is all about *up*. We prayed before we went, while we were there, and gave glory to God as we viewed the unparalleled skyline from the Empire State Building using the above steps and in the restaurant on the 101st floor of the ill-fated twin towers—*one week before 9/11!*

Our next vacation took us to the Lewis and Clark exposition in St. Louis, where we visited the Arch. When Keith saw the small egg-shaped six-seated elevators, he said, "I'm not sure I can go in there." My sister, who had come along, said, "Let's pray." So, we huddled in a circle and prayed in front of God and everyone. Years ago, Keith had waited while the kids and I had gone up to the top of the Arch—but not this time.

The gal who took our tickets overheard my sister saying something to Keith about trusting the Lord, and she said, "I'm a Christian too." After hearing our plight, she assigned us to our own elevator, and we sang praise songs all the way up.

> *"The Lord is my strength and my shield; my heart trusted in*
> *Him, and I am helped...and with my song I will praise Him."*
> (Psalm 28:7, NKJV)

Each time Keith saw God in the situation, the strength of the infirmity lessened. He had discovered the "power of Christ" was real as He praised the Lord in his fears and allowed God to make changes in his life.

Most anxiety-related problems spring from something in life that needs to be dealt with. So the next time you ask God to remove an infirmity, and He isn't answering, ask Him to show you *His* way.

Not my way, but Yahweh!

That's what the Apostle Paul did when he wasn't getting the answer he wanted. God gave him an amazing revelation:

> *"My grace is sufficient for you, for My strength is made perfect in weakness."*
> (2 Corinthians 12:9, NKJV)

When Paul understood that God didn't want to deliver him out of his difficulty. Rather, let him experience the "power of God" in difficulty, he exclaimed,

> *"...I will rather boast in my infirmities that the power of Christ may rest upon me. I take pleasures in infirmities, in reproaches, in needs, in persecutions, in distresses, for Christ's sake. For when I am weak, then I am strong."*
> (2 Corinthians 12:9–10, NKJV)

Did you catch that? Paul took "pleasure in infirmities" because he believed (had faith in) what God said: that the "power of Christ" would rest upon him whenever he was weak!

I can hear some of you thinking, "Well, I'm not Paul." Well, neither was my husband, but he praised the Lord until the "power of Christ" rested on him. He said he didn't sense any great presence coming over him. Rather, it was an ordinary quiet peace, the panic was gone, and he could continue doing what he had started.

Interestingly enough, a few years later, I developed something similar to panic attacks, but not nearly as bad. I leaned heavily on Keith's advice as I dealt with the insecurity that plagued me from my youth. I prayed that God would deliver me from my fears, and like my husband, God didn't want to "deliver me out of it," no, He had something better: He wanted to teach me some things in it—first!

Some things Keith and I learned:

- Praise God while walking—rather than just sitting—motion helps to displace anxiety.
- Read His Book. Ask God to give you pertinent verses and repeat them until they become alive inside of you, such as:

"God has not given us a spirit of fear..."
(2 Timothy 1:7, NKJV)

"The Lord is the strength of my life,
of whom shall I be afraid?"
(Psalm 27:1, NKJV)

"Do not fear, little flock, for it is your Father's good pleasure
to give you the kingdom."
(Luke 12:32, NKJV)

- Look up "fear" in a concordance.
- Talk to someone you trust: sometimes, we need to see through the perspective of others—they see things we can't see and can encourage us.
- Talk to Jesus *a lot*, and listen to what He is saying.

"I have learned in whatever state I am, to be content:"
(Philippians 4:11, NKJV)

"I can do all things through Christ who strengthens me."
(Philippians 4:13, NKJV)

66. Altering My Attitude

The Apostle Paul said, "I have learned...to be content." But I'm not quite there. I'm *still* learning "in whatever state I am, to be content" through perseverance and prayer.

I was staying with my eighty-two-year-old mother for a couple of weeks and praying that the Lord would give me grace while my sisters—who take excellent care of her—were on vacation.

After my father went to be with the Lord, my mother was never the same. Theirs had been a "happily-ever-after" kind of marriage, and she was lost without him. She volunteered a couple of days a week at the hospital, visited and picked up people for church, made items for benefits, etc., but I never again saw that light that had been in her eyes.

Several years later, she developed dementia. Sometimes she was sweet, and other times she became suspicious of her daughters, accusing my sisters of being after her money and telling me I was a liar. We learned to accept her condition and disregard the accusations. But it was difficult to see her change from our beloved mother who would do anything for her children to someone who circumvented even the best suggestions.

I asked Mom one morning while I was staying there if she would please buy a new mattress—money was not a problem—but she refused. I was sleeping on an old sagging mattress, spending a couple of hours each night walking the floor with a backache.

I went outside, sat on a lawn chair, and complained to the Lord. I thought I was right; I wasn't asking anything out of line, but as I talked to Him, I felt He was saying I had to give up that right. I had started out asking Him to change my mother, and now He was asking me to change.

After talking to Him a little while longer, I could feel my attitude improving. I knew what Jesus would do—He would sleep on the love seat and not complain—even if His feet hung over the edge. When Jesus left home and started His ministry, He didn't even have a bed. So who was I to complain? Jesus told His followers:

> "Foxes have holes and birds of the air have nests, but the
> Son of Man has nowhere to lay His head."
> (Luke 9:58, NKJV)

I gave up my right to God; it felt good to obey. Mom and I enjoyed the rest of our time together, and I slept fairly well on the love seat. God changed me on the inside to keep peace on the outside.

The next time my husband and I came to stay with her, she blew us away when she volunteered to buy a mattress. God can do amazing things when we follow His leading. A couple of days later, she asked how the bed was that she had paid for, quoting the exact price to the penny! We chuckled because she sometimes had trouble remembering what happened earlier that day.

When Mom could no longer stay alone, we hired trained companions to be with her day and night. She would order them out of the house, try to run away, and thought people were living in her basement.

Mom's dementia progressed, and we put her in a wonderful Alzheimer's Home. Between the medications, the doctor gave her, the friendly staff, and being with people all the time, her disposition changed back to the sweet mother that we had known, even though her mind was still limited.

After she couldn't take care of her daily needs, she was transferred to another nursing home. The food didn't look all that appetizing, so one day, I made her favorite soup—chicken noodles from scratch. Some family members came along, and we found a table next to a sunny window and served the soup. She took a spoonful and remarked, "This is the worst soup I ever had!" Oh well, you had to laugh. If you didn't learn to laugh, you would cry.

When I came to see her, she would raise her arms like a little child, excited to see me—much like the Sunday morning many years ago when I walked into the kitchen and saw her arms waving high, responding to a televangelist's invitation to ask Jesus to forgive her sins and come into her life.

She had always been a faithful church go-er and a pray-er. When my dad contracted the virus in the 1943 epidemic (before antibiotics) and became delirious, Mom prayed all night long; in the morning, he was much improved.

My mother prayed for me endlessly during my rebellious teen years; I believe those prayers were answered years later when I gave my heart to Jesus and then shared with my family what this awesome Savior had done for me.

But knowing Jesus personally brought a new dimension to her life. She began praying daily, reading her Bible, and seeing God work in ways she had never seen before. Whenever I called her with a prayer request, I knew she'd be praying until it was met.

Several years later, my dad was diagnosed with lung cancer and spent most of the day in bed because he didn't feel any pain lying down. But he and Mom wanted to sit at the table and talk like they always had, so they prayed together until the pain ceased for an hour or two.

Mom always loved going to church; she loved singing the old hymns. When she was still mobile, my sister took her to church every Sunday. The girls at the nursing home would make a big deal of fixing her up to go to church—even after she was bed-ridden and couldn't go. One Sunday morning, the same girls were getting her ready for "church" when God decided to take her to a church service beyond description—where the singing never ends, the joy is unspeakable and full of glory—*for the Lord God is there!*

"Then He who sat on the throne said, 'Behold I make all things new.' And He said to me, 'Write, for these words are true and faithful.'"
(Revelations 21:5, NKJV)

Mom lived to be eighty-six. My prayer was always, "Lord, don't let her get to the place where she doesn't recognize me." God was faithful. And like God, I keep only the good memories Mother and I had—and they are abundant!

"But I say to you...do good to those who hate you, and pray for those who spitefully use you and persecute you."
(Matthew 5:44, NKJV)

67. Offended? Take the High Road

Her remark caught me off-guard. It was well below the *spiritual* belt. It had happened before, but this time her put-down was blatant. It hurt. Especially since I had been inwardly praising God that we were conversing so well—and then it happened. I said nothing in defense. That's not surprising since I can always think of what I should have said a day or two later.

After I got home, I replayed the scenario in my mind at least a dozen times. I thought of scenes of conversation that never happened—things I wished I had said. By the third day and too many scenes later, the hurt had turned to anger.

I had an appointment with my Christian hairdresser that day, and as she clipped away, I described the episode to her—expecting her to commiserate—but instead, she encouraged me to "take the high road." "The enemy," she said in part, "is looking for ways to make Christians feel offended. Don't let him! Take the high road..." I latched on to the enemy part, taking only half of what she said, leaving the shop looking better outwardly but inwardly the same.

In the days ahead, I heard the words "Take the high road" frequently, but I didn't have a good grasp on what God was saying. So, when I randomly opened a book of Bible Selections on "Love," and I read,

> *"Bearing with one another, and forgiving one another...*
> *even as Christ forgave you so you also must do. But above*
> *all these things put on love which is the bond of perfection."*
> (Colossians 3:13–14, NKJV)

I knew God was speaking. I'd read those verses before, but that day I heard them. Jesus and I had a long talk. He wasn't excusing my friend's remarks. Rather, He was dealing with my reaction to them. He had told me long ago, "When she puts you down, she is putting Me down." That's how much He identifies with us!

Jesus confirmed that when He appeared before Saul and said, "I am Jesus, whom you are persecuting" (Acts 9: 5). He takes our persecutions personally, and He will deal with them. But first, there were things in me He needed to change first.

> *"Blessed is he who is not offended because of Me."*
> (Luke 7:23, NKJV)

I took the high road. I asked Him to change me and love her through me, and then I expected to "love happily ever after." Not so. Several days later, I regurgitated the scenario playing it in my mind several times. The enemy works through people, even Christians, through their weaknesses, hoping to offend us and render us ineffective. We can overcome the enemy's scheme by listening to God and following His instructions—but I wasn't there yet.

When we make mistakes, God doesn't give up on us; He is teaching us something we need to listen and learn. His next lesson came through another verse:

> *"Pray for those who spitefully use you and persecute you."*
> (Matthew 5:44, NKJV)

I started praying for my friend strictly out of obedience, but as I continued, my feelings began to change. It's hard to think badly of someone you are praying for. Change is a process. It takes time, and rarely is it a once-and-for-all event.

Make no mistake, even after we think we have dealt with it—zing—it comes back. I thought the situation was all sewn up. It started unraveling when I told my sister about the offense. The thought crossed my mind that I shouldn't be rehashing this—I think I knew it was the Lord, but I dismissed it—because frankly, I enjoyed telling it, and I reasoned, *This is my sister; I can tell her anything*. But I had left the door open, and the enemy snuck in.

I recall praying for someone later that day, and as I prayed, the words came out lifeless and succinct. At the time, I wondered what was wrong, but I did not pursue it.

For the next four days, I felt like I had wandered into a desert. I wondered if rehashing the offenses was the cause, but it was easier to blame the malaise on a health problem I was having.

On the fifth day I was close to desperate. I prayed, "Lord, I don't know what's wrong but teach me whatever You want me to learn. I am trusting You to bring me out of this darkness."

To try and get out myself, I have learned, only pushes me in deeper. To do nothing but trust (have faith in) God to get me out—works! I prayed and waited on Him...

> *"For You Lord will light my lamp; the Lord my God will*
> *enlighten my darkness."*
> (Psalm 18:28, NKJV)

On day six, I watched Joyce Meyer with guests John and Lisa Bevere discuss how the enemy uses offenses to trap Christians. When John talked about his book *The Bait of Satan*,[14] I could see how Satan had trapped me when I talked about the offenses and grieved the Holy Spirit.

Jesus warns us not to "give place (an opportunity) to the devil" (Ephesians 4:27). Looking back, I had sensed the Holy Spirit's quiet conviction, how I brushed it aside, "giving place to the devil" and falling right into his trap.

I felt horrible. I prayed; I asked for forgiveness. I repeated this verse:

> *"If we confess our sins, He is faithful and just to forgive us*
> *our sins and to cleanse us from all unrighteousness."*
> (1 John 1:9, NKJV)

---

14 John Bevere, *The Bait of Satan*, Lake Mary, FL: Charisma House, 1994.

I love that verse! It is powerful! God is faithful to forgive us and to cleanse us from all unrighteousness. As I repeated those words, I sensed a "freeing" inside. Then I asked the Lord to refill me with His Spirit. He did. It was s-o-o-o-o-o good to spend time in His presence. I praised Him, thanked Him for the lesson, for His faithfulness, His love, and told Him,

> "Lord, I want to bring every rebel thought into captivity. I want to listen to You the next time I hear Your faithful reminder to keep my mouth shut. Nothing is worth being outside Your presence Lord. *Nothing!*"

When those thoughts come, I am learning to emphatically resist them with statements like: "Lord, I am *not* going there!" "I rebuke those thoughts in the Name of Jesus!" "I refuse to listen to them, Jesus, I put them under your feet," or something similar.

The longer we allow those lawless thoughts to linger, the harder it is to kick them out. It becomes imperative to cast them out as soon as we are aware of them.

> *"Casting down arguments and every high thing that exalts*
> *itself against the knowledge of God, bringing every thought*
> *into captivity to the obedience of Christ."*
> (2 Corinthians 10:5, NKJV)

On day seven, I woke up feeling God's peace, wishing it could always be like this. This is the rest between tests. I know there will be another test around the corner. Who said the Christian life would be easy? But it is worth all the *miserable* moments, knowing that what we gain is worth so much more than what we had to lose.

I began praying for my friend again. As I continued to pray regularly, the Spirit took over, and in time enmity faded, and to my amazement, I found I really wanted the Lord to bless her. That wasn't me, but the "Christ in me, my hope of glory" (Colossians 1:27).

*"All things work together for good to those who love God
and are called according to His purpose."*
(Romans 8:28, NKJV)

68. Even Mistakes, Lord?

I woke up in the middle of the night with pain registering around "eight" on the now-familiar pain scale. I took the well-worn path to the medicine closet while questioning my decision to go to the chiropractor the day before. I thought God said "yes," but now I wasn't sure.

For the past eighteen months and too many doctors later, my chronic neck problem refused to yield, and now my back and legs had joined the melee. I swallowed the pain pills and woke up my husband; he held me close and prayed for me as he had done so many times before.

The next morning brought *another* trip to Urgent Care, *another* doctor, and *another* prescription that put me in a stupor for two weeks. But glory to God, the pain ceased, and my neck began to heal. Keith asked, "Do you think God allowed you to go to the chiropractor so you would end up in Urgent Care?"

I didn't know, but what I did know was God had been working on an area of my life that resisted change. I had been caught in a cycle of walking in victory, then stumbling in defeat. At times I was afraid that God would throw up His hands and give up on me. Then two verses changed my way of thinking:

> *"I did not come to judge the world but to save the world..."*
> (John 12:47, NKJV)

> *"If we are faithless, He remains faithful;*
> *He cannot deny Himself."*
> (2 Timothy 2:13, NKJV)

Even if we are faithless, He still remains faithful. Doesn't that comfort you? It did me. I am touched by His unending and far-reaching love. Surely the nation of Israel tested Him to the nth degree, yet He reached out to them over and over with undying love in many verses:

> *"For all this His anger is not turned away,*
> *but His hand is stretched out still."*
> (Isaiah 5:25, 9:12, 9:17, 9:21 and 10:4, NKJV)

Sadly, no matter how many times He reached out, they did not grasp His hand.

I saw His mercy in the whirlwinds as we traveled across the country to visit family. My neck wasn't doing well. I hardly said a word but laid my head on a pillow. Keith said later he was waiting for me to say, "Let's go home." We had canceled our plane trip several weeks earlier and decided to drive so I could lie down.

We drove into forecasted storms—we prayed—and woke up to learn tornadoes touched down on either side of us the night before. On the third day, a heavy fog settled over the road impairing our vision—we prayed again—I heard Keith catch his breath as the fog lifted, while I "saw" our car moving within two huge extended arms and hands.

"With a strong hand, and with an outstretched arm,
for His mercy endures forever."
(Psalm 136:12, NKJV)

Weeks later, when the pain was more than I could handle, God's overwhelming presence descended on me until the pain receded gradually in a couple of weeks but didn't go away entirely.

No, God wasn't angry with me, He wasn't judging me, but He wouldn't let me go until I learned to do His will, His way.

"Not my way, but Yahweh."

So, was my trip to the chiropractor a mistake? Ecclesiastes 3:1 says, "To everything there is a season. A time for every purpose under heaven." God allowed the right doctor with the right medication according to His timing.

The Lord got my attention through pain, but I was still trying to keep myself from falling—and I failed every time.

"For it is God who works in you both to will
and to do for His good pleasure."
(Philippians 2:13, NKJV)

"Both to will and to do..." is God's job! My part is to believe (have faith) that He will deliver me. But I wasn't there yet. After many failures, I sought God diligently, and He gave me this verse.

> *"Now to Him who is able to keep you from stumbling,*
> *and to present you faultless before the presence of*
> *His glory with exceeding joy."*
> (Jude 1:24, NKJV)

Notice, it is "*Him* who is able to keep me." So, if He will keep me, what is my part? Believing (having faith). It took longer to believe *He* would "keep me from stumbling." But He wouldn't give up until I stopped trying and trusted Him to do what I couldn't. Faith is where the power is! Just like salvation, faith (believing Him) without relying on works is what God requires; *trying* instead of trusting doesn't work—ever.

You say, "That sounds too easy." I say it's not always easy to trust (have faith in) God to do what we can't do—in many ways, yes—but when I came against a stronghold, I tried and tried, failed and failed until I was exhausted, then God gave me the above verse (Jude 1:24) and finally, *through faith*, the bonds were broken.

"He has torn, but He will heal us;
He has stricken, but He will bind us up."
(Hosea 6:1, NKJV)

69. Better Than Ever

I have a friend who is hurting deeply, she and her husband have recently separated, and she is devastated.

Several of us women met together to encourage her. I remember telling her not to give up hope no matter what it looked like because God can make any situation *better than ever*. I felt those words were God-inspired—especially the last three— she probably doesn't remember them. I looked at the situation and saw the potential for positive things. Understandably, she could only feel the hurt.

Years ago, I found myself in a "valley" with very different circumstances. All I saw there was confusion, but God saw potential. I didn't understand how God could use that valley "as a door of hope," but as I read this verse, thought about it, prayed about it, God opened my understanding:

"I will give her...the Valley of Achor (Hebrew word for
trouble) as a door of hope. She shall sing there, as in the

days of her youth, as in the day when she came up from the
land of Egypt."
(Hosea 2:15, NKJV)

He began teaching me that He can take any circumstance and turn it into a "door of Hope" if we put it in His Hands and trust Him with it.

Think back to when God rescued you from Egypt (life before you met Christ). Did you sing after He saved you? I did. Or maybe you just felt peace and joy, but now you are stuck in the Valley of Achor (trouble), and you feel depressed, alone, and wondering what God is saying.

God wants to show you how this valley can become a "Door of Hope." If you'll cooperate with Him and learn what He is teaching, you "shall sing there," like you did when you gave your heart to Jesus and He betrothed Himself to you:

"I will betroth you to Me forever; Yes, I will betroth you to
Me in righteousness and justice, in lovingkindness and
mercy; I will betroth you to Me in faithfulness, and you
shall know the Lord."
(Hosea 2:19–20, NKJV)

What a beautiful promise! Years ago, God gave me a revelation of our marriage that sent me to my knees: our relationship was shallow, we had little in common, and our communication was a little more than "How are you?"

I prayed fervently and frequently, and God answered my prayers. And through a series of circumstances, we fell in love again. But God wouldn't let us stop there—that was only the be-ginning—we had many lessons to learn to give our relationship depth and then to keep it alive and growing.

Some of our lessons were:

- Listening—*really* listening—being open to each other's perspectives.
- Letting God deliver us from: habits, hang-ups, hurts, and fears—by sharing them, talking about them, pray-ing together, and letting God work in us.
- Spout, pout, or the balance—talking it out while staying "in the Spirit."
- Learning that when we try to *be right*, no one wins; *get-ting it right* allows both of us to win. Admitting we were wrong gets easier.
- Lifting up our spouse through encouragement, compli-ments, affection, and prayers.
- Not letting "stuff" crowd out our relationship.
- Our partner doesn't know our needs unless we speak up.
- Forgiving and forgetting—nobody's perfect—except Je-sus, and He forgave us.
- We can't change anyone, not even ourselves—only God can.
- Laughing a lot. Going places, learning something new—just us two. Being together—forever!

God is a patient teacher; He won't let us settle for ordinary when He has *extra-ordinary* in mind. I look at my friend, and I know she has some heart-wrenching weeks and months ahead of her. But as she continues to look to Jesus—in those very struggles—she will find wisdom, growth, and strength. God will lead her. I believe that! I believe God and I (and God and you) can do anything as long as He is leading and we are following.

> *"I am the Lord, the God of all flesh.*
> *Is there anything too hard for Me?"*
> (Jeremiah 32:27, NKJV)

I believe my friend's devastating valley has the potential to make her marriage "better than ever" and that God will fight for her. He "hates divorce" (Malachi 2:16), and that one fine day, she will look back and see the path of God's faithfulness strewn with beautiful promises.

> *"He heals the brokenhearted and binds up their wounds."*
> (Psalm 147:3, NKJV)

> *"He makes peace in your borders,*
> *and fills you with the finest wheat."*
> (Psalm 147:14, NKJV)

Epilogue:

Many years have passed since my friend and her husband reunited, went to counseling, fell in love again, recommitted their lives to the Lord, and began serving Him fervently together. God did it—He made it better than ever!

Dedicated to: A & J.

*"And the Lord said to Moses...lift up your rod and stretch out
your hand over the sea and divide it. And the children of
Israel shall go on dry ground through the midst of the sea."*
(Exodus 14:15–16, NKJV)

70. Doubts

It was during a study of Israel's exodus from Egypt and the subsequent wilderness trials that I began to understand how important it was to have faith in God and not doubt.

*"Thus Israel saw the great work which the Lord had done in
Egypt; so the people feared the Lord, and believed the Lord
and His servant Moses."*
(Exodus 14:31, NKJV)

Oh, that the Israelites would've continued to believe the Lord after seeing the miraculous unfold as the waters divided and they crossed the Red Sea on dry ground—but they didn't. Three days later, they came to the waters of Marah and found them bitter. They complained, and God told Moses to take a tree and throw it into the waters to sweeten it.

> *"There He made a statute and an ordinance for them,*
> *and there He tested them."*
> (Exodus 15:25, NKJV)

They failed the test. God tests us, so we will learn to trust Him. It's the devil who tempts us to doubt, telling us that God doesn't care and that our circumstances cannot change.

The Israelites journeyed from the waters of Marah to Elim, where they found water and palm trees; everything went well until they came to the Wilderness of Sin, and there they complained again,

> *"Oh, that we had died by the hand of the Lord in the land*
> *of Egypt, when we sat by the pots of meat and when we ate*
> *bread to the full! For you have brought us into the wilder-*
> *ness to kill this whole assembly with hunger."*
> (Exodus 16:3, NKJV)

God heard their complaints and rained "bread from heaven" in the morning and "meat to eat in the evening." Every trial they faced duplicated the same response. Instead of trusting God, they complained, tempting the Lord, saying,

> *"Is the Lord among us or not?"*
> (Exodus 17:7, NKJV)

Have you ever wondered that? I have.

God sent them food and water, fought against their enemies, sent a cloudy pillar to guide them by day and a pillar of fire by night,[15] showing them He had the power and the willing-ness to meet their needs. He led them into the wilderness, not to kill them but to prove them and make them strong. Just like He does with us!

In the third month, the children of Israel came to the Wil-derness of Sinai. There God spoke tenderly to them, revealing how much He loved them.

> *"You have seen what I did to the Egyptians, and how I*
> *bore you on eagles' wings and brought you to Myself. Now*
> *therefore, if you will indeed obey My voice and keep My*
> *covenant, then you shall be a special treasure to Me above*
> *all people; for all the earth is Mine."*
> (Exodus 19:4–5, NKJV)

Think of it! God wants us to be His "special treasure." Doesn't it warm your heart as He tenderly describes our salvation—how He "bore us on eagles' wings and brought us to Himself!"

When I first met Jesus, I felt like I was on "eagles' wings." I saw God do some awesome things, but after a while, things quieted down, adverse situations arose, and like the children of Israel who asked, "Is the Lord among us or not?" (Exodus 17:7) I, too, questioned: "Why has He allowed this?" "I'll never get through this." "Does God really care?"

"Oh God, I was just like them!"

There wasn't much teaching beyond salvation. I fell into de-pression because I thought I would never measure up. My life was a series of ups and downs until I made the decision to study

---

15 Nehemiah 9:12.

the Bible, believe God, walk in faith, and be willing to change. I learned I had to trust Him *before* I could see His Hand in my life.

It's easy to believe God when all is going well, but the true test of our faith comes when all is not going well, and we decide to believe He is still in control, that He loves us, and He has a purpose in our wilderness.

Sometimes God showed me that He could change the situation if I believed. Other times, I had to accept the way things were, or He wanted to change something in me so my circumstances would change. As I waited on the Lord in prayer—His timing, not mine—and refused to doubt, I began to understand what it was He wanted me to do.

God was very patient with the children of Israel (as He is with us), but they never stopped doubting, they never learned to believe God, and they never made it to the Land of Promise on this earth.

All of us have a tendency to doubt, but we can't stay there; we must move on. Even John the Baptist doubted. He had seen the Spirit descending and remaining on Jesus. When he saw Jesus coming toward him, he said, "Behold! The Lamb of God who takes away the sin of the world!" He told others, "I have seen and testified that this is the Son of God" (from John 1:29–34).

Yet, after John had been thrown in prison by Herod, he told his disciples to ask Jesus,

> *"Are You the Coming One or do we look for another?"*
> (Matthew 11:3, NKJV)

Jesus told John's disciples to tell him:

*"The blind see and the lame walk; the lepers are cleansed
and the deaf hear; the dead are raised up and the poor have
the gospel preached to them."*
(Matthew 11:5, NKJV)

Then Jesus added,

"And blessed is he who is not offended because of Me."
(Matthew 11:6, NKJV)

When Jesus heard that John the Baptist had been beheaded,

*"He departed from there by boat to a
deserted place by Himself."*
(Matthew 14:13, NKJV)

"A Man of sorrows and acquainted with grief."
(Isaiah 53:3, NKJV)

God gives us extreme examples in Scripture so all of us can
identify with the circumstances that sometimes rage before us.
We need to accept and not be offended by what God puts in our
path; we need to lay our doubts at His feet, tell Him we trust His
decisions, and believe that "all things" really do "work together
for our good," as we look for God in all our circumstances, and
wait while we are tested by various trials—

"...that the genuineness of your faith, being much more precious than that of gold that perishes, though it is tested by fire, may be found to praise, honor, and glory at the revelation of Jesus Christ..."
(1 Peter 1:7, NKJV)

*"But you Bethlehem, in the land of Judah, are not the least
among the rulers of Judah; for out of you shall come a Ruler
who will shepherd My people Israel."*
(Matthew 2:6, NKJV)

71. The Maidservant of the Lord

"Please, Lord, let the next place have a room available."

"Sorry."

"Lord, I'm putting this in Your hands; I know that You've led us here."

"Nothing here."

"Lord, You know the lateness of the hour; You know how tired I am."

"Try down the road."

"Lord, You have promised to supply all our needs..."

"All filled up."

"Doesn't God see how uncomfortable I am? Oh, Joseph, surely He knows we need a place to stay *tonight.*"

The above conversation is not based on fact. The Inn was the only place recorded in the Bible that Mary and Joseph inquired (Luke 2:7). But I wonder, did Mary question her circumstances that night? It seems incongruous that His royal coming, announced by the angel, would begin in *a barn*?

After all, the angel said her Son would be:

- "Great,"
- "Called the Son of the Highest,"
- "Given the throne of His father, David,"
- "Reign over the house of Jacob forever" and of
- "His kingdom there will be no end" (from Luke 1:32–33).

Then again, perhaps she recalled her surrender to God when she responded to the angel Gabriel:

> *"Behold the maidservant of the Lord!*
> *Let it be to me according to your word."*
> (Luke 1:38, NKJV)

Mary may have been perplexed, but this was no ordinary woman God chose to birth His Son. She was, as the angel said, "highly favored" and "blessed among women." She may not have understood everything that was happening, but it was said,

> *"Mary kept all these things and pondered*
> *them in her heart."*
> (Luke 2:19, NKJV)

All of us experience circumstances in our lives that we don't understand. Sometimes they are the exact opposite of what we expected, prayed and trusted God for. It is then we have a choice to make:

1. We can question God's provision, or
2. We can tell God we don't understand, but we accept what's happening, believing He has a good reason for allowing unsettling situations.

The latter is called faith, and faith is what God requires. There is no compromise. He asks for our unconditional trust.

Mary was "highly favored," but she wasn't perfect. To be chosen and awarded with such a great gift, God knew she needed to stay humble. I doubt if she told anyone what the angel Gabriel told her—would they have believed her? It appears that Joseph didn't believe her, for he was "minded to put her away secretly" (Matthew 1:19) before an angel of the Lord appeared to him in a dream and told him to take Mary as his wife.

The angel Gabriel had told Mary that her relative Elizabeth (mother of John the Baptist) was expecting in her old age. Mary visited her, and when she entered her home Elizabeth was filled with the Holy Spirit and began prophesying...ending with:

> "Blessed is she who believed, for there will be a fulfillment
> of those things which were told her from the Lord."
> (Luke 1:45, NKJV)

Mary believed, and God fulfilled His promise—

> "And she brought forth her first-born Son, and wrapped
> Him in swaddling cloths, and laid Him in a manger, be-
> cause there was no room for them in the inn."
> (Luke 2:7, NKJV)

How we believe determines our outcome! Mary believed.

When Joseph and Mary brought Jesus to the temple to present Him to the Lord, Simeon, a man who was waiting for the Lord's Christ, began to prophesy while Mary and Joseph "marveled at those things which were spoken of Him" (from Luke 2:25–34). In the middle of the prophecy, Simeon turned to Mary and said,

> *"Yes, a sword will pierce through your own soul, also."*
> (Luke 2:35, NKJV)

Did Mary "ponder that in her heart?" Did she wonder why Simeon didn't include Joseph? The woman who was "blessed among women" and "highly favored" lived through the loss of a spouse, became the head of the house, urged Jesus into His ministry, and then had to release Him to His ministry so she could embrace Him not only as a Son but as a Savior.

I can't even begin to imagine Mary's agony as she witnessed her beloved Son nailed to the cruel cross; it was there she felt the "sword piercing through her own soul." Yet, through it all, she did not withdraw her unconditional commitment to God:

> *"...Let it be to me according to your word."*
> (Luke 1:38, NKJV)

Lord, help us to believe and have faith like the mother of Christ, and through every confusing, difficult, or painful situation You allow, let us repeat,

"Behold the maidservant[16] of the Lord! Let it be to me according to Your word."
(Luke 1:38, NKJV)

---

16 Or *manservant*

"For though we walk in the flesh, we do not war according to the flesh. For the weapons of our warfare are not carnal but mighty in God for pulling down strongholds..."
(2 Corinthians 10:3–4, NKJV)

72. Strongholds!

The Old Testament pictures a stronghold as a "castle," "fortress," or a "place of safety," whereas "stronghold" appears only once (above verse) in the New Testament and portrays an opposing view.

I didn't know what a stronghold was until God showed me I had one. I tried fixing it on my own, but my "carnal" weapons were ineffective, and I was stuck in an endless scenario of walking in victory—then stumbling, repenting with tears, receiving forgiveness—totally convinced I wouldn't fall again, only to repeat the cycle weeks or months down the road.

Did you catch that statement in the last paragraph—*"totally convinced I wouldn't fall again"*—can you see how I was subtly relying on myself instead of relying on God to deliver me? I wanted to be free, but I didn't know how even though I had trusted God in other situations to deliver me.

A stronghold can be an addiction, an ingrained habit, an overly dependent relationship, irrational fears, pride, to name a few. Even things that are good can be overindulged in like money, food, sex, work...whatever *demands* our attention more than God.

Sometimes a stronghold hides behind an unmet need. We try to meet it *our way* and end up listening to the enemy. We wrestle with God as He tries to make us willing to give it up so He can meet our need *His way*—providing it is His will—but in our insecurity or rebellion, we are convinced we need it, fight to keep it, and hang onto it like a too-old child clutching an old-tattered blanket.

Before I knew I had a stronghold, there were two verses that I turned to frequently—it wasn't coincidental—God was speaking, but I wasn't listening. Then God sent two "mountains," one to get my attention and the other to make me willing—*and then I listened!*

God's plan to deliver me started with a neck injury. He got my attention after it progressively got worse, and I woke up in pain in the middle of the night and began reading Beth Moore's *Breaking Free*[17] while waiting for the pain pills to kick in. After several nights I was convinced that God was speaking.

> *"I will bless the Lord who has given me counsel; my heart*
> *also instructs me in the night seasons."*
> (Psalm 16:7, NKJV)

I wanted to break the stronghold, but I didn't know how. At one point, I feared I had fallen too many times. Fear overwhelmed me, and I began desperately seeking the Lord through His Word—and His word convinced, comforted, and brought a flood of relief that drowned out my fears:

---

17 Beth Moore, *Breaking Free*, B&H Publishing Group; Nashville, TN; 2000.

"The Lord will perfect that which concerns me;"
(Psalm 138:8, NKJV)

Notice it says: "the *Lord* will perfect...me." I don't have to do it; I have to be willing and cooperate. I need to believe that He will work in me through trials, tribulations, or whatever it takes until my will becomes His will.

"For it is God who works in you both to will and to do for
His good pleasure."
(Philippians 2:13, NKJV)

I thought His mercy would cease because I had blown it so many times. But when God says "forever," He means forever!

"Your mercy, O Lord, endures forever;"
(Psalm 138:8, NKJV)

I had seen God do so much for me. I had gone through so many trials; I didn't want it all to be in vain. But I still had more to learn. I was scaling my second "mountain," walking back and forth throughout the house one day, praying and bemoaning another failure over the stronghold that plagued me.

"O God, You are my God; early will I seek You; my soul
thirsts for you; my flesh longs for You in a dry and thirsty
land where there is no water."
(Psalm 63:1, NKJV)

I stopped in the hallway, leaned against the wall, and said, "God, I need some answers, *now!* I've been doing all the talking; do You have something to say?" Immediately, I heard a verse:

"Now unto Him who is able to keep you from falling, and present you faultless before the presence of His glory with exceeding joy."
(Jude 1:24, NKJV)

His answer came with fresh revelation in a verse I hadn't read in years. *That's it! I'm relying on myself to keep me instead of trusting God to keep me from falling.* I've learned to trust Him in other areas. Why should this situation be any different?

Then He showed me how I give the enemy a foothold by listening to his way of meeting my needs, and when it didn't work, I would kick myself, saying, "Didn't you know it wouldn't work?" I answered my own question, "No, I thought *this time* it would," even though I was doing the same dumb thing over and over and...

Several verses confirmed that just as I trusted Him to save me, I should trust Him to deliver me. God wasn't about to let me get away with "trying-and-praying-really-hard-to-be-victorious." He wanted to teach me His way—the way of God's power in me through faith.

"For in it (the gospel) the righteousness of God is revealed from faith to faith; as it is written, "The just shall live by faith."
(Romans 1:17, NKJV)

> *"For we through the Spirit eagerly wait for the hope of*
> *righteousness by faith."*
> (Galatians 5:5, NKJV)

"...by faith." Did you catch that? When I read that verse, it hit me like a velvet-covered brick. I was reminded of how God delivered me from smoking. I had tried and tried, prayed and prayed, and still, I could not stop until He convinced me that He was the deliverer and that I was to trust *Him* (believe, have faith) that He would deliver me. I believed, and He delivered me from smoking and gave me the strength and power to deal with the temptations that followed.

Recently I heard a song that resonated with me deeply about trying to win a battle that God has already won. Jesus settled that at Calvary when He said, "It is finished." Does that sound too easy? Didn't Jesus tell us,

> *"Take My yoke upon you and learn from Me, for I am gentle*
> *and lowly in heart, and you will find rest for your souls. For*
> *My yoke is easy and My burden is light."*
> (Matthew 11:29–30, NKJV)

We make it heavy by trying to do things in our own strength, even though we've prayed and prayed; too often, we aren't relying (believing by faith) on Christ alone to deliver us.

> *"For though we walk in the flesh, we do not war according*
> *to the flesh. For the weapons of our warfare are not*

carnal (the flesh), but mighty in God for pulling down
strongholds..."
(2 Corinthians 10:3–4, NKJV)

So, you think I finally got it together? Not quite. I fell again. But this time, I didn't wail and whine, nor did I fall into condemnation. Instead, I asked God for forgiveness and said calmly but decisively, "Lord, *You* have to keep me; I cannot keep myself. *You* have to work in me deeper than You ever have, and I am trusting You to do it!" And He did! That was many years ago, and He is still keeping me.

"He is able to keep what I have committed to Him
until that day."
(2 Timothy 1:12, NKJV)

The weapons of our warfare that are "mighty in God" and can "pull down strongholds" is Christ—alone. He is God's mighty weapon of warfare. Jesus is the only One who can deliver us—that's His part. And my part? Things I can do:

- Search for verses that fit my situation. Write them on paper and in my mind:

"The Word of God is living and powerful,
sharper than any two-edged sword..."
(Hebrews 4:12, NKJV)

- When the enemy tries to get me to think thoughts contrary to God's, I kick them out and bring them "into captivity" to Christ.

> *"...casting down arguments and every high thing that*
> *exalts itself against the knowledge of God, bringing every*
> *thought into captivity to the obedience of Christ..."*
> (2 Corinthians 10:5, NKJV)

- I tell Jesus something like, "Lord, I know you are faithful, and I believe that you will deliver me. I'm not going to try anymore; I am going to *trust You* to do what I can't." When doubts or questions come, I kick them out and tell Jesus again, *"I am trusting You!"*

There is a stronghold that is out of control today—obesity. Years ago, I watched on the 700 Club a woman who lost 150 pounds by faith, trusting God to do what she couldn't. She had prayed, tried numerous diets, and some of them worked *for a while*. But when she gave up trying and started trusting God to deliver her, He gave her the power to resist overeating.

When I see people who are struggling with their weight, I think: If only they knew that Jesus can give them the power to deliver them by faith.[18]

Years ago, we listened to a pastor who said he was walking throughout the pews the night before, praying for the Sunday Service when God spoke to him, telling him how it grieves Him that His children lean on their own strength instead of His. God was talking about all their weaknesses, not just strongholds. I wonder how many Christians know that Jesus wants to deliver them from their weaknesses and their strongholds by trusting

---

18 See Devotional #2: God's Way & God's Timing.

Him to do what they can't. The only thing that will hold us back is—if we don't want to give it up—but God can deal with that too. I've done it. I tell Him, "Lord help me to *want to*, 'work in me both to will and to do for Your good pleasure'" (from Philippians 2:13). And when He works in me, I find myself wanting to—absolutely amazing!

"Fear not for I have redeemed you; I have called you by your name; you are Mine...When you walk through the fire, you shall not be burned, nor shall the flame scorch you. For I am the Lord your God, the Holy One of Israel, your Savior;"
(Isaiah 43:1–3, NKJV)

73. Encountering God's "But If Not..."

You've prayed and prayed; others have prayed for you. You are asking God to miraculously take away this present, heavy load. You believe He could, but will He? You are trying with all your heart to believe, to have faith...then the test comes back, and it's not good; the job falls through; the relationship breaks; the unforeseen happens...

It's always good to trust God. It's not always wise to trust God to do a certain thing—unless you have a definite word from Him. We can ask for the miraculous—and I do—but more often than not, I have encountered God's "But if not..." as did our three Jewish friends in the days of the Babylonian captivity.

When King Nebuchadnezzar decreed that everyone should fall down and worship the gold image he had made, Shadrach, Meshach, and Abed-Nego—in charge of the affairs of the province of Babylon—refused to obey. The king gave them another chance, warning them of the fiery furnace awaiting them. "And who," the king asked, "is the god who will deliver you from my hands?" (Daniel 3:15)

Who indeed! They answered him,

> *"Our God whom we serve is able to deliver us from the burning fiery furnace, and He will deliver us from your hand, O king. But if not, let it be known to you O king, that we do not serve your gods, nor will we worship the gold image..."*
> (Daniel 3:17–18, NKJV)

God could have plucked the three men out of the king's hands immediately, but He chose to let them go through the *"But if not..."* He had His reasons. King Nebuchadnezzar was furious and ordered them bound and cast into the furnace. But when he looked into the fire, he was astonished—

> *"Look!...I see four men loose, walking in the midst of the fire; and they are not hurt, and the form of the fourth is like the Son of God."*
> (Daniel 3:25, NKJV)

What a divine revelation! Jesus, the Son of God, walking in the fire with them. What a comfort for God's people down through the ages: God will walk through the fire with us, and we will not be burned. Have you noticed that God records extreme examples in His Word so that all of us can identify and say?

"God, if you can do that for them, I believe You will take me through my fire. I am trusting You that it will not burn me, nor will the flame scorch me. I will look for Your hand, and I believe

I will come out closer to You, more like You, and with greater faith."

His reasons for allowing us to go through the fire are diverse. Some might be:

- He may want to show us His glory, what He can do;
- Increase our faith,
- Draw us closer,
- Change something in us,
- Some or all the above.

We may not sense God's presence immediately, but if we persevere, have faith, we will see His right hand—Jesus.

> *"Do not cast away your confidence, which has great*
> *reward. For you have need of endurance, so that after you*
> *have done the will of God, you may receive the promise:"*
> (Hebrews 10:35–36, NKJV)

Before I understood God's ways, I would fall into condemnation when trials came. Most of them, I reasoned, were caused by my own stupidity, weakness, or sinfulness. In the middle of my misery, God spoke to me from Jeremiah. It was years ago, but I still sense the strength of that verse as though it were yesterday; I can still see my surroundings as that verse was read from a stage and etched itself in my mind.

> *"I know the thoughts that I think toward you,*
> *says the Lord thoughts of peace and not of evil,*
> *to give you a future and a hope."*
> (Jeremiah 29:11, NKJV)

Another verse confirmed the above and brought reason to my thoughts:

*"God did not send His Son into the world to condemn the
world, but that the world through Him might be saved."*
(John 3:17, NKJV)

If Jesus wasn't condemning me, why should I? He was sending trials to help me, not to harm me. I found a poem that explained some of the "whys?"

Is there no other way, O God,
Except through sorrow, pain, and loss,
To stamp Christ's image on my soul
No other way except the cross?
And then a voice stills all my soul,
As stilled the waves on Galilee;
"Canst thou not bear the furnace heat?
If 'mid the flames I walk with thee?"
"I bore the cross, I know its weight,
I drank the cup I hold for thee;
Canst thou not follow where I lead?
I'll give the strength—lean thou on me."[19]

Author Unknown

The last "fire" I encountered didn't burn me, but it did burn out some things in my life that hindered my growth. It's amaz-

19 From *Springs in the Valley*, Mrs. Charles Cowman, Zondervan Publishing House, Grand Rapids, MI 1968

ing how my ears are attuned to hearing His voice and how willing I am to give up what I've held onto so tightly as the "flames" dance around my feet.

My trials have deepened my faith, as I have been forced to draw closer to God by searching His word, spending time in prayer, and learning to trust Him more.

We were praying for one who was in our Bible study group and going through what I would call a "four-alarm" fire. As I prayed in our group, I quoted Isaiah 43:2, "When you walk through the fire, you shall not be burned, nor shall the flame scorch you."

Fast forward about three months: my husband was still fuzzy from the medical procedure He had just gone through. We were listening to the doctor explain the test results—it wasn't good. After the doctor left, the nurse who had been taking notes reiterated what the doctor had said. To which I replied, "We'll have to take it a day at a time—with a lot of prayer."

She responded, "I guess he'll have to go through the fire." *Everything seemed to stop. I sensed God was speaking.*

The verses I prayed for our friend were now for us, and so was God's promise:

> *"When you walk through the fire, you shall not be burned,*
> *nor shall the flame scorch you. For I am the Lord your God,*
> *the Holy one of Israel, your Savior;"*
> (Isaiah 43:2–3, NKJV)

An outpouring of well-wishes and promises to pray for my husband came in the days ahead, one of which was an email from our friend we prayed for in our Bible study (in part).

"We will continue to pray for Keith's healing. We
know that God is faithful to His word and will walk
with Keith through the fire; we have learned this
first-hand. This journey has taken our faith to a new
level that we have not experienced before and has
opened so many doors for us to give God the Glory
He deserves for the blessings He has given to us and
others through us..."

Keith and I are trusting God that our "fire" will continue to
accomplish whatever He pleases and that it will be good! Our
faith has been stretched and strengthened as He leads us step
by step. Would we change it? And not have seen His hand in so
many situations? Or learned more of His awesome ways? And
not have been lovingly forced to walk closer to Jesus than ever?
Never!

For some, the "But if not..." doesn't work the way we think
it should. I recall an author who wrote, "God keeps Himself a
sovereign two percent," referring to those situations that don't
seem to fit the promises, circumstances that seem impossible
to comprehend and difficult to accept.

 Our friend, who encouraged us and many others with his
life, stayed strong in the faith to the end. When he was unable to talk, he would smile and give us a "thumbs up" when we
mentioned the name of Jesus.

Today he is talking with Jesus!

Dedicated to our dear friend, "Larry."

> *"The eternal God is your refuge,*
> *and underneath are the everlasting arms."*
> (Deuteronomy 33:27, NKJV)

74. Safe & Secure

It was around nine o'clock in the morning when my husband said he had chest pains and couldn't breathe well. We headed for the ER in town because he didn't think he could make it to the hospital thirty-five miles away, where he had undergone an esophagectomy four weeks earlier.

Keith was anxious. I tried encouraging him, but it wasn't helping, so I started singing an old hymn, "Leaning on the Everlasting Arms." I don't know if it helped him, but it did me.

At the ER, they asked a lot of questions, hooked him up to the machine that takes the necessary vitals, took blood samples, and gave him an EKG. Then the nurse gave him a nitroglycerin tablet *just in case*. The doctor had not come in yet.

I sat down in a chair attempting to call our son when I glanced at Keith. He was staring intently at the wall directly above me. I looked at the wall and then back at him; he was still staring with eyes wide open and fixed. *Something wasn't right! It looked like a death stare.* I jumped up, and his eyes went back into his head. All I could see were the whites of his eyes. I yelled, "Do something—NOW!"

The nurse looked at Keith, gasped, and said, "I'll get the doctor," and ran out.

I put my arms around Keith and prayed desperately, *"Jesus, You have to do something."* Immediately, I thought of Elijah and the widow's son of whom "there was no breath left in him," and I lifted Keith up, pulled him tightly to me, and prayed, *"Lord, breathe Your life into him. Jesus! Jesus! Jesus!"*

I laid him down. His eyes were closed but no longer bulging. I cupped his face in my hands and said, "Keith, you can't leave me. Do you hear me?" He opened his eyes ever-so-slightly, then closed them again. "Keith, stay with me. You *have* to stay with me, okay?" He nodded a little. I felt somewhat relieved but unable to assess the situation—it shook me to the core.

The nurse came back and started an IV, lifted his legs with pillows, telling me that would help his blood pressure rise. The nitroglycerin had dropped his blood pressure dangerously low. We waited as his blood pressure crawled up, then down, back and forth. I kept praying, "Jesus, Jesus, Jesus." The doctor finally came in.

Eventually, Keith's blood pressure rose high enough for them to transport him to the hospital where he had the surgery. Once there, they "tapped" two liters of fluid from his chest, put tubes in his back to continue to drain fluid until he came home six days later.

When Keith had told his doctor that he had vacuumed the day before he came into the hospital, the doctor told him vacuuming a month after this surgery was not good. Keith looked at me, smiled, and said, "I told you I shouldn't be vacuuming!" We needed a little levity.

I had told him he *shouldn't* be vacuuming, even though he was progressing well, but he insisted he was fine. The recovery from side effects of that particular surgery is only nine to eleven percent. That is not funny at all.

(I hope this warning will help others in a similar situation. If you have had surgery, check with your doctor exactly when and how much you can exert yourself even if you feel you are doing well.)

It took several days to shake the ER scene from replaying in my head—it was surreal. But the words of the familiar chorus comforted me, and I sang it often: "Leaning on the everlasting arms."

Thinking back, I believe Keith knew something was wrong when he looked at me for help. His blood pressure tapes from the room where the machines monitored him showed it went below the graph, so it wasn't readable. The young nurse ran out of the room instead of checking to see if he was breathing. When she came back, she said, "I've never seen anything like that." When the doctor finally came in, he held his hand out to shake mine. I said, *"Forget about me, take care of my husband,"* who at the time did not have his eyes open yet.

Even though it seemed like everything was out of control that morning in the ER, God showed me He was *still* in *control*. To Him be all the glory. We may never know exactly what happened that morning, but we praise our awesome God that nothing is too hard for Him and that Keith is alive today.

"With men it is impossible, but not with God;
for with God all things are possible."
(Mark 10:27, NKJV)

With all my heart, I thank you, Jesus!!!

"Call to Me, and I will answer you, and show you great and mighty things, which you do not know."
(Jeremiah 33:3, NKJV)

75. His Power and His Promises

Jesus was adamant about teaching His disciples an important principle before He was crucified. He repeated the words, "If you ask anything in My name, I will do it," or very similar in seven different verses in the book of John: 14:13 & 14 (below), 15:7 & 16; 16:23, 24 and 26.

"And whatever you ask in My name, that I will do, that the Father may be glorified in the Son. If you ask anything in My name, I will do it."
(John 14:13–14, NKJV)

Last week I was sweeping up seeds on the front sidewalk when a large dog I'd never seen before came running across the street, barking at me. I knew I'd never make it to the house. My next thought was: *Jesus has to help me.* So I shook my hand at the dog and said, "In the name of Jesus, get out of here." The dog stopped, started to turn around, then came at me again...I repeated the same words a little louder, and the dog turned, took a step or two, and for the third time, started coming at me barking. I shook my hand and said even louder, "In the name of *Jesus*," and he ran away.

God puts us in situations where we have to trust Him—and when we do—He always comes through! I, who have a fear of dogs, felt no fear at all! I didn't realize that until afterward. God was truly in control. I learned later the dog was part boxer, part pitbull, and who knows what else, and was fairly new to the neighborhood.

> *"You have put all things under His feet. All sheep and oxen—even the beasts of the field, the birds of the air, and the fish of the sea..."*
> (Psalm 8:6, NKJV)

Yes, even dogs!

A pastor, during his sermon, shared how he was walking throughout the sanctuary praying the night before when God spoke to him, "It grieves Me that too many Christians are relying on themselves, trusting in their own strength, instead of Mine."

I was relying on myself. One day, overwhelmed with responsibility, I cried out to God, "Lord, I *can't* handle this!"

God replied, "You can't, Carole, *but I can!*"

"Oh Lord, I'm leaning on my strength instead of Yours. I receive Your strength, Jesus; I know You will carry me." And He did; God and I can handle anything—when I lean on His strength.

The following verse is my life-line; it covers a multitude of situations as I draw near to God, leaning on His strength.

*"And He said to me, 'My grace is sufficient for you, for my
strength is made perfect in weakness.' Therefore most gladly
I will rather boast in my infirmities, that the power of Christ
might rest upon me. Therefore I take pleasure in infirmities,
in reproaches, in needs, in persecutions, in distresses, for
Christ's sake. For when I am weak, then I am strong."*
(2 Corinthians 12:9–10, NKJV)

When we stop relying on our strength and rely on Christ's strength and His power—by faith—then we will see Him work everyday wonders.

The longer we walk with Him, the more we learn about His ways. Our ways are not God's ways—not even close. His ways are found as we search His Word and step out in faith.

*"For as the heavens are higher than the earth,
so are My ways Higher than your ways,
and My thoughts than your thoughts."*
(Isaiah 55:9, NKJV)

Several years ago, Keith and I were on a plane when the kid in the seat behind him kept kicking the seat. Keith told him to stop twice, but he didn't stop; the person sitting next to him didn't seem to care. I didn't want the situation to go any further, so I began praying, and a verse came to me—one I had read but never thought of using.

"Assuredly, I say to you, whatever you bind on earth will be bound in heaven, and whatever you loose on earth will be loosed in heaven."
(Matthew 18:18, NKJV)

I "bound" the kid's feet in the name of Jesus and "loosed" peace upon Keith. That was the first time I quoted that promise, and I was amazed how quickly God answered it.

My niece and nephew were telling me that their mom (my sister), living in an assisted living home, refused to take a bath. It was unlike her; she has always been cooperative. We prayed the above verse and bound her "stubbornness," and loosed her "cooperation." We were relieved to learn she willingly took a shower.

My grandson was being bullied after he entered ninth grade. I prayed and bound this kid from touching my grandson. The bullying stopped, but he continued to stare eerily at my grandson in the hallways. I bound his eyes from looking at my grandson, and he stopped staring.

The enemy uses ungodly kids to mess with our kids. God tells us, "Fight for them."

"Do not be afraid of them. Remember the Lord, great and awesome, and fight for your brethren, your sons, your daughters, your wives, and your houses."
(Nehemiah 4:14, NKJV)

I added "grandson" in my Bible to the above verse. God is great and awesome, but we have a part in this too, and that is to "fight for your brethren, your sons, your daughters, your wives, and your houses." And He has given us the means and the faith to do it.

> *"Behold, I give you the authority to trample on serpents*
> *and scorpions, and over all the power of the enemy and*
> *nothing shall by any means hurt you."*
> (Luke 10:19, NKJV)

*"Nevertheless, when the Son of Man comes, will He really
find faith on the earth?"*
(Luke 18:8, NKJV)

76. According to Your Faith

When I read the above verse in the Parable of the Persistent Widow (Luke 18:1–8), I wondered, *What does that have to do with the Parable, and what was God saying?* Then I lived it last week and learned through experience what I believe God meant.

It all started when my niece texted me about her mother (my sister) that her kidneys had fallen from seventeen percent to ten, then six, and now she was in Hospice, not doing well. I was planning on going there in a couple of days but decided to leave right away. I packed fast and started the four-hour trip, praying that she would be alive when I got there.

Twenty-five miles into the trip, I missed a turn on the Interstate and spent the next forty minutes in a large city trying to find my way back. I was praying desperately, wondering why God wasn't helping me. I finally pulled over, got my phone out, and googled a map to the interstate, and when I saw a sign that the interstate was six blocks away, I breathed a sigh of relief—*until I looked at the nearly empty gas tank.*

I decided I wasn't going to panic this time; I *had* to trust God. "Lord, I am trusting You. I believe there will be a gas station before I get on the Interstate." I said it calmly. I praised Him and thanked Him all the way to the Interstate, and there it was! I filled up the tank praising the Lord. "Oh, God, You are so good to me," I said over and over. But the lesson was not finished. As I drove along, I heard:

> "It is *not* according to your panic;
> it is according to your *faith!*"

God's Word tells us unequivocally,

> *"Without faith it is impossible to please Him, for he who*
> *comes to God must believe that He is, and that He is a*
> *rewarder of those who diligently seek Him."*
> (Hebrews 11:6, NKJV)

I think I hold the record for getting lost. God has come to my rescue more times than I can count when I trusted Him to help me find my way, but that morning I left the house in an anxious state. I didn't take time to pray. I should have trusted Him after I made the wrong turn, I usually do, but that day I didn't...until I looked at the near-empty tank, I knew I had to have faith, and the Lord responded.

God saw the mess I got myself into and, through an empty tank, pointed out how crucial it is to always have faith. When I was lost that day, I asked the Lord for help—but not in faith—rather from a panic-driven, *"Lord help,"* to*"Why aren't you helping me, God?"*

That reminded me of what a pastor said in his sermon as he walked throughout the church the night before, praying for those who would be there Sunday morning, when the Lord spoke to him and said, "It grieves Me because too many of My children are leaning on their own strength, instead of Mine." Leaning on God demands faith.

Back to the Parable. The persistent widow kept coming to the judge asking for justice from her adversary, and because he was wearied by her continual coming, he decided to avenge her. The Lord said,

> *"And shall God not avenge His own elect who cry out day*
> *and night to Him, though He bears long with them? I tell*
> *you that He will avenge them speedily..."*
> (Luke 18:7–8, NKJV)

"Speedily?" If His elect "cry out day and night," and Jesus "bears long with them," does that describe the word "speedily?" Crying out day and night sounds like the persistent widow. So, what is His lesson?

That day on the road, my crying out to Him didn't bring His response, but when I exercised faith—decided to believe, began to thank Him, His response was "speedily."

Luke 18:8 (NKJV) (the end of the above verse) asks a thought-provoking question:

> *"Nevertheless, when the Son of Man comes,*
> *will He really find faith on the earth?"*

The Lord continues to lead me into situations that test my faith. Like the night, I tossed and turned, fell asleep, and woke up several times, worrying about the MRI I was having the next morning. I wasn't worried about the outcome. It was the hour I would be stuck in the cave-like machine. One of the many questions the hospital person had asked me over the phone the day before was: "Can you stay in the machine for an hour?"

I got up the next morning, determined to deal with the situation. I prayed and told the Lord over and over that I trusted Him. I opened the Bible and started to read—and there was Jesus walking on water, saying,

> *"Be of good cheer! It is I; do not be afraid."*
> (Mark 6:50, NKJV)

I repeated that verse over and over, believing it was for me. Then I said emphatically, "Lord, I believe," and all my fears fell at His feet. I felt like I was walking on water the rest of the day. I was on the table for only twenty-five minutes, of which I talked and sang inwardly to Jesus the whole time.

> *"According to your faith let it be to you."*
> (Matthew 9:29, NKJV)

"Who shall separate us from the love of Christ? Shall tribulation, or distress or persecution, or famine or nakedness, or peril, or sword?"
(Romans 8:35, NKJV)

"Yet in all these things we are more than conquerors through Him who loved us."
(Romans 8:37, NKJV)

77. Panic Attacks

I read that sometimes the after-effects of coronavirus can come back weeks or months later. It was confirmed when I went to ER with low oxygen, fever, and spent four days in the hospital. While I was there, I prayed daily. On the third day, I prayed intensely—I was scared. I heard the Lord say, "You have to trust Me more."

I always thought I had trusted God, but I hadn't been ill for years and years. Then I started having panic attacks when I couldn't breathe well, which made it worse. I went to the ER twice because I couldn't breathe, had a lung infection, and was told it would last three weeks—it lasted four; then, I contracted two more infections.

I have always been healthy. I take no pills—just vitamins and memory—and can't remember the last time I was ill (besides

COVID). One of my devotionals is titled The First Step: Accept. I found that hard to do. I thought I had a lot of faith, but at the time, it felt like I had none.

I listen daily to contemporary Christian songs on YouTube. I love Phil Wickham's song "The Battle Belongs to the Lord." It helps me put my fears at the Lord's feet, but first, I have to accept what is happening, believe that God is allowing this for my good and that I need to learn to trust Him more. He's not done with me yet.

Perhaps, it is because this world is not going to get better, so I will need more faith to deal with whatever happens in the future.

> *"For when Your judgments are in the earth, the inhabitants of the world will learn righteousness."*
> (Isaiah 26:9, NKJV)

Yes, God will take care of His children, and I need to trust that He will.

> *"Behold, I have refined you, but not as silver; I have tested you in the furnace of affliction."*
> (Isaiah 48:10, NKJV)

"For when Your judgments are in the earth, the inhabitants of the world will learn righteousness."
(Isaiah 26:9, NKJV)

78. Praying for Our Country and Our Kids

Our country was filled with disasters this year. Each time I prayed for the good of our country, the thought would come to me, *What if God is allowing calamity to continue because the United States has pulled away from God in so many ways?* Then I added, "Your will be done, Lord."

A few weeks later, I opened my Bible and turned to Ezekiel, Chapter 14. Later that day, I opened my Bible to the same place, and I thought, *Lord, is there something on this page you want me to read?* I read Ezekiel 14:12–23, how God uses disasters to bring back His children—and our children—to Himself.

"The word of the Lord came again to me, saying: 'Son of man, when a land sins against Me by persistent unfaithfulness, I will stretch out My hand against it;" (14:12–13). "Even though Noah, Daniel, and Job were in it...they would deliver neither son nor daughter; they would only deliver themselves by their righteousness." (14:20). "Yet behold, there shall be left in it a remnant who will be brought out, both sons and daughters; surely they will come out to you, and you will see their ways and their doings. Then you will be comforted concerning the disaster that I have brought..." (14:22).

As parents it is difficult for us to see our children going through tribulation, but that might be just what is needed to bring them to the Lord, which is what God is saying in the Ezekiel 14:22–23. "...and you shall know that I have done nothing without cause that I have done in it, says the Lord God" (14:23).

Even though the judgments are on the earth, we as Christians have to deal with the situations, too, knowing that God will use those situations to bring people to Himself. When all is going well, people don't see a need for God, but when the earth is overcome with problems—as it is beginning now—many will listen to God's people, like you and me!

I have talked with many Christians who have been praying for revival. In reading books, I have noticed that when people pray fervently for revival, God answers. Let's join them. Prayer is powerful!

> *"O Lord, revive Your work in the midst of the years!*
> *In the midst of the years make it known; in wrath*
> *remember mercy."*
> (Habakkuk 3:2, NKJV)

Amen!

Endnotes

1. Rachel Carson, *Silent Spring*, Fawcett World Library, New York, 1962

2. David Reuben MD, *The Save Your Life Diet*, Random House, Inc., New York. 1975

3. Eileen Renders MD, *Food Additives*, Nutrients & Supplements A-Z, Clear Light Publishers, Santa Fe, NM. 1999

4. *George Washington Carver*, Doubleday & Co. Inc., Garden City, NY 1943

5. Care Net Family Resource Center: An international Christian organization for women who are pregnant and/or have children under two, providing classes with dozens of teaching DVD's, peer counseling and spiritual encouragement for mothers; clothing and material items for children. For a center near you: www.care-net.org

6. Charles Stanley, *God's Power through Prayer*, J. Countryman Publishers, Houston TX

7. Patsy Clairmont, *Under His Wings*, Focus on the Family Publishing, Colorado Springs, CO 80995, 1994

8. Dialogue is author's perception of Hannah taken from 1 Samuel Chapters 1–4

9. Dialogue is author's perception of Hannah from 1 Samuel, Chapters 1–4
10. Dialogue is author's perception of Hannah taken from 1 Samuel Chapters 1–4
11. Ibid.
12. Dialogue is author's perception of Hannah from 1 Samuel, Chapters 1–4
13. Ibid.
14. John Bevere, *The Bait of Satan*, Lake Mary, FL: Charisma House, 1994
15. Nehemiah 9:12
16. Or manservant
17. Beth Moore, *Breaking Free*, B&H Publishing Group; Nashville, TN; 2000
18. See Devotional #2: God's Way & God's Timing
19. From *Springs in the Valley*, Mrs. Charles Cowman, Zondervan Publishing House, Grand Rap-ids, MI 1968